Televising Restoration Spain

David R. George, Jr. · Wan Sonya Tang
Editors

Televising Restoration Spain

History and Fiction in Twenty-First-Century
Costume Dramas

palgrave
macmillan

Editors
David R. George, Jr.
Department of Spanish
Bates College
Lewiston, ME, USA

Wan Sonya Tang
Department of Romance Languages
and Literatures
Boston College
Chestnut Hill, MA, USA

ISBN 978-3-319-96195-8   ISBN 978-3-319-96196-5   (eBook)
https://doi.org/10.1007/978-3-319-96196-5

Library of Congress Control Number: 2018950508

Cover credit: Lul De Panbehchi/Eye Em/Getty Images
Cover design by Ran Shauli

This Palgrave Macmillan imprint is published by the registered company Springer Nature
Switzerland AG
The registered company address is: Gewerbestrasse 11, 6330 Cham, Switzerland

ACKNOWLEDGEMENTS

We are most grateful to the contributors to this volume, whose enthusiasm for the project made it possible. We are likewise appreciative of our editor Shaun Vigil and assistant editor Glenn Ramirez for their guidance and support throughout the publication process.

Wan Sonya Tang extends sincerest thanks to Boston College for the Research Incentive Grant, which allowed her to workshop her chapter in a conference setting and to Timothy Fair for his unwavering moral support.

David George thanks colleagues at Bates College and in the field for their encouragement and feedback.

Finally, we would like to thank research assistant Lauren Mushro, a tireless expert in formatting bibliographies in Chicago Style.

CONTENTS

NOTES ON CONTRIBUTORS

Elena Cueto Asín is Professor of Hispanic Studies in the Department of Romance Language and Literatures at Bowdoin College, USA. She is author of several articles on modern Spanish literature, film, and television and of the books *Autos para siluetas de Valle-Inclán* (2005), *Reconciliaciones en escena. El teatro de la Guerra Civil* (2008), and *Guernica en la escena, la página y la pantalla* (2018). She is also co-editor of the volume *Historias de la pequeña pantalla. Representaciones históricas en la televisión de la España democrática* (2009).

Mónica Barrientos Bueno is Associate Lecturer in the Universidad de Sevilla, Spain's School of Communication, in the Department of Audiovisual Communication and Advertising. She is author of *Inicios del cine en Sevilla (1896–1906)* (2006), *Celuloide enmarcado. El retrato pictórico en el cine* (2009), and *Dentro del cuadro. 50 presencias pictóricas en el cine* (2017). Her research interests include the social functions of television, transmedia storytelling, early cinema history, and the relationship between cinema, television, and painting.

Ángeles Martínez García is Assistant Lecturer in the Universidad de Sevilla, Spain's School of Communication, in the Department of Audiovisual Communication and Advertising. She is author of several books: *Mito, cine, literatura. Laberinto y caos en El tercer hombre* (2006), *Laberintos narrativos. Estudio sobre el espacio cinematográfico* (2012), and *La imagen cinematográfica. Manual de análisis aplicado* (2015). Her research interests include cinematic imagery, image composition, and social media.

Iván Gómez García is Associate Professor in the School of Communication at Universitat Ramon Llull, Spain, where he teaches History of Film, Audiovisual Narrative, New Media, and Cinema Genres. He holds a Ph.D. in Literary Theory and Comparative Literature from the Universitat Autònoma de Barcelona, Spain, and degrees in Law (ESADE-Universitat Ramon Llull), Literary Theory and Comparative Literature (UAB), and Audiovisual Communication (Universitat Ramon Llull). He has published four books: *Adaptación* (2008), *Ficciones Colaterales: Las huellas del 11-S en la ficción televisiva norteamericana* (2011), *El sueño de la visión produce cronoendoscopias: tratamiento y diagnóstico del trampantojo digital* and *Bullitt. Un policía llamado Steve McQueen. Historia, análisis, mito* (2016).

David R. George, Jr. is Senior Lecturer in Spanish in the Department of Spanish at Bates College, USA. He has published articles and book chapters on a variety of aspects of nineteenth- and twentieth-century Spanish literature, film, and television. He is co-editor of *Historias de la pequeña pantalla. Representaciones históricas en la televisión de la España democrática* (2009), and author of annotated editions of Leopoldo Alas's *Doña Berta* (2008) and Benito Pérez Galdós's *Tormento* (2012).

Leslie J. Harkema is Associate Professor of Spanish in the Department of Spanish and Portuguese at Yale University, USA, where she teaches courses on the literature and culture of post-Enlightenment Spain. She is author of *Spanish Modernism and the Poetics of Youth: From Miguel de Unamuno to La Joven Literatura* (2017), a re-examination of early twentieth-century Spanish cultural production in light of the emergence of youth culture in Europe and its influence on European modernism. Her scholarship has appeared in *Anales de la Literatura Española Contemporánea*, *Bulletin of Spanish Studies*, *Revista Hispánica Moderna*, and elsewhere.

Francisca López is Professor of Spanish in the Department of Spanish at Bates College, USA. She specializes in contemporary Spanish literary and cultural studies, paying particular attention to politics of representation in narrative fiction, film, and television. She has authored and co-edited several books. The most recent are: *Global Issues in Contemporary Hispanic Women's Writing* (2013) and *Cartografías del 23-F: Representaciones en la prensa, la televisión, la novela, el cine y la cultura popular* (2014). Her articles have appeared in edited volumes and in such journals as *The Arizona Journal of Hispanic Cultural Studies, Letras Peninsulares,* and *Dissedences/Disidencias: Hispanic Journal of Theory and Criticism.*

María Gil Poisa is Resident Director at Educational Services Abroad in Barcelona, Spain. Her research deals with Hispanic horror film and minority European film. She received her Ph.D. from Texas A&M University in 2017, and her doctoral dissertation "Nuevos monstruos en el cine español contemporáneo" proposes a new conceptualization of the monster illustrated through the comparative analysis of contemporary Spanish genre films.

Wan Sonya Tang is Assistant Professor of Hispanic Studies in the Department of Romance Languages and Literatures, and affiliated faculty of the Women's and Gender Studies Program at Boston College, USA, where she teaches courses on nineteenth- to twenty-first-century Spanish literature, visual arts, and culture, with an emphasis on gender studies. Her current book project examines fantastic short fictions from nineteenth-century Spain as a repository of cultural anxieties. She has published in edited volumes and journals such as the *Revista de Estudios Hispánicos* and *Anales Galdosianos,* among others.

Concepción Cascajosa Virino is Senior Lecturer in the Department of Journalism and Audiovisual Communication at the Universidad Carlos III de Madrid, Spain, where she is a member of the research group TECMERIN and also director of the MFA in Film and TV Screenwriting. She has written or edited nine books and more than forty papers about television fiction and media history, including articles in *Studies in Hispanic Cinemas, Journal of Spanish Cultural Studies,* and *VIEW Journal of European Television History and Culture.*

Linda M. Willem is the Betty Blades Lofton Professor of Spanish in the Department of Modern Languages, Literatures and Cultures at Butler University, USA. She received her Ph.D. from the University of California, Los Angeles, USA, and is a four-time recipient of National Endowment for the Humanities awards. Her area of specialization is nineteenth-century Spanish literature, with a secondary focus on Spanish cinema. She currently is the President of the Asociación Internacional de Galdosistas, Inc. and has also served two terms as its Secretary–Treasurer. She has published books with the University of North Carolina and the

University of Mississippi presses, edited a collection of short stories by Emilia Pardo Bazán, and authored over thirty scholarly articles.

Nicholas Wolters is Assistant Professor of Spanish in the Department of Spanish and Italian at Wake Forest University in Winston-Salem, NC, USA. His teaching and research currently focus on modern Spanish peninsular literature and visual culture, with a particular emphasis on cultural constructions of manhood and masculinity. Nicholas's current book project examines and historicizes representations of masculinity in nineteenth-century novels and visual culture (fashion, illustrated press, painting) and their role in shaping discourses of modernity, nationalism, and regional identity.

LIST OF FIGURES

CHAPTER 1

Introduction

David R. George, Jr. and Wan Sonya Tang

In episode 32 "Tiempo de Verbena" of Televisión Española's sci-fi history series *El Ministerio del Tiempo* (TVE, 2015–2017), the character Angustias (Francesca Piñon) takes a break from her post as secretary in the Ministry of Time to travel back to 1894 in hopes of landing tickets for the premiere of her favorite *zarzuela, La verbena de la Paloma*. Having missed the show because of her mother's illness, she is profoundly dismayed to discover upon arriving at the defunct Teatro Apolo in Madrid that the performance has been canceled. Angustias returns to the present and persuades the ministry to send her back in the company of special agents Lola (Macarena García) and "Pacino" (Hugo Silva) to ensure that the show goes on to make history. Within the structure of the series, this particular mission serves as a comic digression from the main plotline, but nonetheless falls within the purview of the government ministry charged with safeguarding the course of Spanish history against the meddling of rival secret societies. The agents initially question the importance of saving a *zarzuela*

D. R. George, Jr. (✉)
Bates College, Lewiston, ME, USA
e-mail: dgeorge@bates.edu

W. S. Tang
Boston College, Chestnut Hill, MA, USA
e-mail: Wan.tang@bc.edu

© The Author(s) 2018
D. R. George, Jr. and W. S. Tang (eds.),
Televising Restoration Spain,
https://doi.org/10.1007/978-3-319-96196-5_1

1

for posterity, yet, following the established pattern of the series that gives equal weight to political and cultural artifacts, figures and events in the preservation of national heritage, the trio is assigned the task. Through the depiction of the moment of gestation of what remains one of the most popular pieces of the Spanish *género chico* (light-opera) repertoire, the trope of time-travel consecrates the work, and more important still, the period of the Restoration (1874–1931) in which it was produced, as fundamental in the trajectory of Spain's past as represented in the series.

El Ministerio del Tiempo traffics in historical *tableaux vivants* that entertain and instruct by recreating recognizable episodes of Spanish history for twenty-first-century audiences (Rueda Laffond et al. 2016, 98). The opening sequence of "Tiempo de verbena" exemplifies the *modus operandi* of the series: Angustias finds herself on stage on the night of the opera's debut improvising the role of Tia Antonia, backed by Lola and "Pacino," dressed in traditional Madrid garb. The comic sequence recreates a plausible yet irrecoverable moment of cultural history through a medley of the *zarzuela*'s most familiar scenes and tunes—"Por ser la Virgen de la Paloma," "Coplas de Don Hilarión," and "Donde vas con mantón de Manila"—in uncanny fashion that interpolates the audience's memories of performances preserved and replayed on film and video. As a result, the historical context becomes available for fabulation: History and fiction playfully mix when fictional agents track down the librettist Ricardo de la Vega (Manuel Brun) and composer Tomás Bretón (Bruno Oro) in a café conversing with novelists Benito Pérez Galdós (Jorge Basanta) and José Echegaray (Pedro Garcia de las Heras). While the musical figures are less known, the time-travelers, and viewers of a certain age, recognize the writers as cultural icons whose faces once adorned 1000 pesetas notes issued in the 1970s and 1980s.

Within the scope of the series, this comic episode is loaded with self-referential winks to avid fans, since this is not the only instance in which ministry agents intervene in the period spanning the turn-of-the-twentieth century over the course of three seasons. By and large, more than as history, the Restoration functions as story in *El Ministerio del Tiempo*, either as a plot point of origin, or as a convenient retreat into the past, as in the case of Angustias's "vacation" to 1894. Consequently, the epoch appears prominently, and so not insignificantly, in agent biographies developed both on-screen and in the web of transmedia stories spun on the Internet and social media. Together with Angustias, who was born in the 1870s, all four of the series' female characters hail from the years of the Restoration: Amelia Folch (Aura Garrido) was born in 1857; Lola, around 1920; and Irene Larra (Cayetana Guillén), in 1930. This gendered treatment of the Restoration is fitting, as it was during this period that the modern Spanish feminist movement was consolidated. Of the four female characters, the popular agent Amelia best embodies the period: Born to an upper-class family in Barcelona, she was supposedly among the first women to graduate university and became active in the anti-slavery movement of the 1880s before her recruitment to the ministry. Her departure from *El Ministerio del Tiempo* in episode 27 ("Tiempo de esclavos") occurs significantly after ministry agents foil a wholly fictional plot to assassinate King Alfonso XII in 1881, which would have fundamentally altered the history of the period by leaving the throne without a male heir (Alfonso XIII). Notably, the ministry's recruitment officer Irene brushes with death when she travels back to 1918 in episode 13 ("Un virus de otro tiempo") to assist the birth of historic flamenco dancer Carmen Amaya "La Capitana" and becomes a victim of the Spanish flu pandemic; she is rescued by colleagues and returned to the present to be cured. Perhaps the most emblematic historical events of the Restoration figure in the biography of Amelia's male cohort Julián Martínez (Rodolfo Sancho): Halfway through season two, he abandons his post and is eventually tracked down in 1898 serving as volunteer field doctor during the Spanish–American War, first in Cuba (episode 15 "Tiempo de Valientes I"), and finally in the Philippines (episode 16, "Tiempo de Valientes II"). True biography also works as an indirect mode of representing the era in the form of references to mostly cultural figures whose works are emblematic of Restoration Spain as the hatching ground for successive movements of artistic innovation. In addition to the historical characters in "Tiempo de Verbena," who represent the Realist Generation of 1868, the Generation of 1898, Modernism and the Avant-Garde are evoked in cameo appearances by the likes of Pablo Picasso, Federico García Lorca, Luis Buñuel, and Ramón del Valle-Inclán, among others.

The recurrence of the Restoration in *El Ministerio del Tiempo* puts the show in dialogue with various recent costume dramas set in the era, as well as with the longer tradition of literary adaptations that have brought to the small screen numerous works of literature from the time. Whereas the vignettes of the sci-fi series transport the agents of the ministry back to the period and engage audiences as voyeuristic spectators who derive pleasure from the characters' game of dress up, recent series that recreate the age promise to transport viewers themselves through original fictions that directly involve them in stories that are historically plausible and visually pleasurable. These full-fledged recreations of the Restoration are not incompatible with the brief encounters offered by *El Ministerio del Tiempo*; on the contrary, both formats complement each other in the production of a more complete rendering of an age that, for all its tele-visual presence, still remains a largely misunderstood chapter in contemporary Spanish history.

THE RESTORATION IS HISTORY

Following the airing of episode 27 "Tiempo de esclavos" on July 7, 2017, Aurelio Pimental posted a feature on TVE's *El Ministerio del Tiempo* webpage titled "Las diez cosas que España no tendría si Alfonso XII hubiera muerto en el atentado de *El Ministerio del Tiempo*" (Pimental 2017). In the introduction to the list, the writer assures fans that, had the mission failed, the course of Spanish history would have been fundamentally altered. The enumeration is little more than a hodgepodge of trivia that at best undermines the historical plausibility of the episode set in 1881; most of the events and outcomes listed predate the supposed setting and so would have happened anyway. This aside, the register of things that would be missed today includes the playground song "¿Dónde vas, Alfonso XII?," the popular boating pond in Madrid's Retiro Park and the king's torrid affair with opera diva Elena Sanz, alongside the 1876 Constitution, the end of the Carlist Wars and the institution of the Bourbon monarchy itself. By referring to random events and outcomes of Alfonso XII's reign, and more generally, of the Restoration of the monarchy he symbolized, the page and viewers' commentary and rankings of the items provide insight into the place both the period and the monarch occupy in popular historical imaginary.

For television viewers, part of the appeal of the Restoration as a historical setting is that it constitutes an aesthetically attractive period that is recognizable yet about which audiences retain relatively little real knowledge. In 2014, the online version of conservative newspaper *ABC* published a short quiz titled "¿Aprobarías un examen de la Restauración borbónica?" (Would you pass an exam on the Bourbon Restoration?). In it, author Manuel Villatoro challenges *ABC*'s online readers to outperform high school students, for whom the Restoration comprises a unit of the state-mandated history curriculum, on a ten-question, largely multiple-choice quiz (2014). Villatoro prefaces the questions by stating that

"Su extensión, su cercanía en el tiempo a nuestra época (menos de dos siglos) y sus grandes repercusiones políticas han hecho de este periodo uno de los más reseñables de la Historia de España" (its extension, its temporal proximity to our time [less than two centuries], and its great political repercussions have made of this period one of the most noteworthy in the history of Spain), and yet his challenge to readers seems to suggest that the average Spanish adult will in fact fail to correctly identify key elements, characters, and policies of the Restoration. Ironically, Villatoro himself seems shaky on the period, as his subtitle incorrectly states "En el S.XVIII se instauró en España un sistema basado en el poder de la corona y el 'turno de partidos'" (In the eighteenth century, a system was established in Spain based on the power of the crown and alternation between parties).

In comparison with the Spanish Civil War, Franco's dictatorship and the Transition to democracy, which are still heatedly discussed in public fora, the Restoration is studied in schools, only to be relegated to the recesses of memory. Thus, whereas Spanish history post-1931 remains mired in political controversy and debates over historical memory, the Restoration appears to be a safe, relatively peaceful and uneventful period, in spite of the localized violence of the final Carlist civil war, spurts of anarchist terrorism and colonial conflicts in the Caribbean, Philippines and North Africa that marked the 1874–1931 period. As a result, the Restoration becomes a floating signifier of sorts, onto which television producers and viewers might project present-day social concerns such as class conflict, gender norms and political divides. Working-class struggles, restrictive models of masculinity and especially femininity, and polarized political ideologies are common threads running through the majority of the series discussed in *Televising Restoration Spain*. To be sure, these issues likewise permeated the public consciousness during the Restoration itself, particularly toward its end, when public figures like politician Clara Campoamor clamored for women's suffrage, and the 1909 Tragic Week in Catalonia pitted striking workers against the Spanish Civil Guard in violent confrontation. Like Victorian England, then, Restoration Spain can be considered a birthplace of modernity, both in terms of the political and social problems that came to the fore, and the scientific and technological advances that were implemented. As Iris Kleinecke Bates states in *Victorians on Screen: The Nineteenth Century on British Television, 1994–2005*,

The period is both close to our own and associated with a perceived loss, a fall from grace, while the technological advances that mark the period and signal the birth of the modern industrial world create an ongoing affinity which denies the satisfaction of a clearly defined boundary between past and present. The resulting blurring of the margins of either means that the period is perceived as at once distant and modern. (2014, 5–6)

Although Bates speaks here of England's Victorian period, the Spanish Restoration could be described in similar terms. It, too, is perceived as simultaneously remote and proximate, such that audiences of Restoration period dramas can both recognize their roots in the society portrayed on-screen and appreciate how far Spain has come, particularly in terms of questions of social justice. This joint dynamic of audience identification and separation applies to many of the series we analyze here.

RESTORING THE RESTORATION

The Restoration as a historical setting and a source of adaptable stories for series and telefilms has been present on TVE almost from the moment public broadcast television was launched in Spain in 1956. By the end of the 1960s, as José Carlos Rueda Laffond and María del Mar Chicharro Merayo observe, TVE had become "una verdadera factoria de adaptaciones y traslaciones teatrales" (a veritable factory of adaptations and theatrical revivals) based on works of classic and contemporary literature (2006, 201). In program spaces reserved for fiction, most prominently *Estudio 1* (TVE 1965–1984) and *Novela* (TVE 1962–1979), the Golden Age figures large for obvious reasons, yet there is also an overwhelming presence of works by writers of the late-nineteenth and early-twentieth centuries, including Benito Pérez Galdós, Emilia Pardo Bazán, Pío Baroja and Ramón del Valle-Inclán. Cervantes and the authors of the *comedia* clearly fulfilled the requisites of heritage and the didactic mission of the public service broadcaster, whereas figures like Galdós, Juan Valera and Leopoldo Alas ("Clarín") more often than not offered stories suited for melodrama, which were readily made visually appealing through inexpensive costuming and set designs. Over the course of the decade, production values increased thanks to the incorporation of multiple cameras, more sophisticated mise-en-scène and the introduction of videotape editing, yet remained deficient by international standards (Rueda Laffond et al. 2006, 202). Indeed, as Luis Miguel Fernández notes, by the early 1970s the proliferation of series based on nineteenth-century novels with little technical innovation would contribute to the crisis experienced by Spanish television producers, who were unable to compete with the superior quality of offerings arriving from the USA and the UK (2014, 126).

The miniseries *La saga de los Rius* (TVE), filmed in 1975 but aired in 1976–1977, and based on Falangist writer Ignacio Agustí's pentalogy *La ceniza fue árbol*, established the paradigm for television serials in the 1970s and 1980s. Filmed in color and with high production values, the program continued the reliance on the format of the nineteenth-century novel established in the previous decade, as Fernández observes (2014, 194). Even so, Rueda Laffond suggests that, in the context of the Transition, the Restoration was evoked in television series as a generic setting for exploring the values of participative democracy (2009, 99). Between 1976 and 1982, television in Spain underwent a fundamental transformation in terms of mission, function and financing that parallels the vast political and social changes wrought by the transition to democracy. Changes in administration and legislation of TVE, Palacio points out, aligned the medium with the political process and positioned the entity to play an active role in the democratic socialization of the Spanish population (Palacio 2001). Citing the success of *Los gozos y las sombras* (TVE, 1982) and *La plaza del Diamante* (TVE, 1982), Palacio goes on to highlight the importance of productions that treat themes of the Civil War as evidence of TVE's explicit pedagogical mission to cement political cohesion and "incidir en el imaginario de hechos constitutivos de la vida colectiva contemporánea de los españoles" (Palacio 2002; influence the imaginary of constitutive acts of the Spaniards' contemporary collective life). While the predilection for the war and postwar period is undeniable in adaptations made for TVE after 1982, in the prime time slot reserved for miniseries, it is the Restoration that is revisited with the most consistency (Rueda Laffond 2009, 99). *La saga de los Rius*, along with adaptations of Vicente Blasco Ibáñez's *Cañas y barro* (TVE, 1978) and *La barraca* (TVE, 1979), Galdós's *Fortunata y Jacinta* (TVE, 1980), Juan Valera's *Juanita la larga* (TVE, 1982) and Emilia Pardo Bazán's *Los Pazos de Ulloa* (TVE, RAI, 1985), comprise a cycle of high-quality miniseries that, under the guise of bringing to life some of the great works of Spanish literature, recreate in a visually pleasing manner the sociopolitical milieu of the late nineteenth and early twentieth centuries. For Palacio, the primary contribution of these programs is the cultivation of a broader sense of the national past that resides primarily in the prestige of the original works and their authors in the literary heritage of the nation. However, as Carmen Peña Ardid and David George have studied, notwithstanding the consistency of the cycle and the types of novels chosen, these adaptations offered television viewers from the Transition through the 1980s something more than simply a dose of culture in the dulcified form of visually pleasing costume dramas (Peña Ardid 2010; George 2009, 2011). Under the guise of popularizing literary classics, these miniseries restore the social consciousness of the original Realist and Naturalist texts with the result of projecting the Restoration, in spite of its shortfalls, within a prehistory of liberalism and constitutional government in Spain.

From the second half of the 1980s to the early 2000s, the Restoration, in the form of literary adaptations and otherwise, disappeared from the small screen in the same measure that TVE lost audience share to regional broadcasters, private national channels and most recently streaming services. Certainly, the drift away from Realist novels as a source of history tracks political and social changes in the period: Rueda Laffond notes that, while the nineteenth century had served the purposes of the Transition by projecting pertinent issues of political socialization, following the electoral victory of the PSOE in 1982, attention progressively shifted to deal with more recent history, first the Civil War and then the Franco dictatorship and the process of democratization itself, as material for television historical fictions (2009, 98). No doubt, throughout the period of TVE's hegemony from 1956 until 1990, the treatment of history on television was in almost all cases an indirect effect of the public entity's foundational pedagogical mission. Yet, according to Palacio and Carmen Ciller, in the present context, television's mode of looking to the past is determined as much by altruistic goals as by the demands of the market, brand image, financing and ever-shifting patterns of consumption (2010, 38).

Changes in Spanish period dramas, indeed, reflect the global move away from the classic adaptation in the 1990s and the emergence of "quality" original series in the mid-2000s (De Groot 2016, 225). With certain exceptions, most notably the miniseries based on Alas's *La Regenta* (TVE, 1995) and Blasco Ibáñez's *Arroz y tartana* (TVE, Intercartel, 2004), the Restoration disappears as a setting for costume dramas until the 2008 premiere of *La señora* (Diagonal, TVE, 2008–2010). The aspiration to "quality," which historian Jerome De Groot deciphers as a generic "air of the adaptation," distinguishes the various *telenovelas,* miniseries and made-for-TV movies set in the Restoration that have debuted on Spanish television over the past ten years (2016, 235). The original teleplays produced by private producers Diagonal, Bambú and Boomerang in collaboration with national broadcasters TVE and Antena 3, as well as streaming services, purport to offer an authentic recreation of the past, yet because their primary goal is first and foremost to entertain, the treatment of history and historical detail are almost always a function of melodrama, as argued in many of the essays that follow.

The image of the Restoration resulting from the cycle of classic adaptations in the 1980s is tethered to the perceived pedagogical value of the source texts, but at the same time, these works and their authors represented a cultural heritage that begged to be recovered following 40 years of dictatorship. The act of vindication in the form of commemoration is a further determining factor of how the period has been re-presented on Spanish television. While it is true that the taste and marketability for literary adaptations of Realist novels has waned, the shift toward original scripts also reflects a progressive interest in the events of a century ago, based on the "centenary" as a generic commemorative marker. To a certain extent, what historian William Johnston describes as Europe's "cult of anniversaries" drives this recent television production in as much as it participates in a larger "commemoration industry" that coordinates across various entertainment and cultural sectors the events and figures of the past to be revisited as part of local, regional or national identity-building initiatives (1991, 63). For the most part, producers and writers of these recent television fictions have not ventured into the temporal territory already covered and recovered by the classic adaptations in the 1980s given that they fall outside the limits of the commemorable. The tendency, instead, has been to focus on the turn of the century, the reign of Alfonso XIII, and in particular, the decade of the 1920s. This is clearly reflected in the programs studied in the present volume: With the exception of *Bandolera* (Diagonal TV, 2011–2013) and *Víctor Ros* (New Atlantis, Telefónica Studios, TVE 2014–2016), all are set in the twentieth century and deal with aspects of the Restoration that have remained heretofore unknown and unfamiliar to audiences because they have yet to be the subject of commemoration.

Palacio and Ciller are correct to caution against the pitfalls of reading too much into the versions of the past offered by television when they affirm, "todo programa televisivo histórico es antes que nada televisión" (2010, 39). Even so, as Samuel Raphael posits, "television ought to have pride of place in any attempt to map the unofficial sources of historical knowledge" (1994, 15). Fictionalized histories on television, for all of their potential shortcomings, impact the popular imagination, determining the ways in which we think and learn about the past, as well as how "history" itself is constructed as a cultural production (De Groot 2016, 4). The prevalence of representations of the Restoration in programs like *El Ministerio del Tiempo* confirms that the period still matters, if only as a consumable object. The programs examined here reflect the fundamental paradigm shifts that have reconfigured the past as a commodity in a globalized entertainment industry. Great works of nineteenth-century literature have given way to intimate stories of everyday life in the past, and the authors of these texts are now more apt to appear on-screen as characters themselves.

NATIONAL TELEVISION IN A GLOBAL DEBATE

In his recent volume *Dramatized Societies: Quality Television in Spain and Mexico*, Paul Julian Smith contends that "Over the last decade Spain and Mexico have both produced an extraordinary wealth of television drama and are among the leaders in their respective continents" (2017, 1), yet most Hispanists at home and abroad have failed to recognize "that television has displaced cinema as the creative medium that shapes the national narrative" (3). Generally speaking, cinema still maintains an aura of cultural prestige denied to television production in the Spanish context, despite the fact that "the nightly audience for a single Spanish show. .. is greater than the annual audience for all Spanish feature films" (Smith 2007, 1). While Smith was thinking of the Spanish series *El comisario* (Bocaboca, Estudio Picasso, Telecinco, 1999–2009), his comments could well be generalized to many of the Restoration period dramas discussed in the present collection, which have ranged from moderately to spectacularly successful in terms of audience share. The relatively scant amount of academic publications dedicated to Spanish television series thus belies both the quantity and quality of programs on offer.

The essays collected in *Televising Restoration Spain*, then, seek to help address the critical silence surrounding Spanish television products, particularly period dramas. Within Spain, Manuel Palacio pioneered television studies with his *Historia de la televisión en España* (2001), but it is only in the past decade or so that the analysis of television content has provoked sustained interest in Spanish researchers, as evidenced by the 2006 creation of the research group Televisión y Cine: Memoria, Representación e Industria (TECMERIN). Led by Palacio, and based at the University of Carlos III in Madrid, the TECMERIN research group has examined such topics ranging from on-screen gender representations to Spain's audiovisual diversity (Grupo de Investigadores TECMERIN 2015). Nevertheless, this important body of work has largely been published in Spanish, thus limiting its audience and ability to enter into dialogue with media scholars elsewhere in Europe, the Americas and beyond.

As Smith notes in the introduction to *Dramatized Societies*, "even outside the US, TV studies and criticism are overwhelmingly biased toward US and English-language production" (2). In contrast, Spanish television is hardly referenced in English-language television studies, with Smith's work standing out as a notable exception. The general silence surrounding Spanish television becomes increasingly problematic in consideration of the growing international popularity of Spanish series. Broadcasting rights to the shows discussed in this volume have been sold around the globe, not to mention their success on international streaming services such as Netflix. Notably, of the twelve Spanish television series currently available on Netflix, three are set in Restoration Spain: *Gran Hotel* (*Grand Hotel*; Bambú, 2011–2013), *Las chicas del cable* (*Cable Girls*; Netflix, Bambú, 2017–) and *Tiempos de Guerra* (*Morocco: Love in Times of War*; Bambú, 2017–). As previously discussed, recent Netflix acquisition *El Ministerio del Tiempo* likewise engages episodically with the 1874–1931 period. This Netflix sampling is indicative of the plethora of recent original television offerings that depict the Restoration period, a corpus that has remained largely ignored in scholarly circles.

TELEVISING THE RESTORATION

As Villatoro's *ABC* quiz suggests, the Restoration has been ignored for too long. In Spain, it has been overshadowed by discussions of the Civil War and postwar society, and outside of Spain, non-Hispanists often have no concept of the Restoration at all. This volume then plays an important pedagogical role in introducing English-speaking audiences both to an important period of Spanish history and to the series that represent it on-screen. As such, it complements the flurry of recent publications centered around the televisual depiction of Victorian or Edwardian England (see, for instance, Bates 2014 or Byrne 2015) and allows for comparative study and discussion. This volume aids particularly in introducing Spanish-language series into the college classroom, whether it is in the context of Hispanic or media studies. In Spanish literature and culture courses, the series under study allow students to improve their listening comprehension skills while immersing themselves in the world of late nineteenth- and early twentieth-century Spain. Because so many Restoration-era authors are canonical staples of Spanish literature (such as the aforementioned Pérez Galdós, Pardo Bazán and Alas), assigning students episodes of television series set in the period can be an invaluable tool in promoting a more complete vision and comprehension of the Restoration as sociohistorical context. Additionally, these series, many of which are available with English subtitles, can be introduced into English-language courses on television or heritage cultural production to broaden the predominantly Anglo-centered focus of media studies and provide material for a more comprehensive, comparative analysis. For classroom usage, the essays collected in the present volume aid in focusing the study of each series, drawing out relevant aesthetic and cultural issues and questions for further debate.

To facilitate comparative discussions of the series studied in *Televising Restoration Spain*, chapters are divided into five parts that reflect similar themes and shared historical and theoretical concerns. Under the heading of "Producing Heritage," the two chapters of Part I discuss how diverse television programs designate the Restoration period and its posterior televisual depictions as "heritage." In "Fortunata's Long Shadow: the Restoration as Televisual Heritage in *Acacias 38* and *El secreto de Puente Viejo*," David George proposes a reading of afternoon costume serials *Acacias 38* (Boomerang TV, 2015–) and *El secreto de Puente Viejo* (Boomerang TV, 2015) as "heritage revival" in the sense that both bring the past back to life in a format that substitutes surface spectacle for historical knowledge. Understanding the possible significance of the late Restoration for contemporary audiences, he argues, involves a consideration of how *Acacias* and *Puente Viejo* revivify the period as televisual heritage. His "close-reading" of storytelling and historical references reveals how these daily serials appeal to collective memories of depictions of the period as preserved not only in canonical literary works, but also in their television adaptations created for TVE during the Transition and Post-Transition. In George's reading, the series of the late twentieth century, including Mario Camus's adaptation of *Fortunata y Jacinta* (TVE, 1980) and Fernando Méndez-Leite's *La Regenta* (TVE, 1995), ultimately comprise a televisual heritage that confers a seal of quality upon the twenty-first-century shows that reference them in terms of narrative or production.

In Chapter 2, "Profane Unions: Constructing Heritage from Anarchist-Bourgeois Romances in *Ull per ull* and *Barcelona, ciutat neutral*," Elena Cueto Asín turns to look at the construction of heritage in Catalonia. She critically examines the integration of anarchist history into Catalan heritage through the trope of anarchist-bourgeois romances in two Televisió de Catalunya (TV3) miniseries: *Ull per ull* (TVE, TV3, Roda y Rodar Cine y Televisión, 2010) and *Barcelona, ciutat neutral* (TV3, Radio e Televisão de Portugal, Stopline Films, 2011). In both dramas, set in 1919 and 1914, respectively, a rebellious child of Barcelona's industrial bourgeoisie renounces money and privilege to identify with the circumstances and ideology of an anarchist ennobled by a strong work ethic and filial piety. Although the two miniseries differ in their presentation of political and social struggles, Cueto proposes that both programs participate in a shared project of uncovering a heritage of social cohesion based on the union between two diametrically opposed forces in Catalan society of the late Restoration period. Cueto ultimately argues that these narratives mark anarchism as a historically defined and "museumizable" ideology, conveniently absorbed as national heritage, and so as available for incorporation into contemporary concepts of class and Catalan identity.

Similarly concerned with the way in which the past is packaged for present-day consumption, Part II "Imagining Technologies" examines the use of period technologies and modern-day media platforms to connect twenty-first-century viewers to on-screen depictions of the Restoration period. First, Mónica Barrientos Bueno and Ángeles Martínez García explore the Internet and social media's role in attracting, maintaining and educating audiences in "New Technologies and Transmedia Storytelling in *Víctor Ros*: Captivating Audiences at the Turn of the Century." From the authors' perspective, *Víctor Ros* stands out among other Restoration period dramas for its multimedia strategy. They argue that the series' creative team strategically deploys different media platforms such as Twitter or interactive websites to expand the world of protagonist Víctor and connect him to contemporary audiences by immersing viewers in the show's setting of turn-of-the-century

Madrid and Andalusia. Barrientos Bueno and Martínez García observe in particular the mix of authentic and fictional period materials featured across the various media, which they contend invites viewers to actively participate not only in following Víctor Ros on his adventures, but also in reconstructing Restoration history.

Technology is likewise the focus of Wan Sonya Tang's chapter, "From Photos to Forensics: Technology, Modernity, and the Internationalization of Spanish History in *Gran Hotel*." Here, she looks at the prominent role played by turn-of-the-century technologies within the narrative and staging of the international hit series *Gran Hotel* (*Grand Hotel*; Bambú Producciones, 2011–2013). From its initial episode, Tang observes that *Gran Hotel* is steeped in period-specific technology: Viewers are privy to the arrival of electricity to the hotel and later witness such developments as cinematography, psychoanalysis and the use of forensics in law enforcement. As she argues, the prominent role played by these advances within the series extends beyond that of the plot device. Instead, period technology serves to familiarize global audiences with Restoration Spain in three key ways: firstly, by refuting the long-standing stereotype of Spain as a historically backward nation; secondly, by highlighting universally familiar themes of Restoration society, such as class conflict or the modernizing impulse; and finally, by appealing to twenty-first-century technophiles who recognize the indispensable role played by technological innovation in our everyday lives. Tang ultimately concludes that through these three functions, the technology featured in *Gran Hotel* serves to present the Restoration period as a universally appealing setting, particularly in visual terms.

Turning from the material advances of the period and their consumption in the present, the chapters in Part III "Constructing Genders" look at the way in which series set in the Restoration represent the era's shifting gender dynamics from a contemporary perspective. Both authors concur that the period is largely characterized by gender inequity, but nevertheless recognize that it marks the birth of Spain's modern feminist movement. In "Dresses, Cassocks, and Coats: Costuming Restoration Gender Fantasies in *La Señora*," Nicholas Wolters analyzes the wardrobe used to "dress up" the protagonists and narrative of TVE's award-winning series *La Señora (2008–2010)*. As Wolters argues, the show reanimates the 1920s in the form of well-established gender tropes like the fashionable heiress and the enamored priest canonized in texts like Leopoldo Alas's novel *La Regenta*. By focusing on mise-en-scène and dialogues with Restoration texts, Wolters concludes that the TVE period drama candidly transforms nineteenth- and early twentieth-century aesthetics to satisfy the expectations of its twenty-first-century audiences. However, as the author contends, even while *La Señora* revises and reimagines stereotypical Restoration gender tropes, the show's creators still nostalgically embrace their literary–visual precedents.

Linda Willem also explores the tensions between historical accuracy and presentism in "'Las normas son para romperlas': Emilia Pardo Bazán, Carmen de Burgos, and the Unruly Women of *Seis Hermanas*." In this chapter, Willem examines how the daily serial *Seis hermanas* (Bambú Producciones, 2015–2017), set in Madrid from 1913 through 1916, draws on the lives and writings of two of the era's strongest proponents of women's rights, authors Emilia Pardo Bazán and Carmen de Burgos, to explore the social and legal situation of women in Restoration society, and to raise such issues as gender and class barriers, spousal abuse, infidelity, divorce and lesbianism. Exploring this intertextuality, she contends that the writings of Pardo Bazán and Burgos justify the transgressive actions of the fictional sisters as they defy social and legal norms in pursuit of personal freedom and self-actualization. She furthermore argues that these women writers serve as a bridge to today's television viewer whose twenty-first-century perspective validates Pardo Bazán and Burgos's feminist ideas that were once considered radical but are now accepted.

The two contributions gathered in Part IV "Restoring the *Telenovela*" examine the generative potential of the Restoration as a period to which producers turn in an effort to renew, reinvigorate and nationalize the formulaic Latin American genre of the *telenovela*. In "*Bandolera*: Limits and Possibilities of Period *Telenovelas*," Francisca López establishes connections between *Bandolera* (Diagonal TV, 2011–2013), set in late nineteenth-century Andalusia, and the evolution of the *telenovela* genre within the global entertainment market of the twenty-first century. She identifies the ideological thrust—liberal social politics—driving the story as well as conspicuous thematic parallels between the time represented (1882–1887) and that of the show's broadcast (2011–2013). López demonstrates that while the Restoration setting provides a credible background for the *bandolero* theme and drives some narrative arcs, *Bandolera* does not engage the past significantly. Instead, she argues, the past functions mostly as a visually appealing backdrop for traditional *telenovela* conflicts that draw large audiences, securing marketability for the product.

In "Creating Locally for a Global Audience: *Seis hermanas* and the Costume Serial Drama as Quality Television," Concepción Cascajosa Virino concurs with López's assessment of the visual appeal of the Restoration as a contributing factor to the marketability of period serials. Like Willem, Cascajosa also studies *Seis hermanas* (Bambú Producciones, 2015–2017) with an eye on gender issues, but considers the program more broadly as a case study of a new kind of "quality" daily serial that looks to British heritage dramas as a reference for fusing the conventions of melodrama with the production values of a prime-time series, largely contingent upon historically accurate mise-en-scène. She additionally examines how the local production context determines its treatment of the historical period, altering British models to reflect a progressive vision of social change, which contributed to the show's popularity among the LGBTQ community.

In Part V, "Sensing the Ending," the final three chapters of the volume evaluate how series have depicted the end of the Restoration by reflecting on the progress (or lack thereof) made during the period in terms of political and social change. In "Commercializing Nostalgia and Constructing Memory in *As leis de Celavella*," María Gil Poisa discusses a Galician production set in a rural town in the 1920s during the dictatorship of Miguel Primo de Rivera. The series *As leis de Celavella* (TVG, Voz Audiovisual, 2003–2004) deploys the tropes of the detective, fantastic and period drama genres to construct a nostalgic vision of the late Restoration that, according to Gil Poisa, resonates with modern Galician audiences through an appeal to regional identity. Focusing on the portrayal of a typical Galician community as immutable in spite of changing times and technologies, Gil Poisa further analyzes the appearance of a sympathetic young Francisco Franco on the show, concluding that the series establishes a fictitious continuum between the late Restoration and Francoism, building a new, manipulated collective memory for television audiences.

Leslie Harkema's chapter, "'*Felices años veinte?*': *Las chicas del cable* and the Iconicity of 1920s Madrid," likewise examines the televisual representation of the Primo de Rivera dictatorship. However, rather than a regional production with a rural setting, Harkema delves into the first Spanish Netflix original series, set on the bustling streets of Madrid. In her analysis, Harkema compares *Las chicas del cable* (Bambú Producciones, Netflix, 2017–) with the dominant image of 1920s Madrid preserved in Spanish cultural memory as associated with the mostly male Generation of 1927 and the ideas of modernity, experimentation, liberation and transgression. Harkema argues that, unlike other recent Spanish dramas, the Netflix original engages critically with the historiographical representation of the period in which it is set, subverting the mythologization of a decade often remembered as the last, idyllic moment of cultural openness before the Spanish Civil War. By depicting pervasive sexism, domestic violence and the precarious political order of the 1920s in Spain alongside references to the elite cultural circles most commonly associated with these years, *Las chicas del cable* offers a new perspective that complicates Spanish culture's nostalgia for *"los felices años veinte"* (Spain's so-called Happy Twenties).

Whereas Gil Poisa and Harkema discuss the final moments of the Restoration, Iván Gómez García offers a retrospective evaluation of the period in "The End of the Restoration: A Vision from the Early Second Republic in *14 de abril. La República.*" In this chapter, Gómez questions the historical accuracy of the short-lived series *14 de abril. La República* (Diagonal TV, 2011), whose second season was never broadcast in spite of solid viewer ratings. Gómez discusses the show's various characters largely as stock types inherited from the Restoration era: the landowner, the anarchist or the military man, among others, and examines the reaction of each to the proclamation of the Spanish Second Republic. As Gómez asserts, the show portrays the Republic as plagued by the Restoration's legacy of unresolved problems and political and social divisions. He concludes that whereas the Restoration is generally romanticized on television, the Republic continues to be seen as problematic, both for the series' characters and for some modern audiences.

Salient in the last three essays of the volume is how assessments of the social, political and cultural legacies of the Restoration are a function of regional, national and global broadcast contexts and the politics mandating the television marketplace in Spain from 2000 to 2017. Although the series studied engage with historic happenings of the period to differing degrees, all authors acknowledge a common impulse to view the period as synonymous with glamour and intrigue. Indeed, what these eleven chapters jointly demonstrate is that the Restoration still beckons to twenty-first century audiences, be it as part of a national origin story, as an era of social growth or technological modernization, or simply as a beautiful backdrop. As the setting of daily serials, miniseries, and dramas, the Restoration invites reflection on Spain's political and cultural evolution (or lack thereof), the establishment of feminism, and the appearance of new social classes, political parties and interest groups. In its many contradictions and complexities, the Restoration remains a generating matrix for new and novel television productions.

BIBLIOGRAPHY

Byrne, Katherine. 2015. *Edwardians on Screen: From Downton Abbey to Parade's End*. New York: Palgrave Macmillan.

De Groot, Jerome. 2016. *Consuming History: Historians and Heritage in Contemporary Popular Culture*. New York: Routledge.

Fernández, Luis Miguel. 2014. *Escritores y televisión durante el Franquismo (1956–1975)*. Salamanca: Ediciones Universidad de Salamanca.

George, David R., Jr. 2009. "Restauración y Transición en la Fortunata y Jacinta de Mario Camus." In *Historias de la pequeña pantalla: Representaciones históricas en la televisión de la España democrática*, edited by Francisca López, Elena Cueto Asín, and David R. George, Jr., 53–71. Frankfurt: Iberoamericana.

————. 2011. "Cañas y barro de Vicente Blasco Ibáñez: La adaptación oportuna." *Hispania* 94: 577–588.

Grupo de Investigación Tecmerin. 2015. *Tecmerin.es*. Accessed February 21, 2018.

Johnston, William. 1991. *Celebrations: The Cult of Anniversaries in Europe and the United States Today*. New Brunswick: Transaction.

Kleinecke-Bates, Iris. 2014. *Victorians on Screen: The Nineteenth Century on British Television, 1994–2005*. New York: Palgrave Macmillan.

Palacio, Manuel. 2001. *Historia de la televisión en España*. Barcelona: Gedisa.

Palacio, Manuel. 2002. "Notas para una comprensión sinóptica de la televisión en la transición democrática." *Área Abierta* 3 (July): 1–6. https://revistas.ucm.es/index.php/ARAB/article/view/ARAB0202230004A. Accessed February 27, 2018.

Palacio, Manuel, and Carmen Ciller. 2010. "La mirada televisiva del pasado. El caso español (2005–2010)." In *Memoria histórica e identidad en cine y televisión*, edited by Juan Carlos Ibáñez and Francesca Anania, 38–58. Seville: Comunicación Social.

Peña Ardid, Carmen. 2010. "Las primeras grandes series literarias de la Transición: 'La saga de los Rius' y 'Cañas y barro'." In *Televisión y literatura en la España de la transición (1973-1982)*, edited by Antonio Ansón Anadón, 71–96. Zaragoza: Institución "Fernando el Católico".

Pimental, Aurelo. 2017. "Las diez cosas que España no tendría si Alfonso XII hubiera muerto en el atentado de *El Ministerio del Tiempo*." http://www.rtve.es/television/20170706/diez-cosas-espana-no-tendria-si-alfonso-xii-hubiera-muerto-atentado-ministerio-del-tiempo/1575827.shtml.   Accessed February 27, 2018.

Rueda Laffond, José Carlos. 2009. "¿Reescribiendo la historia?: Una panorámica de la ficción histórica televisiva española reciente." *ALPHA* 29 (December): 84–104.

Rueda Laffond, José Carlos, and María del Mar Chicharro Merayo. 2006. *La televisión en España, 1956–2006: política, consumo y cultura televisiva*. Madrid: Fragua.

Rueda Laffond, José Carlos, and Carlota Coronado Ruiz. 2016. "Historical Science Fiction: From Television Memory to Transmedia Memory in El Ministerio del Tiempo." *Journal of Spanish Cultural Studies* 17, 1: 87–101.

Samuel, Raphael. 1994. *Theatres of Memory*. London: Verso.

Smith, Paul Julian. 2007. "Introduction: New Approaches to Spanish Television." *Journal of Spanish Cultural Studies* 8, no. 1: 1–4. https://doi.org/10.1080/14636200601148710. Accessed February 21, 2018.

———. 2017. *Dramatized Societies: Quality Television in Spain and Mexico*. Liverpool: Liverpool University Press.

Villatoro, Manuel P. 2014. "¿Aprobarías un examen de la Restauración borbónica?" *ABC.es*, November 15. http://www.abc.es/vuelta-al-cole/20141125/abci-vuelta-cole-restauracion-borbonica-201411241557_1.html. Accessed February 22, 2018.

PART I

Producing Heritage

Fortunata's Long Shadow: The Restoration as Televisual Heritage in *Acacias 38* and *El Secreto de Puente Viejo*

David R. George, Jr.

In the summer of 2017, actor–singer Ana Belén addressed a group of scholars during the inaugural session of the XI Congreso Galdosiano, a conference dedicated to the study of the literature of Realist novelist Benito Pérez Galdós in Las Palmas, Gran Canaria. The iconic celebrity of the Transition recalled the experience of playing Fortunata in the 1980 Televisión Española (TVE) adaptation of Galdós's *Fortunata y Jacinta*, insisting on the continued relevance of the author and his novels as a rich source of material for twenty-first-century dramas (Hernández 2017).[1] The actor's comments were tinged with nostalgia for the period between 1978 and 1982 when miniseries based on works of Spanish literature figured prominently in the public broadcaster's program schedule and played a part in the consolidation of democracy. Her words also rang pessimistic when she contrasted the "quality" programing of the past with that of the present, echoing the disdain for Spanish television

D. R. George, Jr. (✉)
Bates College, Lewiston, ME, USA
e-mail: dgeorge@bates.edu

© The Author(s) 2018
D. R. George, Jr. and W. S. Tang (eds.),
Televising Restoration Spain,
https://doi.org/10.1007/978-3-319-96196-5_2

often voiced by intellectuals on the Left. The panegyric reaffirmation of Galdós's relevance as a narrator of contemporary Spanish society is indisputable, yet the idea that his works have been overlooked as potential sources for television fictions in the new century ignores the very impact of her own performance celebrated by scholars at the conference. The fact that the appearance was covered in the press as if Fortunata herself had come to inaugurate the event, evidences the extent to which the 1980 television miniseries, more than the 1887 novel, has come to be inscribed in Spain's popular cultural heritage and continues to function as a point of reference for depictions of the Restoration period.

At the 2014 Vitoria FesTVal, private broadcaster Antena 3 (Atresmedia) announced the project for a remake of TVE's *Fortunata y Jacinta* in collaboration with BoomerangTV (El Mundo 2014).[2] The "update" of the series based on Galdós's masterpiece has yet to materialize; however, the report is sufficient to associate Boomerang and its other productions set in the Restoration with the benchmark for "quality" adaptation and historical authenticity established by the classic miniseries (Antena 3 2014). In 2014, on the eve of the airing of episode 300 of *El secreto de Puente Viejo*, produced for Antena 3 by Boomerang, the station's webpage feted the milestone with a gloss of the show's impressive audience statistics and high production values. The program's success is attributed to a meticulous set design and elaborate wardrobe, including costumes apparently used in earlier period dramas, including a previous version of *Fortunata y Jacinta* (Antena 3 2014).[3] The following spring, ahead of the premiere of TVE's *Acacias 38*, Boomerang producer Luis Santamaria summarized the primary source material and inspiration for the new afternoon serial by affirming, "aquí hay mucho de *Fortunata y Jacinta*" (RTVE 2015; there is a lot of *Fortunata and Jacinta* here). In the same interview, co-producer and writer Josep Cister describes how the series relies on Galdós novels like *Fortunata y Jacinta* or *Misericordia*, and other turn-of-the-century works by Emilia Pardo Bazán and Vicente Blasco Ibáñez to maintain the tone of the period (RTVE 2015). Although Cister and Santamaria emphasize the influence of literature, the mention of Realist novelists more vividly taps associations derived not from books, but rather from their television adaptations.

The insistence on connecting *Acacias 38* and *El secreto de Puente Viejo* to the Restoration by way of earlier televisual representations of the time uncovers how both function as a revised mode of heritage television. Unlike the 1980s adaptations in which prestigious literary sources and historical settings fulfilled a dual mission to inform and entertain with the purpose of recovering a heritage repressed under the Franco dictatorship, it can be argued that the two recent series bring the past-as-heritage back to life in a format that privileges surface spectacle over deeper historical understanding. The possible significance of the Restoration as a useable past for contemporary audiences, I contend, involves a consideration of how *Acacias* and *Puente Viejo* revivify the Restoration not as history but as a part of what can be called televisual heritage. Through the examination of aspects of plot development and engagement with the past common to both afternoon serials, in this chapter I analyze how both appeal to collective memories of the television series set in the late nineteenth and early twentieth centuries created in the Transition and Post-Transition (1975–1992).[4]

TELEVISION AS HERITAGE

Historian David Lowenthal points out that heritage is "not an inquiry into the past, but a celebration of it... a profession of faith in a past tailored to present-day purposes" (1985, x). Heritage is a discourse projected through a variety of cultural products and practices that, as Eckart Voigt-Virchow describes, "re-establish the past as a property or possession, which... 'belongs' to... certain interests or concerns in the present" (2007, 123). It is therefore unequivocally national and political in its underlying intention to identify and preserve a stable and "desirable past" (Voigt-Virchow 2007, 123). In the field of television studies, the concept has evolved as a critical genre category used to describe historical fictions as well as costume dramas and literary adaptations that convey a nostalgic image of the past that stands in for actual historical knowledge or understanding of periods or figures represented (Vidal 2012, 1). Such programming is generally marked by high production values, historicity, and period authenticity and replicates the formal narrative conventions of the classic Realist text derived largely from the nineteenth-century novel. Sarah Cardwell emphasizes how affect and emotions in the form of nostalgia are deployed as the primary mechanism of engagement between audiences and the story and past represented in television series (2002, 142). In the heritage context, production design, mise-en-scène, and storytelling are combined to create an overall mood of nostalgia that elicits not a desire to return to the past, but rather a more complex reflection on it as something separate from the audience's present-day collective self (Cardwell 2002, 203).

In 2009, on the occasion of its fiftieth anniversary, Radio Televisión Española (RTVE) announced the release of thirteen "classic series" on its "A la carta" streaming platform. The press note announces: "Las series clásicas de Televisión Española, que forman parte de nuestra memoria colectiva, podrán verse a partir de ahora, de manera gratuita y permanente, en Rtve.es" (Rtve.es 2009; Televisión Española's classic series, which form a part of our collective memory, can now be seen free of cost and permanently on Rtve.es). In effect, the broadcaster reclaims the collection of miniseries produced in the Transition and Post-Transition and based on "classic" works of Spanish literature, like *Fortunata y Jacinta*, or depicting the lives of cultural icons, such as Miguel de Cervantes, as heritage by asserting their central place in the collective memory.[5] The categorization of these programs as "heritage television," strictly along the lines of similar British serials made in the conservative climate of the 1980s, may be difficult given the distinct Spanish production context marked by the political and social changes of the democratic Transition. Nonetheless, the essential qualities of the "heritage aesthetic"—nostalgia, fidelity, and quality—are easily identified in their repackaging as part of a shared past for consumption in the present (Cardwell 2002, 112). The advertising campaign announcing the earlier DVD release of the same group of series in 2002 promises a new way to enjoy great actors and directors in high budget productions that "han hecho historia" (have made history). The collection of programs clearly combines the qualities of the typical heritage production—a prestigious literary or historical source text, a cast of well-known actors, a veteran director, and high production values—and establishes the prestige of the TVE brand. However, also apparent is the way in which these "classic series" come to represent a desirable televisual past, dominated by the public service broadcaster as the sole source of "quality" television programing.

FOLLETÍN AS HERITAGE

Randolph Popes suggests that through the recurring character of crackpot *folletín* (feuilleton) writer José Ido del Sagrario, Galdós distances his fiction from other inferior forms of writing such that his version of the well-tread plot of *Fortunata y Jacinta* appears to be more real (2003, 217). Likewise, the desire to produce "quality" television for an emerging democratic polity in the Transition similarly imbued the literary adaptation with an aura of superiority over other kinds of television programming available at that time. Jerome De Groot points out that classic serial adaptations possess an instant cultural value conferred by the source material, and in the case of the UK's BBC, functioned "to establish the cultural hegemony and standing of the channel" (2016, 224). The same might be said of the adaptions produced by TVE in the late 1970s, which established the public broadcaster's reputation for "quality" that continues to this day. The announcement of the Antena 3 new adaptation of *Fortunata y Jacinta* emphasizes the prestige of the source novel as one of Galdós's best and most popular works and highlights its status as representative of Realism in Spain (Antena 3 2014). Clearly, by alluding to the project as "una actualización" (an update), the primary source text is both the 1880s novel and the 1979 television adaptation. The connection is subtle, but nonetheless present, such that placement of the description of the project on the station's website redoubles the status of the private channel's push to compete with TVE.[6]

The press release for Antena 3's *Fortunata y Jacinta* remake summarizes the plotline as one telling the story of the love of two women from different social classes for the same man (Antena 3 2014). Outwardly, the description would appear to betray the aspiration to "quality" by punctuating the melodramatic appeal of the literary and televisual source material, though it can be argued that this is precisely the intention of the broadcaster: The association between the remake and the original is extended to other similar costume dramas set in the same period and that rely on a similar mode of storytelling. In the spirit of the original TVE adaptation, the update promises to be a faithful recreation of the historic novel in terms of plot; however, from the outset, it appears to reduce the potential for a deeper engagement with the historical period to surface features that translate into mere elements of melodrama rather than social critique. Melodrama and the serialized format of the *folletín*, however, are also relics of the cultural heritage of the nineteenth century that persist in contemporary culture through the form of the *telenovela*.

The dramatic premises of *Acacias 38* and *El secreto de Puente Viejo* echo *Fortunata y Jacinta*: The subtitle of the Galdós novel "Dos historias de casadas" (two stories of married women) could be attached equally to the two serials. *Acacias* originates with the confrontation between the lower-class Carmen Blasco (Sheyla Fariña), alias "Manuela Manzano" who escapes an abusive marriage by fleeing to Madrid and changing her name. Like Fortunata, Manuela also bears a child, which she is forced to put up for adoption in order to save herself. Upon arriving in the capital, Manuela crosses paths with the upper-class Cayetana Sotelo-Ruz (Sara Miquel) when she becomes involved with the lady's husband, Doctor Germán de la Selma (Roger Berruezo). The foundling narrative pattern structures Manuela's search for her lost child and also explains Cayetana's malicious acts, which include killing her own child, when it is revealed that she herself was adopted by an aristocratic family. *Puente* also begins with the rivalry between two women: Midwife Pepa Aquirre (Megan Montaner) and Doña Francisca Montenegro (María Bouzas), the widow of the local *cacique*, clash when the former becomes involved with the latter's son Tristán Ulloa (Álex Gadea). Here too, the central conflict turns around children begotten from a tangle of illicit affairs that cut across class boundaries. The anguish of maternal loss, which ultimately creates a space of understanding between Fortunata and Jacinta in Galdós's novel, in the twenty-first-century soap opera becomes a continuous source of antagonism between female characters that persists through various generations and renews each television season.

The narrative arcs of both Boomerang series are multiple and sprawling and reflect the *telenovela* format that both exploit to capture audience share in the competitive after-lunch time slot. However, while *Acacias* and *Puente Viejo* certainly make use of many tropes derived from the Latin American soap opera, it can be argued that both more purposefully replicate the kind of literature Galdós and his contemporaries sought to undermine through their embrace of Realism: the *folletín*. The logic driving the stories of both series is very similar to the market-oriented storytelling practiced by Ido del Sagrario in Galdós's novel: After the filming of episode 1000, *Puente Viejo* creator Aurora Guerra admitted the ending had yet to be planned and that it would continue for as long as commercially viable (Figueroa 2015). The openness of the multiple-episode serial is fundamentally different from the formal unity sustained by the closed structure of the miniseries format of the classic adaptation, where the beginning and ending are predetermined by the source text. Plot development in *Puente Viejo* and *Acacias* is largely a function of positive audience ratings, and as a result, the conflicts that set both dramas in motion have been resolved and absorbed into new tensions at the macrolevel as their respective networks have renewed contracts and purchased additional blocs of episodes.

At over 1700 episodes, *Puente Viejo* is the longest running series in the history of Spanish television (Antena 3 2017).[7] The story, set in an invented rural locale in northwestern Spain, begins in 1902 and continues through the late 1920s. Since its debut in February 2011, the plot has evolved through nine multi-episode arcs, each built around revelations, that is, *secretos* (secrets), about the past and present lives of characters. On the macrolevel, the town and its residents ground the multiple subplots and lend continuity and coherence to the groupings of episodes into seasons, while the character arc of Doña Francisca and her lifelong pining for Raimundo Ulloa (Ramón Ibarra)—her first love—vertebrates the overarching story line, as all intrigues eventually lead back to her. The conniving "cacica" (female *cacique*) is cast from the same literary mold as Galdós's Doña Perfecta of the eponymous 1876 novel and recalls the malicious Angela Channing of the globally popular 1980s US series *Falcon Crest* (Antena 3, 2011–2013).[8] The story line that runs through the first and second seasons, titled "Pepa, la partera" and "La verdad de Gonzalo," respectively, indeed shares many plot points with *Doña Perfecta*, but also taps the audience's familiarity with other nineteenth-century texts derived from televisual adaptations. While the likenesses are too many to list, a few examples illustrate the point. In terms of setting, the town and, particularly, Doña Francisca's manor house recall that of Gonzalo Suaréz's 1985 televisual rendering of *Los Pazos de Ulloa*. At the level of story, the character arcs of Doña Francisca's daughter Soledad (Alejandra Onieva), and her granddaughter María Castañeda (Loreto Lauleón), each evoke aspects of Galdós's Rosario from *Doña Perfecta*, but also bear similarities to Nucha (Victoria Abril) in *Los Pazos*, as well as Ana Ozores (Aitana Sánchez-Gijón) in Fernando Méndez-Leite's version of Leopoldo Alas's *La Regenta*, and Pepita (Tina Sanz) in the 1978 adaptation of Juan Valera's *Pepita Jiménez* (TVE). In the same grain, the handsome priest Gonzalo (Jordi Coll) is strikingly similar in appearance to Luis (Jaime Blanch) in the TVE version of the Valera novel, not to mention Fermín de Pas (Carmelo Gómez) from *La Regenta*, and also recalls the more recent figuration of the priest Ángel (Rodolfo Sancho) in TVE's *La señora* (Diagonal, TVE, 2008–2010).

On a more modest scale, *Acacias* clocked more than 700 episodes after three seasons on the air. The plot begins in 1899 and has evolved more or less in real time, through three phases centered on intersecting character arcs that converge around the vengeful machinations of Cayetana. If Doña Francisca is a Spanish Angela Channing, then Cayetana is the Alexis Carrington, the female villain of 1980s evening soap *Dynasty* that Deo Aquilar of *Harper's Bazaar Spain* calls "la mejor *bitch* de la historia" (Aguilar 2016; the best bitch in history).[9] Like her American televisual model, her scheming carries the plot from the pilot episode until her fiery death in episode 576, and her trail of destruction continues to structure the story from beyond the grave.[10] Like *Puente Viejo*, the narrative arc of *Acacias* is anchored in an invented space indicated by the title. Here, the modern upscale apartment building on Acacias Street and the surrounding businesses constitute the nasty protagonist's field of operations. The spatial configuration of the neighborhood is typical of the fin-de-siècle *ensanches* (expansions) that reorganized the urban spaces of most Spanish cities and provides a contained fictional space that facilitates the introduction of new characters into the story line as neighbors. Whereas *Puente Viejo* references classic television serials through individual character arcs and characterization, *Acacia* evokes televisual heritage through production design and mise-en-scène. The combination of street and interior scenes where the action unfolds sequentially, instead of simultaneously as in conventional telenovelas, recalls the rendition of late-1860s Madrid created for Camus's *Fortunata*. In a very similar manner, the street is populated by extras engaged in the routines of daily life in turn-of-the-century Madrid and functions as a place for encounters among characters from different social classes; the key relationships of the first season, between Manuela and Germán, and Leonor Hidalgo (Alba Brunet) and Pablo Blasco (Carlos Serrano-Clark), have their plausible starts on the sidewalk. Interior scenes, by contrast, take viewers into the public and private spaces mostly frequented or inhabited by the bourgeoisie and middle-class residents. The Viuda de Selér tailor shop and La Deliciosa café, where the neighbors gossip, recalls the businesses visited in the televised *Fortunata y Jacinta*, while the homes clearly evoke the likes of the Santa Cruz residence or the humbler abodes of Evaristo Feijoo or Maxi Rubín as portrayed on-screen.

The story line of Galdós's novel is focused and contained: In spite of its length—the four-volume first edition comprised almost 1800 pages— and large number of characters, the story line follows Fortunata's struggle, and how her life and death impacts Jacinta and her husband, Juanito. The same is true of the ten-episode miniseries: Mercedes López-Baralt praises the strict fidelity of the series to the novel and the author's originality, as triumphs over the dangers posed by the process of televisual adaptation to the literariness of the Realist masterpiece (1993, 98). The sentiment echoes the critical recognition of Galdós's artistry itself as a victory of verisimilitude over imagination as the most expeditious way to overcome the purely narrative form of the popular *folletín* (Martí 2003, 67). Similar to how the Realist novel displaces mere storytelling by privileging aesthetic presentation, so too the classic television adaptation attempts to offer more than a televisual rendering of the plot of the source text through the careful reconstruction of the historical period.

According to De Groot, classic serial adaptations convey knowledge about the past by relying on the viewers' acceptance of the narrative as fiction while embracing the mise-en-scène and historical setting as truth (2016, 255). The case of the literary adaptation is, in essence, very simple because the fictional component is historic rather than historical: Even though Galdós's novel is set almost 20 years before the time of composition, *Fortunata y Jacinta* is to be taken as a truthful representation of present-day Spanish society (George 2009, 58). With the narrative firmly grounded in the past, the only challenge the adapter faces, then, is the careful reconstruction of the period represented in the source text. By contrast, costume dramas based on adaptation of contemporary historical novels as well as original scripts written for television lack the gravitas instilled by a prestigious historic source text (De Groot 2016, 225). Thus, whereas the authenticity and historicity of fictional narratives derived from classic works of literature stand unquestioned, costume dramas must employ alternative strategies in order to achieve a similar level of perceived historical accuracy in both narrative and mise-en-scène. As the recent worldwide success of the British series *Downton Abbey* (Carnival Films, Masterpiece, 2010–2015) has proven, the issue can be solved by adopting "an air of the classic adaptation" in terms of production values, and through the deployment of similar generic narrative tropes and formulas (De Groot 2016, 225). *Downton Abbey*'s period setting and the plotline built around master–servant relationships invited comparison with the popular 1970s drama *Upstairs, Downstairs* (London Weekend Television, 1971–1975).[11] Ahead of the debut of *Acacias*, Boomerang producers cite both *Upstairs, Downstairs* and *Downton Abbey* as key points of references for the narrative and visual "universe" they sought to create (RTVE 2015). The director of *Puente Viejo* follows suit by citing the influence of the nineteenth-century novel, and in particular Galdós, on the construction of the plot: "la idea era hacer un folletín clásico" (Dufour 2012; the idea was to create a classic *folletín*).[12] The Boomerang creative teams behind both series limit mention of Spanish influences to nineteenth-century literature without acknowledging the 1980s television adaptations. They also elide obvious comparisons with contemporary television series set in the Restoration and structured around the relationship between masters and servants in an environment dominated by a powerful woman, such as *Gran Hotel* (Bambú Producciones, 2011–2013) or *La Señora*. However, if the goal is to imbue *Acacias* and *Puente Viejo* with an aura of "quality" in order to appeal to a young audience perhaps unfamiliar with Spanish miniseries of the 1970s and 1980s, it is logical to aspire to the production values of British series, which continue to set the global standard for period dramas.

Originally, *Puente Viejo* was conceived as a weekly evening prime-time drama, but was transformed into a daily after-lunch serial at the behest of the broadcaster, and the change meant a complete overhaul of the plot and subplots in order to sustain the narrative and dramatic rhythm (Dufour 2012). The description of *Puente Viejo* as "folletín clásico" reflects how an early nineteenth-century mode for distributing literature to a burgeoning mass readership has eventually come to be considered a genre in its own right (Martí 2003, 68). Indeed, in contemporary usage, *folletín* refers to any type of serialized melodrama, whether for television, literature, cinema, or theater. Yet, by connecting *Puente Viejo* to Galdós and the *folletín* via the notion of the "classic," Guerrero seems to want to ground the series in the cultural heritage of the Restoration. At the same time, if the word "classic" describes a foundational moment that sets the standard for subsequent artistic productions, then the category of "folletín clásico" also refers to the tradition of the "quality" miniseries.

Literary critics are careful to recognize and then distance Galdós and Alas from the *folletín* as a genre by observing that their works were published in the slightly less nefarious *por entregas* format, either chapter by chapter or in several parts. As already mentioned, scholars also emphasize how these nineteenth-century writers implicitly and explicitly criticize the popular literary form through characters who are engaged in this kind of writing, such as Ido del Sagrario or Petra in *La Regenta*. It is doubtful that Guerrero and his colleagues had in mind that several of Galdós's novels, including *Doña Perfecta*, were first published in serialized format; however, the mere mention of the author in the context of Puente Viejo seems sufficient to connect the series to the main plot points and structural elements of the 1876 novel that lent the work to serialization. Victor Manuel Amela, television critic for *La Vanguardia*, makes the connection explicit in his review of the pilot episode of *Puente Viejo* when he describes the program as a potent cocktail of clichés and archetypes common to both the *folletín* and the writings of Pardo Bazán, Alas, Galdós, and Pedro Antonio de Alarcón (2011, 11). By collapsing the categories of high and low culture of the Restoration period, the critic exposed how the two are combined in the construction of Spanish televisual heritage, and illuminates the way in which Realist literature has come to be associated with the *folletín* by virtue of its early and frequent serialization for television. *Puente Viejo*, and *Acacias*, taps a longer tradition of costume drama on Spanish television that is directly connected to the way in which images, stories, and the history of the Restoration have been transmitted to viewers via weekly programs from the 1960s, like *Novela*, which presented mostly literary adaptations.[13] The format no doubt opened the way for the classic miniseries of the 1970s by providing Spanish television audiences with the necessary viewing experience and familiarity with the narrative tropes of nineteenth-century literature to gauge truthfulness in terms of period reconstruction and fidelity to the source material.

A similar connection to the *folletín* as cultural heritage is made to *Acacias*: TVE director for fiction programming Fernando Puig López describes the series as, "una telenovela que tiene la vocación de folletín decimonónico" (Agencia EFE 2015; a *telenovela* [soap opera] with a vocation to be a nineteenth-century *folletín*). Significant here is the identification of the "original" nineteenth-century *folletín* as the standard to which *Acacias* aspires and how the connection functions to distance the new series from the *telenovela* of Latin American origin with which it was designed to compete for audience acceptance in the afternoon time slot. While in *Puente Viejo* the link to the *folletín* is never made explicit in the plot, in *Acacias* both high and low forms of the nineteenth-century novel are central to the drama in the first season, when the young Leonor Hidalgo (Alba Brunet) first appears seated on a street bench reading *La Regenta*. The scene provides a literary context and narrative frame for the love-at-first-sight encounter with shop clerk Pablo Blasco (Carlos Serrano-Clark). The love story between the upper-class girl and working-class boy unfolds along predictable lines, but the initial reference to Alas's novel intervenes in the form of reality checks that deflate the ecstatic romanticism of their first meeting and force them to find practical, verisimilar solutions to overcoming the social opposition to their relationship.

Pablo and Leonor take turns pointing out reality to each other, but the lessons derived from the story of Ana Ozores are reserved for the young woman: In the first scene, Leonor describes the predicament of Alas's protagonist and shows a strong identification with her search for happiness. The connection between Leonor and Ana is further developed when the television character reveals her literary aspirations: Like Ana, she too writes verses and short stories and even imagines a writing career as a solution to her family's financial woes. Pablo channels his drive to ascend the social ladder, understood to be much more difficult given the circumstances of the time, by encouraging Leonor to deliver her writings to the director of the local newspaper *El adelantado*. In episode 13, the newspaper's director reprimands Leonor with a piece of advice that echoes the scene in *La Regenta* in which Ana is ridiculed for her literary "vices." Folding under social pressure, Leonor accepts a marriage of convenience with wealthy Claudio Castaño (Jaime Olias), covering up his homosexuality in exchange for his helping her publish her stories under the male pseudonym "Leopoldo Safo."[14] While the young Ana suffers for her literary inclinations when she is nicknamed *Jorge Sandio* (George Sand) by her male and female cohorts, Leonor's *folletín* titled *La encrucijada* triumphs when published under the pseudonym. The neighbors at Acacias 38 celebrate "Safo" and his novel, and the work eventually catches the critical eye of Leopoldo Alas himself, who happens to be passing through Madrid. In episodes 42 and 43, Alas is introduced as a character, first, when he is lured to a literary *tertulia* at the Hidalgo home by the promise of meeting "Safo," and later, when he meets Leonor at a local café. The novelist praises "Safo"'s work stating: "Joven, no sea usted modesto, porque *La encrucijada*, a pesar de ser por entregas, es un gran texto" (Young man, don't be so modest, even though *La encrucijada* is a serial novel, it is great piece of writing). Even so, he is thoroughly unimpressed by Claudio's clumsy intellect, more proper to the image of a *folletín* writer than a budding Realist novelist. Nonetheless, he is enchanted by Leonor's knowledge of literature, and in particular, her familiarity with his own writings; so much so, that he promises to share with her his latest story. Figure 2.1 Leonor and Alas meet again and he hands her a copy of "El gallo de Sócrates," one of the last works written before the writer's death in 1901.[15] The brief conversation concludes when the novelist reverses the editor's earlier condemnation of women writing by declaring that Leonor could be the next Pardo Bazán.

The two encounters on-screen between Leonor and the historical character Alas ground *Acacias* in the literary heritage of the Restoration and reinforce the association between the Realist novel and the *folletín* by weaving into the fiber of the narrative structure a reflection on how stories are constructed. José Manuel González Herrán notes the way in which the fictional Ana Ozores is both the subject and object of the literary work in which she appears since she both writes and reads, as she herself is written (2005). The initial romance between Leonor and

Fig. 2.1 *Acacias 38* (Boomerang, TVE, 2015–): Episode 43—Leonor meets Leopoldo Alas

Pablo, and the continuation of her character arc over the course of more than 700 episodes, similarly injects a note of autoreflexivity that enhances claims to historical accuracy. In the final scene in which Alas appears, Pablo reveals that Leonor is "Safo" in order to save *La encruci-jada* from the scathing critique the novelist had promised to write after having met Claudio. He also shares that she has been using *La Regenta* to teach him to read, to which the flattered Alas responds: "Intuyo que la suya es una bonita historia que merecería ser, si no contada, al menos vivida" (I get the feeling that yours is a beautiful story, which if not told at least deserves to be lived). The inclusion of Alas in the story line, if only briefly, validates truthfulness by imprinting the series with the Realist mantra of art imitating life. The commentary thus projects Leonor as the implied author of her love story with Pablo, which is based on lived experience, rather than merely a tale embellished by picturesque details for dramatic effect.

The novelist and the reference to his masterpiece further embeds *Acacias* in televisual heritage by making an indirect reference to the popular 1995 TVE three-part miniseries based on *La Regenta*. If Camus's *Fortunata y Jacinta* marked the zenith of the classic adaptation in Spain, then Méndez-Leite's careful transposition of the 1886 novel closed the cycle as the last program to merit the classification of "quality television" in terms of production design and historical rigor. No doubt, just as Fortunata has become inseparable from the image of Ana Belén, so too has Ana Ozores come to be connected with the face of actor Aitana Sánchez-Gijón, and *Acacias* seeks to activate both associations among the collective memory of its target audience. The novelist's presence lends historicity to the series, but also reveals how both the author and his work have come to be consecrated as cultural heritage via television. His image on-screen not only gives the show the air of an adaptation, but also adds an additional seal of quality in the absence of a historic source text. William Guynn notes the way in which historic figures impose limits on the fictional texts in which they appear because of the traces of their existence that remain in the popular imaginary (2013, 103). So, Alas's intervention can be said to bolster the pretense to authenticity by aligning his interactions with fictional characters within the realm of the historically plausible. Therefore, the performance, although a falsification, enhances the overall presentation of "pastness."

¿DÓNDE VAS, ALFONSO XIII?

In classic adaptations, the decision to recreate historical events on-screen obviously depends on the presence of such scenes in the source text, but also on the perception of a need to supplement the viewers' knowledge of the period in order to make the story understandable. Furthermore, reenactments can make a direct link between the past and the present by facilitating the visual extrapolation of imagery from one period to another. In the context of 1980, the recreation of raucous events that announced the liberal revolution of September 1868 and the triumphal entry of Alfonso XII represented in Camus's *Fortunata y Jacinta* had clear resonances for viewers living through the democratic Transition (Smith 2006, 36). As in the novel, however, the social and political reality of the Restoration envelops the lives of characters who remain anonymous observers of the processes shaping the nation.

Similarly, across the multiple character and narrative arcs of both *Acacias* and *Puente Viejo*, historical events unfold in the background and serve to anchor the plot in the Restoration. History per se, however, rarely figures directly in either program; in other words, historical events are not recreated on-screen, but they are mentioned and commented by characters, and sometimes even experienced by them, however always off-screen and beyond the enclosed dramatic space of the serial fiction. The time frame of *Acacias* progresses almost in real time and therefore reduces the possibility of incorporating historical events to the three-year period in which the story line from season one to three takes place, from 1899 to 1903. The choice of a rather uneventful moment of the Restoration is perhaps not accidental since it frees the TVE costume drama from the burden of having to represent the past in terms of events and allows it to focus almost exclusively on the recreation of the past as lived experience. To date, the only significant event covered by the show is the coronation of Alfonso XIII in 1902, and even here, as discussed below, *Acacias* avoids direct reenactment. By contrast, the temporal frame in *Puente Viejo* spans from 1896 to the late 1920s, and over the course of various seasons the story line skips forward such that it encompasses a broader array of historical events, including: the wars in Cuba and North Africa, in 1898 and 1909–1927, respectively; the coronation of Alfonso XIII in 1902 and royal wedding in 1906; the assassination of Prime Minister Eduardo Dato in 1921; and the *coup d'etat* carried out by General Miguel Primo de Rivera in 1923 (BoomerangTV 2016). Some characters participate in the events offscreen and then comment on the experiences or weave them into their personal narrative as justifications for past and future actions. Such are the cases of Tristán, who fought in Cuba, or Isidro Buendía (Javier Abad), who marches off to fight in Morocco. Over the years, violent episodes involving anarchists cause a stir in Puente Viejo: The mayor Pedro Mirañar (Enric Benvent) and his wife travel to Madrid for Alfonso XIII's wedding and witness the attack on the royal procession; later, the Dato assassination raises fears that Doña Francisca might be a victim of kidnapping or worse (BoomerangTV 2016).

Alongside events, the names of key historical figures of the Restoration are also frequently dropped in *Acacias* and *Puente Viejo* to further enhance the texture of the period recreation. More significantly, though, on several occasions in both series, famous people from the worlds of politics and culture become characters in the plot by visiting the Acacias neighborhood or Puente Viejo. As observed in the case of Alas in *Acacias*, such appearances constitute a different sort of event that converts history into a controllable past by subjecting it to the laws of the fictional world of the series. Hence, instead of having the characters go out into the historical reality, in these instances, representatives of the tangible past enter the fiction and determine in some way the development of the story line. For the ploy to function, the historical characters must somehow already exist in the viewer's imaginations as recognizable representatives of the period. Herein, the existence of earlier or contemporaneous televisual characterizations is essential: In the case of Alas, his on-screen presence in *Acacias* is predicated on the television adaptation of the *La Regenta* as well as documentary series about his life and times also produced for TVE over the years.[16] For other figures, such as painter Joaquín Sorolla, who intervenes directly in *Puente Viejo* in the second season, the representation relies on a combination of dramatic recreations involving the historical character and references to his life and work across different media platforms and genres.[17] No doubt, Sorolla is connected to televisual heritage based on his association with Valencia and the classic adaptations of Blasco Ibáñez's "Valencian novels" *Cañas y barro* and *La barraca*, and the more recent version of *Arroz y tartana* (TVE, 2004), all of which rely on Sorolla's paintings to visualize the literary settings. The painter's personal relationship with the novelist has also given rise to on-screen characterizations in the TV movie *Cartas de Sorolla* (Canal 9, 2006) and Luis García Berlanga's made-for-television biopic *Blasco Ibáñez, la novela de su vida* (TVE, 1998).

Another instance of historical figures being introduced as characters in both *Acacias* and *Puente Viejo* involves members of the Royal Family. Javier Moreno-Luzón points out that the Restoration monarchy envisioned by Antonio Cánovas del Castillo utilized the royal visit as an instrument for fomenting national identification with the institution (2017, 88). Both *Acacias* and *Puente Viejo* take advantage of the well-documented historic tours around Spain and frequent public appearances in the Spanish capital made by King Alfonso XIII and his mother, Queen-Regent María Cristina de Habsburgo, to introduce the figures into their fictional worlds by simply having them pass through the imaginary spaces in which the dramas unfold. Here, the falsification of historic details proves to be riskier than when less high-profile historical characters like Sorolla and Alas are made to appear on-screen, given the greater potential for scrutiny and fact checking. Yet, as De Groot writes, "Reenactment and performance history within a heritage context… can demonstrate the uncanny, peculiar, odd way in which we relate to the past, and undermine controlling and disciplining claims of an all-encompassing, authoritative historical mainstream" (2016, 109). In neither case does the treatment reflect the revised image of the king and his reign proposed by Moreno-Luzón and other historians, like

Carlos Seco Serrano. Instead, the respective presentations replicate long-held views of Alfonso XIII, which are either critical and antimonarchical or defensive and nationalist, while simultaneously making him relatable to the contemporary Spanish monarchy.

Set in the last two years of her reign as queen regent, the widow of Alfonso XII and mother of Alfonso XIII, María Cristina, is given a key role in the development of the *Acacias* plot. The sequence in episode 191 in which both the Queen and the soon-to-be-crowned heir to the throne show up on Acacias Street, begins with a conversation among the ladies of the district in front of La Deliciosa. The neighborhood gossip about the true reason for the visit to the home of Cayetana initiates the process of weaving the historical characters into the fictional plot and mixes with press coverage of the event when Manuela, now working at a newspaper kiosk, comments to a passing client that the item is in all the papers, and then the camera focuses on the headline of *El Adelantado* that reads "La reina visitará Acacias" (The Queen Will Visit Acacias). The image of the front page of the fictional newspaper situates the event within the realm of the historically plausible by simulating the existence of documentary evidence. The authentic look of the newspaper calls attention to the "constructedness" of the past visualized on-screen in *Acacias* and can been interpreted as an invitation to viewers to play along with the ludicrous and implausible scenes involving María Cristina that follow.

Recalling Camus's recreation of the entry of Alfonso XII in Madrid in *Fortunata y Jacinta*, the arrival of María Cristina is prefaced by the surprise appearance of the young Alfonso XIII, who awaits his mother among the crowd gathered in front of Acacias 38. Here, Camus's long shot of Alfonso XII on horseback moving along a festooned avenue is replaced by a close-up of the young monarch's face, although the camera similarly simulates the gaze of an onlooker: Leonor recognizes the silent figure at the same time as viewers, and his identity is confirmed when she calls him "Don Alfonso." Figure 2.2 Alfonso XIII's still countenance and silence facilitates his recognizability by evoking period photographs and so limits his narrative function to merely that of a period signifier. By contrast, María Christina is taken over by the historical imagination such that she can be more thoroughly integrated into the story line. The characterization of the Queen evokes a variety of sources, but perhaps most obviously the various portraits executed by Sorolla.[18] The figure perhaps lends to a greater degree of fictionalization given her rather limited televisual presence over the years.[19] Although perhaps less well known to

Fig. 2.2 *Acacias 38* (Boomerang, TVE, 2015–): Episode 191—María Cristina and Alfonso XIII

younger viewers, the image of María Cristina in *Acacias* is most strikingly reminiscent of Argentinean actor Marga López's portrayal in the 1960 film *¿Dónde vas, triste de ti?* (Bálcazar), which along with *¿Dónde vas, Alfonso XII?* (Interpeninsular, 1959) has been regularly run on TVE since the 1980s. To the consternation of Cayetena, the sovereign gracefully engages the rowdy group of servants, who shower her with *vivas* (long-lives), and she ironically excuses the general ignorance of protocol as notes of the neighborhood's *castizo* (authentic) and picturesque charm. In episode 194, María Cristina calls again at Acacias, however this time the scene introduces the twist that eventually closes the first phase of the series' narrative arc focused on Manuela and Germán. Informed by an unknown source of Cayetana's machinations, the sovereign publically humiliates the villain to the great satisfaction not only of her on-screen adversaries, but also of many fans on Facebook and Twitter.

The absurd role María Cristina plays in the plot is wholly accepted by the fans who commented on the episode in the Foro Acacias on the *FormulaTV* website and on the Twitter account #Acacias38. Her intervention in the series confirms the popular image the widow of Alfonso XII enjoyed throughout her reign as queen-regent and reinforces comments already made by bystanders who defend and praise her as a pillar of stability of the Restoration political regime against antimonarchical skepticism voiced by some male characters. The authority of the institution is wielded through her actions against the villain of the series: María Cristina's position as the absolute embodiment of law and order gives her exclusive power to punish Cayetana for her unsavory actions. Conversely, the on-screen Alfonso XIII cannot overcome the negative image of his ensuing reign that persists in popular memory. In episode 191, the overexcited servant Casilda (Marita Zafra) shouts "¡Viva el príncipe de Asturias!" (Long live the Prince of Asturias) as he follows his mother into the apartment building. The reference, which sparked much discussion on the message board "Gazapos" (Mess-ups) on *FormulaTV* dedicated to fishing out inaccuracies and bloopers, is inaccurate since Alfonso had inherited the title "King of Spain" at birth in 1885.[20] Remaining completely silent indeed allows the king's character to retain an aura of historicity, but paradoxically, it also causes his representation to become the subject of fact checking by avid fans. The message board discussions expose the cracks in claims to historical accuracy in *Acacias* precisely at a juncture when creators appear to make an effort to portray the figure in the least intrusive, that is, historically "correct" fashion.

In *Acacias*, the uncanny aspect of heritage observed by De Groot undermines the illusion of authenticity when connotations other than those intended by *Acacias* creators are conjured by the appearance of the king. In the collective imaginary, reinforced by televisual images, the figure of Alfonso XIII is either vilified or caricatured as the incarnation of all the shortcomings of Restoration society, but hardly ever represented merely as an innocent-looking 16-year-old boy, as in the series. The king has been the subject of several television documentaries, including *Paisaje de la Historia—Alfonso XIII, redentor de cautivos* (TVE, 2012),and *Memoria de España—Alfonso XIII* (TVE, 2004), and he has been characterized in various fiction series, including *Gran Hotel*, the never-broadcasted *Tres días de abril* (Boomerang, TVE, 2011–), and the recent Netflix series *Las chicas del cable* (Bambú Producciones, Netflix, 2017–).

The young king also makes an appearance in episodes 27 and 28 of *Puente Viejo* aired in March 2012. Similarly, much fuss is made over news that his visit to the region will include a stop in the town. Instead of heightening melodrama as in *Acacias*, though, here the appearance of the historical character is set in the background as a comic subplot centered on shop owner and mayor, Pedro Mirañar, and his wife, Dolores (Maribel Ripoll), and son, Hipólito (Selu Nieto). In a clear homage to

Luis Berlanga's 1953 comedy *Bienvenido, Mr. Marshall* (UNICI, 1953), Don Pedro hypes the visit by inviting citizens to submit written requests to the king, and he and his wife become so wrapped up in the excitement that Alfonso XIII appears to them in daydreams. Figure 2.3 First, the mayor imagines meeting the king and being called to his side in Madrid to occupy an important ministerial post, and then Dolores fantasizes about being seduced by the young man, who is rumored to be looking for a bride. In the two separate sequences, the handsome and silent Alfonso XIII of *Acacias* is replaced by the googly-eyed child star Javier Bódalo, famous for roles on television comedy series like *Cuéntame cómo pasó* (Grupo Ganga Producciones, TVE, 2001–) and *Los Serrano* (Estudios Picasso, Globomedia 2003–2008). The absurd dialogue and droll characterization, while wholly part of the fictional characters' fantasies, fulfills the caricaturized image of Alfonso XIII and his reign as corrupt and perverse even before he took over the throne.

As in *Acacias*, *Puente Viejo* does not expand knowledge of the leaders of the Restoration, but merely confirms existing images already residing in discourses of national history. The final sequence depicting the royal visit to Puente Viejo makes another nod to the Berlanga classic and its bittersweet denouement: In a festooned central square with a banner

Fig. 2.3 *El secreto de Puente Viejo* (Boomerang, Antena 3, 2011–): Episode 28—Alfonso XIII meets the mayor of Puente Viejo

reading "Bienvenido, Alfonso XIII," the mayor makes a bumbling speech to animate the townspeople, who have grown tired of waiting for the royal entourage, and ends when a telegram arrives announcing a change of itinerary and the cancelation of the visit. Here, history intervenes as a joke, that is, as something to be taken in jest in the context of the daily afternoon series, by way of the explicit reference to the classic film so often used as a parodic referent for political satire on television after 1978. Under the veil of comedy, the use of Berlanga's film functions as a mechanism to sidestep the Restoration as history and instead merely makes a nostalgic appeal for viewers to embrace it as a recognizable period setting within Spain's televisual heritage. Yet, unavoidable in the evocation is also the transfer of the irony that accompanies nostalgia for the 1953 film: Puente Viejo as a site of historical reenactment is revealed to be similar to the version that the town of Villar del Río reconstructs of itself in *Bienvenido, Mr. Marshall* in order to satisfy the stereotyped image of Spain expected by the American visitors. Whereas the treatment of historical figures in *Acacias* appears to hang onto an ideal of authenticity, the subtle ironizing of nostalgia in *Puente Viejo* undermines the burden of truthfulness since it leaves intact preconceived images of the Restoration (Richardson 2012, 39).

CONCLUSION

On February 23, 2016, Antena 3 marked the fifth anniversary of the debut of *Puente Viejo* with a new theme song. The instrumental piano that had played under the episode preview and through the opening credits is now supplemented by a contemporary vocal tune vaguely reminiscent of the original, but clearly aimed at striking a nostalgic chord for viewers who have faithfully followed the series from the beginning. The voice of the singer is immediately recognizable as belonging to Ana Belén. Nostalgia as a key component in the construction of heritage is about recognition and is often triggered by theme song music that evokes in the audience a retrospective awareness of things-past in the present. The first line of the song "Después de tanto vivido" (After experiencing so much) potentially calls forth collective memories of five years of series content, and, for viewers receptive to the prompt, almost 40 years of history that have passed since the actor–singer incarnated Fortunata in the classic TVE series.

In the two episodes dedicated to the Restoration in the 2004 TVE history documentary series *Memoria de España*, director Fernando García de Cortázar makes extensive use of scenes of historical reenactment from various films and television series as a means of bringing to life the events of the period for contemporary viewers. The color sequence used to represent the start of the Restoration shows King Alfonso XII entering Madrid on January 14, 1875 amid fanfare and pageantry. The documentary engages in a creative game of sleight of hand: The image is not identified as a reenactment, but it obviously cannot be authentic since visual memory of the actual procession only exists in lithographs. All the while, the scene could be confused for Camus's recreation of Galdós's text in the televisual adaptation of *Fortunata y Jacinta*. Close examination, however, reveals that the scene was actually lifted from the 1959 film *¿Dónde vas, Alfonso XII?*, which director Luis César Amadori had carefully reconstructed from period lithographs. The materials recycled for *Memoria de España* take on the air of archival sources when mixed with the authoritative voice-over narration, real documentary footage, and still images, and so, evidence how knowledge of the past is difficult to dissociate from televisual representations given the power of moving images to shape perceptions of history.

A similar layering of authentic and fictional footage is used in the music video for the theme song posted on the *Puente Viejo* website the day of the debut of the new title sequence (Antena 3 2016). Employing a familiar technique, the clip opens with an image of a forlorn Pepa in the craggy landscape surrounding the fictional Puente Viejo and then cuts to the real Ana Belén in a recording studio donning headphones and starting to sing. In a video montage against a backdrop of images recalling key moments of the series, Ana Belén stands alongside Fortunata's contemporaries Pepa and Doña Francisca, and by extension Manuela and Cayetana, who ostensibly inhabit the same historical space in collective memory. The same can be said of the historical characters of the Restoration who intervene and impact the lives of the inhabitants of *Acacias 38* and *Puente Viejo*: In the imagination of television viewers they are just as real as the rest of the characters on-screen. Through the reuse of images of the early twentieth century that recall those produced for classic adaptations, the Restoration becomes an accessible and useable past for the purposes of the present, which may or may not have anything to do with historical lessons. In 1980, the image of Fortunata incarnated by Ana Belén ostensibly sought to open the world of Galdós's fiction to a generation of television viewers, and in the process, bring into public discourse a reflection on how the novelist's portrayal of late-nineteenth-century society might inform and shape the present process of democratic transition (George 2009, 62–63). By contrast, instead of a dialogue with history, the costumed characters who inhabit Acacias 38 and Puente Viejo invite twenty-first-century audiences to enter a ludic space where the present projects as past through a game of dress up. Even so, the game is still ruled by expectations of authenticity and historicity, though now derived from televisual rather than literary sources. Ultimately, *Acacias 38* and *Puente Viejo* demonstrate how the Restoration can now only be knowable through television fictions that have taken over the narrative function of the nineteenth-century novel and its derivatives, and therefore only exists as televisual heritage.

NOTES

1. All translations from Spanish to English are by the author unless otherwise noted.
2. FesTVal is a radio and television festival celebrated annually in September; in addition to various awards, new programs are previewed and programming concepts are vetted in roundtable discussions with producers and journalists.
3. From the press release, it is not clear whether the costumes from the Galdós adaptation originated with the TVE series or Angelino Fons's 1969 version starring Emma Penella, but for most television viewers the reference most certainly evokes an image of Ana Belén; the note also mentions wardrobe recovered from *55 Days in Peking* (Samuel Bronston, 1963), shot in Spain and starring Charlton Heston and Ava Gardner.
4. Given the breadth of both series (at the time of writing *Acacias 38* has surpassed 700 episodes, and *El secreto de Puente Viejo*, 1700), and that both are still currently on the air, the analysis and comments herein are limited to the first three seasons of each program.
5. *Fortunata y Jacinta*, along with other adaptations, such as the televised versions of Blasco Ibáñez's *Cañas y barro* (1978) and *La barraca* (1979), Pardo Bazán's *Los Pazos de Ulloa* (1985), and Leopoldo Alas's *La Regenta* (1995), as well as biopics like *Teresa de Jesús* (1984) and *Lorca* (1987–1988), had previously been available on VHS and DVD, however, making them available free of charge, and for posterity, further underscores their patrimonial status.

6. The new adaptation was announced together with the soon-to-be-debuted original drama series *Mar de Plástico* (Antena 3, 2015–2016) and a planned eight-episode miniseries based on Idelfonso Falcones's 2006 novel *La catedral del Mar*.

7. On December 12, 2017, Antena 3 aired episode 1718, making it the longest running fiction series in terms of number of episodes in the history of Spanish television (Antena 3 2017).

8. *Falcon Crest* (CBS, 1981–1990) debuted on TVE in January 1985, in the afternoon slot, and ran until 1991; various later Spanish series featuring a powerful matriarch have been compared to the show including *Herederos* (TVE 2007–2009) starring Concha Velasco and the recent *Traición* (TVE, Bambú, 2017) starring Ana Belén; see (Labastida 2018); following the debut of *Puente Viejo*, María Bouzas stated that she was flattered to be compared to Angela Channing (*Diario de Navarra* 2011).

9. *Dynasty* debuted on TVE in 1986 under the title *Los Colby*; it first replaced *Falcon Crest* in the TVE program grid and then was moved to the mid-morning (see Aguilar 2016).

10. In a symbolically charged scene, when the villain realizes she cannot escape the fire that has broken out at Acacias 38, she strips her red dress and lets herself be consumed by the flames; see (RTVE 2017).

11. The global success of *Downton* spurred a revival of *Upstairs, Downstairs* (BBC, Masterpiece, 2010–2012), which continues the story line where it left off in the 1930s.

12. Here, the word *folletín* is interchangeable with soap opera as well as simply serial.

13. *Novela* aired on TVE from 1962 to 1979 and presented adaptations of European and Spanish nineteenth-century novels, including Charles Dickens's *David Copperfield* and Honoré de Balzac's *Père Goriot*, as well as Galdós's *El amigo manso* and Juan Valera's *Juanita La Larga*, in serialized thirty-minute episodes taped on a soundstage.

14. The treatment of Claudio's sexuality has sparked commentary on social media, and comparisons with the character Celia in the series *Seis hermanas* (Bambú, TVE, 2015–2017). See Concepción Cascajosa and Linda Willem in this volume, and Pérez (2015).

15. The piece is also the title of the author's last collection of short stories.

16. For instance, *El arte de vivir—Leopoldo Alas* (1984) or *La mitad invisible—La Regenta* (2014).

17. Sorolla's *Visions of Spain* have been the subject of recent exhibitions, and centenary celebrations have spawned telefilms and documentaries like *Cartas de Sorolla* (Canal 9, 2006) and *La mitad invisible—Paseo a orillas del mar. Sorolla* (TVE, 2013), as well as theater productions such as Antonio Najarro's *Sorolla* for the Ballet Nacional de España (2014).

18. Sorolla painted María Cristina and Alfonso XIII on several occasions, including the group portrait *La Regencia* finished in 1906 that represents the pair at the time of the 1902 coronation.
19. For instance, the 2003 TVE documentary *Mujeres en la historia-María Cristina de Habsburgo, la extranjera virtuosa*, and more recent short-subject films dedicated to Alfonso XIII.
20. Himawari. 2012. *Gazapos* (message board), January 11, 2016 (5:43 p.m.). http://www.formulatv.com/series/acacias-38/foros/13/3/gazapos/.

BIBLIOGRAPHY

Agencia EFE. 2015. "*Acacias 38*, un folletín decimonónico para las tardes de La 1." *El Diario*, March 3. http://www.eldario.es/cultura/Acacias-folletin-decimononico-tardes_0_370026364.html. Accessed September 20, 2017.

Aguilar, Deo. 2016. "*Dinastía* sigue molando 35 años después." *Harpers Bazaar España*, June 14. https://www.harpersbazaar.com/es/cultura/ocio/a255149/dinastia-serie-35-aniversario/. Accessed February 24, 2018.

Amela, Victor Manuel. 2011. "Tiempo de folletín." *La Vanguardia*, February 25.

Antena 3. 2014. "Grandes éxitos para sorprender." http://www.antena3.com/objetivotv/actualidad/espana/grandes-exitos-sorprender_20140909579114f-e6584a8b7b42a6c85.html. Accessed September 29, 2017.

———. 2016. "Ana Belén interpreta la nueva sintonía de *El secreto de Puente Viejo*." http://www.antena3.com/series/el-secreto-de-puente-viejo/5-aniversario-puente-viejo/ana-belen-interpreta-nueva-sintonia-secreto-puente-viejo_20160221571a4db46584a8abb57f7445.html. Accessed February 28, 2018.

———. 2017. "'El Secreto de Puente Viejo' se convierte en la serie de emisión nacional más longeva al alcanzar los 1.718 capítulos." http://www.antena3.com/series/el-secreto-de-puente-viejo/eres-fan/%E2%80%98el-secreto-puente-viejo%E2%80%99-convierte-serie-emision-nacional-mas-longeva-alcanzar-1718-capitulos_201712115a2e7edb0cf249d880623aa1.html. Accessed February 24, 2018.

BoomerangTV. 2016. "*El secreto de Puente Viejo* celebra su 5o aniversario." https://www.grupoboomerangtv.com/noticias/el-secreto-de-puente-viejo-celebra-su-5-aniversario. Accessed November 17, 2017.

Cardwell, Sarah. 2002. *Adaptation Revisited: Television and the Classic Novel.* Manchester: Manchester University Press.

De Groot, Jerome. 2016. *Consuming History: Historians and Heritage in Contemporary Popular Culture.* London: Routledge.

Diario de Navarra. 2011. "Es un honor parecerme a Angela Channing." *Diario de Navarra*, June 20.

Dufour, Nuria. 2012. "*El secreto de Puente Viejo*. Cruce de sueños y destinos en la España novecentista." *AISGE*, October 24. http://www.aisge.es/el-secreto-de-puente-viejo.

El Mundo. 2014. "Atresmedia realizará una serie basada en 'Fortunata y Jacinta'." *El Mundo*, September 4. http://www.elmundo.es/television/2014/09/04/54087ed-de2704e03188b458f.html. Accessed September 20, 2017.

Figueroa, Verónica. 2015. "Mil tardes en Puente Viejo." *El País*, February 4. http://elpais.com/cultura/2015/02/03/television/1422966149-741168.html. Accessed September 20, 2017.

George, David R., Jr. 2009. "Restauración y Transición en la *Fortunata y Jacinta* de Mario Camus." In *Historias de la pequeña pantalla: Representaciones históricas en la televisión de la España democrática*, edited by Francisca López, Elena Cueto Asín and David R. George, Jr., 53–71. Madrid: Iberoamericana.

González Herrán, José Manuel. 2005. "Ana Ozores, La Regenta: Escritora y escritura." In *Lectora, Heroína, Autora (La mujer en la literatura española del siglo XIX). III Coloquio de la Sociedad de Literatura Española del Siglo XIX (Barcelona, 23–25 de octubre de 2002)*, edited by Luis F. Díaz Larios, et al., 159–171. Barcelona: Universitat de Barcelona/PPU.

Guynn, William. 2013. *Writing History in Film*. New York: Routledge.

Hernández, Diego F. 2017. "Fortunata se reencuentra con Galdós." *La Provincia*, June 21. http://www.laprovincia.es/cultura/2017/06/20/fortunata-reencuentra-galdos/951369.html. Accessed February 28, 2018.

Labastida, Mikel. 2018. "Ana Belén no es Angela Channing." *La Provincia*, January 31.

Lowenthal, David. 1985. *The Past Is a Foreign Country*. Cambridge: Cambridge University Press.

Martí, Elisa. 2003. "The *Folletín*: Spain Looks to Europe." In *The Cambridge Companion to the Spanish Novel: From 1600 to the Present*, edited by Harriet S. Turner and Adelaida López de Martínez, 65–80. Cambridge Companions Online. Cambridge: Cambridge University Press.

Moreno-Luzón, Javier. 2017. "The King of All Spaniards? Monarchy and Nation." In *Metaphors of Spain: Representations of Spanish National Identity in the Twentieth Century*, edited by Javier Moreno-Luzón and Xosé M. Nuñez Seixas, 84–104. New York: Berghahn.

Pérez, Ángel. 2015. "Claudio y Celia frente a la homofobia 'de época.'" http://www.rtve.es/television/20151002/claudio-acacias-celia-seis-hermanas-homofobia/1229020.shtml. Accessed February 20, 2018.

Pope, Randolph. 2003. "Writing About Writing." In *The Cambridge Companion to the Spanish Novel: From 1600 to the Present*, edited by Harriet S. Turner and Adelaida López de Martínez, 264–282. Cambridge Companions Online. Cambridge: Cambridge University Press.

Richardson, Nathan E. 2012. *Constructing Spain: The Re-imagination of Space and Place in Fiction and Film, 1953–2003*. Lewisburg: Bucknell University Press.

RTVE. 2009. "RTVE.es recupera para los internautas trece clásicos literarios emitidos por Televisión Española." http://www.rtve.es/television/20090331/rtvees-recupera-para-internautas-trece-clasicos-literarios-emitidos-television-espanola/257526.shtml. Accessed February 28, 2018.

———. 2015. "*Acacias 38*—La serie." http://www.rtve.es/television/acacias-38/la-serie/. Accessed September 20, 2017.

———. 2017. "*Acacias 38*—Cayetana queda atrapada entre llamas." http://www.rtve.es/alacarta/videos/acacias-38/acacias-38-cayetana-queda-atrapada-entre-llamas/4154944/. Accessed February 28, 2018.

Smith, Paul Julian. 2006. *Television in Spain: From Franco to Almódovar*. London: Tamesis.

Vidal Villasur, Belén. 2012. *Heritage Film: Nation, Genre and Representation*. London: Wallflower.

Voigts-Virchow, Eckart. 2007. "Heritage and Literature on Screen: Heimat and Heritage." In *The Cambridge Companion to Literature on Screen*, edited by Deborah Cartmell and Imelda Whelehan, 123–137. Cambridge Companions to Literature. Cambridge: Cambridge University Press.

CHAPTER 3

Profane Unions: Constructing Heritage from Anarchist-Bourgeois Romances in *Ull per ull* and *Barcelona, ciutat neutral*

Elena Cueto Asín

In conjunction with the publication of his book *L'anarquisme, fet diferencial català. Influència i llegat de l'anarquisme en la història i la societat catalana contemporània*, Xavier Díez declared "the Catalan anarchist movement to be a consciously silenced history" (Esteban 2013). The explanation for this silencing, according to the author, resides in the generally negative image of anarchism held by elites of every political color, including progressive liberals, and with the insistent identification of Catalans with the decidedly bourgeois values of a strong work ethic, law and order, and thrift. These traits overshadow the tradition of resistance and revolution that truly differentiate the region from other parts of Spain. Xavier Theros, 2017 winner of the prestigious Josep Pla Prize for prose, reiterates the idea when he observes that Barcelona has typically been explained through the lens of the bourgeoisie, such that nineteenth-century Catalonia, apart from the final decades

E. Cueto Asín (✉)
Department of Romance Languages and Literatures, Bowdoin College, Brunswick, ME, USA
e-mail: ecueto@bowdoin.edu

© The Author(s) 2018
D. R. George, Jr. and W. S. Tang (eds.),
Televising Restoration Spain,
https://doi.org/10.1007/978-3-319-96196-5_3

51

of the period, remains an "untold story" with enough material to inspire several television series (Geli 2017). The allusion to television fiction as a vehicle for projecting history cannot be ignored, especially in light of the perceived lack or lacunae in understandings of the Restoration's role in the formation of Catalonia's cultural landscape. In effect, television offers a platform for imagining the past and, in the last decade, the history of anarchism specifically. It does so by employing novel plot structures that allow the movement to be folded into Catalan identity as a component fully compatible with the bourgeois attributes noted above. Two miniseries created for Televisió de Catalunya (TV3), *Ull per ull* (Televisión Española, TV3, Roda y Rodar Cine y Television, 2010) and *Barcelona, ciutat neutral* (TV3, Radio e Televisão de Portugal, Stopline Films, 2011), can be analyzed in terms of how each imagines the alliance and/or compatibility between the anarchic tradition and the set of values proper to the bourgeoisie. In doing so, it can be argued both series reflect the symbiotic relationship between the two worldviews that, as Manuel Morales Muñoz points out, cannot be understood historically in isolation from each other (2002, 32).

The solution to the conscious silencing of the history of the anarchist movement, alleged by Díez, would be to vindicate it as heritage, that is, as a past legacy that holds currency for the present. Heritage, comprised of a collection of historical referents that aid in the construction of cohesive identities in the present, is typically projected by dominant institutions with the means and credibility to influence the majority of the population. Mass media, no doubt, play an indispensable role in commemorative activities, events, and practices that create spaces, both intangible and physical, in which to revitalize and display the material traces of heritage. In the case of anarchism, the recreation of public memory in traditional forms turns out to be difficult and complex given the exchange of violence that defines its development; the radical nature and terrorist tactics employed by its adherents were met by severe repression by the state, which is the primary guarantor of national history and cultural heritage. The promotion of previously discredited elements of cultural heritage usually follows in the wake of political evolution and institutional change, as happened in Spain after the democratic Transition. In recent decades, the revaluation of the legacy of certain elements of the past is equally impelled by the growth of a global marketplace for historical fictions to be consumed as entertainment. Andreas Huyssens explains this phenomenon as a social response to the continued failure of technology to make good on its utopic promises in the twentieth century, and as a search for a stable temporal space in which to anchor identity in emotional and aesthetic terms (1995, 6).

Today, plaques, exhibitions, and other forms of recognition mark the sites of violent encounters between anarchism and its adversaries as part of the history of Barcelona, but in a way that counteracts the image of the anarchist as a destructive force. One example of such a designated place of memory is the Montjuic Castle, which had been the setting for military tribunals and executions since it was rebuilt in the eighteenth century. In November 2016, the fort held an exhibition recounting the 1896 trials of anarchists accused of participating in the bombing of a Corpus Christi procession on the Calle Canvis Nous in June of that year. Since 1990, the site has also featured a monument marking the place where libertarian pedagogue Francisco Ferrer Guardia was executed for his involvement in protests against the draft during the Moroccan War, which sparked the violent riots of the so-called Tragic Week in the summer of 1909.

As a model for preserving collective memory and promoting identity, the commemoration of victims of historic trials marks a shift away from the traditional tendency to raise monuments to heroes, achievements, and epic moments in national history (Hite 2013, 13). The designation of official spaces for recognition is accompanied by other modes of memory production, such as spontaneous resistance that, along with art and literature, can be playful and popular, and even irreverent, forms of expression. The Calle Canvis Nous is forever associated with the 1896 bombing that inspired Ramón Casas's renowned 1907 painting *Procesión del Corpus de la Iglesia Santa María del Mar* (The Corpus Christi Procession Leaving the Church of Santa Maria del Mar), displayed at the Museu Nacional d'Art de Catalunya. The ground floor of the building from which anarchist Tomás Asheri threw the bomb is today occupied by a bar named "Salvador," which evokes the memory of Santiago Salvador, the author of the earlier July 1893 bombing of the Teatre del Liceu, a supposed act of vengeance for the capture and execution of his comrade. The Museu de Història de la Ciutat displays the second unexploded bomb that Salvador launched at the theater audience. The names of the victims of both attacks, anonymous in the popular consciousness, are revivified in the historical register of events that lend themselves easily to consumption as media spectacle. The ensemble of commemorative forms, both solemn and ludic, causes the city to undergo a process of "museumization" that develops, according to Huyssens, within as well as beyond designated museum spaces in which cultural materials are always arranged in terms of the predetermined dialectic of hegemonic or counter-hegemonic (1995, 15).

The process of making the past consumable in urban spaces regularly relies on the participation of historical fictions and costume dramas produced for public television, which retains its prestige as promotor of culture and purveyor of heritage and takes advantages of popular trends, such as actors and multimedia platforms to reach a broad cross section of national audiences. Available on DVD and, more recently, through online streaming platforms, television series and TV movies occupy a place alongside traditional narrative forms, primarily novels, as standalone texts detached from their initial broadcast context on the small screen. No longer dominated by literary adaptations, recent series set in the past are based on original scripts that dialogue equally with contemporary and historic texts, including literature as well as earlier televisual representations. The overarching postmodern quality of such programming makes explicit the strategies of dramatization and historical recreation, and, as Jerome de Groot notes, invites the viewer to question the sense of nostalgia they project as heritage (2016, 233).

In recent television depictions of the economic and aesthetic flowering of Barcelona at the turn of the century, anarchism appears as a disruptive force that threatens to derail the process of the mercantilist expansion that underpins the narrative of the Catalan capital's modern identity. The pattern finds its literary roots prior to the democratic Transition, in the writings of Ignacio Agustí, adapted in the 1976 miniseries *La saga de los Rius* by Pedro Amalio López for Televisión Española (TVE), and in Eduardo Mendoza's 1975 novel *La verdad sobre el caso Savolta*, adapted for cinema by Antonio Drove in 1979.[1] Mendoza's 1989 novel *La ciudad de los prodigios*, turned into a feature film 10 years later by Mario Camus, continues the tradition of narrating the expansion of the city through the confrontation between the bourgeoisie and anarchists as a foundational fiction, albeit with less idealism and certain ironic overtones (Oswald). In the twenty-first century, the representation of anarchists persecuted for challenging the dominant social and political order has been the subject of novels like Antoni Dalmases's 2009 *Ull per ull* and Pablo Martín Sánchez's 2013 *El anarquista que se llamaba como yo*. On television, anarchists are central characters in the TVE series *La señora* (Diagonal Television, 2008–2010) and its sequel *14 de abril. La República* (Diagonal Television, 2011), both written by Virgina Yagüe and directed by Jordi Frades. Within this trajectory appear the two miniseries that feature anarchists as the main characters:

the adaptation of Dalamases's *Ull per ull*, directed by Mar Tarragona and written by Isaac Palmiola y Eduardo Rodrigo, and *Barcelona, ciutat neutral*, directed by Sonia Sánchez based on an original script by Mateu Andover and Xesc Barceló.

What distinguishes the two recent television representations is the way in which both invite audiences to empathize with anarchists who hold fast to their radical ideology while becoming romantically involved with members of the bourgeoisie. Framed by this context of irreconcilable political and class differences, the plots of the TV3 miniseries are driven by romantic unions of opposites whose actions and motivations ultimately uncover the common ground between the two: The sons and daughters of industrialists distance themselves from the world of privilege of their families to become involved with individuals of the opposite sex marked by their working-class status and anarchist ideology, but who maintain strong family ties and an unfettered commitment to the values of work and education.

The protagonists are not historic characters but rather are identifiable social types whose actions are limited by the parameters of the period setting. Love relationships complicated by different class origins are staples of bourgeois melodrama and of anarchist literature, which, as Lily Litvak observes, tends to be highly emotional when exploring alternative responses to the moral and ethical dilemmas that characters face (1991, 344). Both series borrow structural and thematic elements from the two historic literary traditions, while taking advantage of the visual appeal of the relationship between *Modernisme* and anarchism to represent the *Belle Époque*, recognized as a moment in which aesthetics become a vehicle for transmitting sensorial experiences and exploring social conditions such as poverty and criminality (Litvak 1991, 18). In this context, anarchists are stylized as they are integrated into an equally sanitized visualization of turn-of-the-century Barcelona that relies heavily on ekphrasis to make the city of the past recognizable as a heritage space. Historical fictions, as a popular genre with clear didactic intentions, channel recognition of the cityscape as a product of the past and as such, a repository of collective historical experience and cultural legacy. The camera imbues the city with an aesthetic dimension independent of physical reality such that the screen image can even come to supersede or substitute it as referent (Koek 2013, 46).

The intersection of ideology and aesthetics that Litvak observes is reflected in Carles Balagué's 2010 documentary *La bomba del Liceu*, which revisits the details of the emblematic 1893 event. Although its premiere coincided with that of the aforementioned miniseries, the latter explores the Catalan anarchist movement in the tense national and European environment of the years between 1914 and 1921 and so avoids the most notorious outbursts of anarchist violence, as well as the notable 1888 and 1929 World's Fairs that showcased the economic prowess of Barcelona. The temporal frame chosen likewise predates the political transformations wrought by the Second Republic and the unfolding of the Civil War. In this way, the plots of the series avoid subjugation to precise historical moments or events, which Pierre Nora defines as the essential units of history as it is typically projected through the channels of mass media (1972, 162). The temporal frame thusly marked by violence and economic development makes the programs' plotlines historically plausible while also allowing them to progress untethered by the aforementioned events and the expectations these impose as the site for anticipated historical and political catharsis.

ULL PER ULL OR ROMANCING A MAN OF ACTION

The coproduced miniseries *Ull per ull* debuted on Catalonia's TV3 on April 30, 2010 in Catalan and played nationally on TVE1 on June 14 in a dubbed version titled *Ojo por ojo*. The collaboration between the Catalan television service and the national public broadcaster exposes the divergent missions of the two entities: The former seeks to offer content that appeals directly to the political and cultural concerns of the autonomous community that does not always satisfy the vision and goals of the latter.[2] The miniseries' unfavorable representation of the reign of King Alfonso XIII echoes a Catalan nationalist perspective and is potentially a cause for suspicion among government-appointed TVE executives similar to that provoked by other series that were modified or canceled following the electoral victory of the Popular Party in May 2011 (de Luna). In the case of *Ull per ull*, however, since broadcast was scheduled months before any politically motivated changes could be implemented at TVE, the two 75-minute episodes were aired on both stations with modest results. The scant references to the miniseries in the press are almost always embedded in features about veteran actor Lluís Homar, who plays

Ricard Torrent, the wealthy factory owner who is willing to dialogue with workers as long as his financial interests are not compromised.[3] The young protagonist Enric Serra (Manu Fullola) gets wrapped up in the conflict when he sees his brother Isidro (Jordi Rico) gunned down in the street by Torrent's henchman, as a reprisal for his activism. Motived by a desire for vengeance, Enric becomes the leader of a clandestine organization called the "Ingovernables" (Ungovernables) and murders Torrent before realizing that it was his son Gregori (Rubén Ametllé) who actually ordered Isidro's death. The group then hatches a plan to kidnap Torrent's daughter Eulalia, but things become complicated when Enric ends up falling in love with her.

The anarchist movement is connected to a notion of heritage in the miniseries beginning with the opening credits that use animation to anticipate the plot: A silhouetted worker morphs into an armed man moving against a background comprised by the Barcelona cityscape, easily identifiable by emblematic buildings, followed by a factory, and finally a traditional *masia* (rural homestead), which links the traditional symbol of rural identity to that of urban modernity. Some of the spaces evoked in the sequence, namely the Estació de França and the Ciutadela Park, later appear as locations for the live action in a highly stylized and artificial fashion. Other moments are more explicitly ekphrastic: Ramon Casas's painting *La carga* inspires the scene of a civil guard dispersing a band of striking workers (Fig. 3.1). It is well known that Casas dated the painting, finished in 1899 and modified in 1903, so that the scene might be associated with the violent strikes in Barcelona of February 1902. The maneuver authorizes the use of the image in *Ull per ull* such that the emblematic image comes to be linked to the series' fictional actions of 1919.[4] The televised repression of protesting workers then becomes an allegory fashioned after the prized masterpiece by one of the most renowned artists of the Restoration period. The enormous painting has been housed in the Museu de La Garrotxa in Olot since 1911 and been moved only twice: once in 1975 for restoration, and in 1982 when it was sent to Barcelona for temporary exhibition in the effort to recover history initiated by the democratic Transition.[5] The series, then, can be seen as another movement of the painting that takes it out of Olot and brings it virtually into the public sphere, at the same time that it situates it in the city as part of a broader process of museumization.

Fig. 3.1 *Ull per ull* (TVE, TV3, 2010): Episode 1—standoff between anarchists and the Civil Guard

Historical reenactment as a derivative of still-imaged ekphrasis is used in the first episode when the workers attend a rally with Salvador Seguí, the historic anarcho-syndicalist known popularly as "Noi del Sucre" (Sugar Boy). The staunch advocate for providing the working classes with access to education was assassinated by gunmen from the rightist Sindicato Libre (Free Union), which was founded in 1919 to combat the union activities of anarchists. The murder of Isidro in *Ull per ull* can be seen as an allegory of Seguí's death, which has been commemorated since 1983 by a plaque in Barcelona's Plaza de San Rafael near where he died, as well as by a plaza bearing his name in the Raval neighborhood.[6]

The series stretches the temporal frame to 1921 in order to make allusions to the assassination of President Eduardo Dato in the same year by including as characters members of the real-life anarchist cell behind the incident. Unlike the gunning down of Torrent, the historic event does not appear on-screen, as this would have meant shifting the action to Madrid. While the death of the industrialist is ultimately presented as an unfortunate revenge killing that turns Enric into a criminal, the death of Dato is celebrated as a victory. The "Ingovernables" congratulate the cell members for their deed upon their return to Barcelona, and the gesture moves the series onto questionable ethical grounds that are difficult to write off ideologically. The murder of the president and the use of kidnappings to secure capital for the purchase of arms are presented as a justifiable response to heavy-handed police repression ordered by Barcelona governor Serveriano Martínez Anido (Álvaro Roig). As one of the most salient historic characters in *Ull per ull*, Martínez Anido incarnates the disproportionate persecution of anarchists under the Dato government, and the consent of Alfonso XIII, whose painting hangs in the office of the governor in the scene where he briefs his officers on their mission.[7]

The introduction of historical elements by employing different degrees of ekphrasis lends credibility to the historical fiction and its characters, even when the series digresses into the epic mode or adventure genre. To the same extent that historic figures are appropriated for the purposes of the fiction, invented characters are assigned attributes of anonymous individuals and groups that make them immediately recognizable in a kind of virtual museum that pays homage to the victims of history. Among those in whose honor neither monuments nor commemorative plaques have been placed, the miniseries chooses to include the bourgeois industrialist, who, despite everything, still represents the mercantilist spirit that contributed to Barcelona's splendor. Unlike younger son Gregori, who is linked to a patriotic and nationalistic conservatism, Ricard Torrent and his eldest son and heir apparent Joan (Albert López-Mutra) are not completely vilified. Gregori risks his sister life by refusing to pay the ransom, and the situation is resolved only when Joan intervenes. The tightfistedness stereotypically associated with Catalans is undone by the Joan's gesture, and at the same time Gregori is scapegoated as an undesirable Catalan. On the other side of the spectrum, but equally noteworthy, the character of "El Murciano" (Andrés Herrera) is introduced as a counterpoint to the more sophisticated Enric: He is simple yet valiant, shaped by the hard life of a peasant laborer before joining the Catalan anarchists. He articulates the political movement as a response to the system of exploitation, and his origins in the southern province of Murcia, as his nickname indicates, invites the identification of viewers with roots outside of Catalonia. In the end, "El Murciano," like so many real-life anarchists, becomes a martyr to the cause when he falls victim to the notorious "ley de fugas" (law of flight) by which prisoners apprehended by police were set free only to be shot in the back.

Within the symmetrical character structure of the series, the bridge between libertarian and bourgeois values is incarnated by Eulalia (Nuria Gago), the educated and freethinking daughter of Torrent. She publishes her progressive ideas in newspaper articles and advocates for social change while living comfortably and harmoniously with her well-heeled family. Her love affair with Enric, which is the narrative focus of the second episode, is not predicated on a process of ideological awakening, but rather on a predictable pattern of sexual tension that builds from the moment she is kidnapped. Locked up in the *masia* as an object of exchange, Eulalia finds herself deprived of the power afforded by her social status and subjected by Enric to a process of ethical reeducation; he reprimands her for throwing her food on the floor and protects her from the sexual aggressions of the other male captors. The uneducated but sensitive Enric aspires to learn from the anarchist literature about which Eulalia is surprisingly well-versed. Books rather than brute force bring the pair together, echoing the anarchist concept of culture as a space for social redemption (Litvak 1991, 336). It should be noted, too, that this also fits within the didactic intention of Dalmases's novel that seeks to promote reading among young Catalan readers. In this context, positions of power are thus neutralized. Eulalia earns Enric's trust such that she no longer needs to be tied up, and the freedom to move about the rural *masia* allows her to witness how her captor also aspires to adopt the practices of personal hygiene valued in anarchist doctrine. She looks on as the naked Enric, drenched in sunlight, bathes bucolically in a barrel of water outside the *masia*; the image offers a sensual contrast to the darkness of the luxurious interiors of the Torrent mansion in which everything is wrapped in rich textiles.

Outside of the literature produced by the anarchist movement itself, the rustic luminosity of the bath scene in *Ull per ull* is a novelty in the representation of the anarchist. Even from the perspective of Restoration-period artists and writers who were more fascinated by the rebellious character of anarchism's adherents than by their motivating ideology, the tendency was to present the figures in romanticized chiaroscuro. For example, Santiago Rusiñol's 1893 charcoal drawing *Cabezas de los anarquistas detenidos con motivo del atentado en el Gran Teatre del Liceu* (anarchist leaders arrested following the attack on the Gran Liceu Theater) can be seen, as Brad Epps suggests, as an attempt to understand an attack on the established order that exceeds the artist's own attempts to question the values of the dominant social class (2005, 121). Rusiñol's sketch in black and white is the equivalent to the literary descriptions by writers like Pío Baroja, Vicente Blasco Ibáñez, or Ramón del Valle-Inclán echoed in Mendoza's contemporary renderings, in which the anarchist is always presented as a dark figure.

In addition to an alternative chromaticism that contests predominant depictions of anarchists, *Ull per ull* incorporates other elements that echo the libertarian literature that developed in the transition from the nineteenth to the twentieth century. As a form of denouncing the injustices of the reigning class structure and fomenting the revolutionary movement, these writings often center on the moral and aesthetic salvation of delinquents who redeem themselves through education, culture, and solidarity; here, the only justifiable crime is tyrannicide (Litvak 1991, 348).

The antagonistic relationship between Catalonia and the Spanish State interpreted in the miniseries through the defense of certain instances of violence and the inventive deployment of historical, artistic, and heritage motifs can be seen in the context of 2010 as an anticipation of future tensions. These aspects can also be accepted as part of a fiction that attempts to conjure in audiences a nostalgia for rebellion. In contrast to the anonymous, uniformed civil guards, the anarchist in shirt sleeves, masculine and independent-minded, is cast in the mold of a tradition that idealizes the man of action in the period after Romanticism and in a historical moment increasingly marked by public protest. The lasting appeal of the figure embodied by Enric is summed up on the miniseries website in a quote by Lluís Homar in which the actor, reminiscing his youth, declares his inclination to identify with the "Ingovernables" (RTVE 2010). The declaration is ironic, but coming from an actor born in Barcelona, it is nonetheless suggestive since his character in the series represents the bourgeois values that are equally essential to the formation of Catalan identity.

Any deeper understanding of anarchism and its complexities announced in the premise of *Ull per ull* is secondary to the expected on-screen consummation of the main characters' relationship. The scene comes once Eulalia has been freed, and she is able to voluntarily give herself to Enric: In the emotionally charged moment, she drops the books she carries and leaves them on the ground to embrace her former captor in the middle of the street. It is difficult to say whether the scene in which intellectual reason appears to succumb to passion is intentionally metaphoric. In didactic terms, the miniseries might have explored in greater depth the set of shared ideals that ultimately bring Enric and

Eulalia together. Likewise, it could have looked into the factors that contribute to the anarchist's complex understanding of communitarianism based on individualism and a faith in science and progress, notions which are otherwise considered the foundations of bourgeois liberalism (Álvarez Junco 1991, 22). Nevertheless, the impossible love is resolved through a sentimental logic that relies on parallelism and a balance of power: Both characters share the experience of witnessing the murder of a loved one as a result of a cycle of revenge violence; Eulalia is the one who enters Enric's world, but when he is arrested and condemned to death, she relies on her social status to have the sentence commuted. The resolution is romantic and marked by sacrifice: Instead of the garrote, he is sent to serve in the army in North Africa. In the last sequence, Enric appears uniformed and marching in lockstep under a fluttering Spanish flag symbolizing the authoritarian state that ultimately impedes the relationship between the young Catalan couple. As Enric marches forth, an epigraph appears recounting the high number of casualties suffered in the summer of 1921 in the disastrous campaign to maintain Spain's colonial toehold in Morocco. By postponing the happy ending, or upending it all together, *Ull per ull* avoids having to explore the potential difficulties of cohabitation faced by the couple as a result of identifying with two different classes that both claim to be a force for change in Barcelona as a center of economic and cultural privilege.

BARCELONA, CIUTAT NEUTRAL OR THE FEMINIZATION OF IDEALS

The miniseries *Barcelona, ciutat neutral* offers a similar emotional journey. The two episodes aired in the evening prime time slot on TV3 on November 28–29, 2011, and then in January 2012 on channel 1 of Portuguese national broadcaster, and series co-producer, RTP under the title *Barcelona, cidade neutral*. The show anticipates by several years commemorations of World War I in which both Spain and Portugal remained neutral. The benefits reaped by Catalan industry as a result of the policy of neutrality between 1914 and 1918 had previously been explored in the novels of Agustí and their TVE adaptation *La saga de los Rius*, as well as in the works of Mendoza and their respective cinematic versions. Those years are also treated as a source of satire in the 1999 historical situation comedy series *La memòria dels Cargols* (TV3, 1999), created by theater group *Dagoll Dagom*, and as material for Antoni Tortajada and Joan Gallifa's documentary series *Històries de Catalunya* (TV3, 2003). Furthermore, World War I serves as a backdrop for the first and second seasons of the global hit *Downton Abbey* (Carnival Film & Television, Masterpiece Theater, 2010–2015), which debuted only one year prior to *Barcelona, ciutat neutral*. Not surprisingly, the centenary offered a pretext for revisiting the Barcelona of the late 1910s as the focal point of the war's impact in Catalonia and Spain. With titles that recall those of the series, Ròmul Broton's 2017 book *La ciutat neutral*, published by the City of Barcelona, examines the history of the period, while Jordi Solé's 2012 novel *Ciutat d'espies* spins a tale of international espionage. The theme of spying embellishes the situation of neutrality with an air of cosmopolitanism and glamorizes the Catalan capital as a center of intrigue and wartime profiteering. It also highlights the growth of the city's industries, in particular, its effervescent musical theater scene.

Commemorations are an industry: Through the promotion of tourism in coordination with other activities showcasing aspects of national heritage, William Johnston explains, anniversaries provide a secular and uncontroversial pretense to foment patriotism and direct public resources to private initiatives (1991, 72). Beginning in 2010, guided tours of sites associated with the Great War in Barcelona began to take advantage of the cultural heritage of the Avinguda del Paral.lel, the center of the capital's early twentieth-century theater industry, to revitalize the blighted area as a tourist and entertainment hub. Like the books by Solé and Broton, the miniseries *Barcelona, ciutat neutral* participates in the project that turns a profit through the coordinated museumization of a variety of activities designed to evoke the past as memory. Allegorical models rather than historical figures inspire the gallery of characters and social types that populate the show. Multilingualism marks the environment as cosmopolitan when figures connected to the international intrigues communicate in German, Portuguese, and Spanish. Against this backdrop, however, the local characters exclusively use Catalan as the vehicle to carry out their daily lives. Anarchism is part of this on-screen mosaic of local experiences, although here it is a facet of the labor movement rather than an ideological movement unto itself. Even though the anarchist character is easily recognizable within the established parameters of the archetype, *Barcelona, ciutat neutral* innovates by casting a woman in the role of the libertarian activist.

The series opens in the summer of 1914 with the young Karl Struch (Bernat Quintana) about to be sent back to Barcelona after a sojourn of debauchery spent in Vienna in the care of his mother's aristocratic family. The architect's artistic inclinations put him at odds with the future laid out for him by his father (Pep Pla), a wealthy industrialist and member of the *Mancomunitat* (Commonwealth), and so he decides to run off again. In the company of the aspiring singer María (Diana Gómez), he drives to the port of Barcelona but the plan is foiled when maritime traffic is suddenly halted by the outbreak of war in Northern Europe. The pair is forced to wait out the situation in the company of a hodge-podge of other travelers including the librarian Glòria (Nausica Bonin), headed to Turin for a women's rights conference, her young companion Cinto (Jordi Pla), and peasant couple, Sebastiá and Caterina (Laura Aubert), emigrating to Puerto Rico to start a new life. The planned journeys of all are eventually canceled because of the deepening conflict; however, the characters are bonded by the night they spend together, and their respective narrative arcs are woven into a complex and uneven plot structure that ends up focusing on the developing relationship between Karl and Glòria.

With the figure of Glòria, *Barcelona, ciutat neutral* examines an intellectual brand of anarchism that is quite different from that explored through Enric in *Ull per ull*. Her eloquence as a public speaker and commitment to education as a vehicle for social justice and gender equality suggest that Glòria is modeled on anarchist leader Federica Montseny, who, unlike contemporaries Seguí or Ferrer Guardia, enjoyed a long career of activism. Like Montseny, Glòria too is the daughter of anarchists who run a libertarian press. The fate of Glòria's father Daniel (Albert Pérez) parallels the story of Ferrer Guardia when he is falsely accused of participating in a terrorist attack and condemned to death following an expeditious trial at Montjuic.[8] The modeling allows the character and her intellectual formation to be linked to an unwavering commitment to family, and to explore the dynamics of the terrorism–repression pairing as a plot structure: A bomb explodes, police forcibly break up meetings of suspected groups, arrests are made, and trials are carried out indiscriminately. Repression takes up more narrative space than the original terrorist act, such that the show can avoid justifying the terrorist action or making it epic.

Glòria departs from her historical model when she comes into contact with Karl, even though he is also loosely based on the rebellious and bohemian sons of industrialists like modernist painters Rusiñol and Casas. The attraction between the pair is spontaneous and mutual, represented on-screen by Karl compulsively sketching a pencil portrait of Glòria, yet it is also conditioned by the unfolding of the case against Daniel. In fact, Glòria initially rejects Karl's advances upon discovering his family connection to the institutions of power, including the Mancomunitat, behind the unjust sentencing of her father. She represses her feelings as irreconcilable with her predicament and her role in the anarchist union. Only when she becomes disillusioned with the members of her collective, who prefer to sacrifice Daniel in order to protect the mission of the organization, does she reconsider her feelings for Karl.

The figure of the union leader Teresa (Laura Conejero) imprints the anarcho-syndicalist movement with a female face and highlights particularly its supposed concerns for the plight of working women. While compelling, as various scholars observe, the image can lead to misperceptions of the historical reality that reflect exaggerations originating in the articulation of feminism by bourgeois women (Nash 2010, 142). The pursuit of women's liberation from a position of privilege, represented by Eulalia in *Ull per ull*, is rejected by anarchist thinkers like Montseny who referred to it as "feminismo de salón" (drawing room feminism). Nonetheless, this attitude is not expressed by the protagonist of *Barcelona, ciutat neutral*; in fact, in the series, the enemy is not the bourgeoisie as such, but rather the institutions of oppression created to defend its interests. Glòria and her family are not poor by any measure, and they even offer to take in the peasant girl Catarina in order to rescue her from illiteracy.

In the home of the anarchist printer, Glòria convenes the ensemble of characters that first met on that fateful day in the harbor to gather around a primly laid table in a convivial and harmonious scene. The eclectic group is shown transiting a variety of recognizable urban spaces apparently unmarked by class divisions. Parks, cabarets, markets, the port, and a *modernista*-styled library comprise an accessible and overly sanitized version of Barcelona that, according to Ferran Monegal, never existed. In his review of the miniseries, he describes the idealization of the cityscape as resulting from "una especie de remilgado narcisismo escenográfico, en donde hasta las partes más humildes y más sucias de la ciudad parecen bonitas" (2011; a kind of fussy narcissistic scenography, in which even the humblest and dirtiest parts of the city look pretty).

The props and wardrobe of female characters, including the clothing worn by the anarchist protagonist, contribute to an attractive image of modernity not restricted to the upper class. Through multiple medium shots and close-ups, the fair complexioned Glòria fills the screen. Her physical appearance, complemented by her prim dress, coordinates perfectly with the emotional and ethical rectitude that defines her character and her pursuits, including the way she adheres to the precepts of the anarchist cause. Glòria's features and dress contrast sharply with Teresa and the other members of the union in a visual strategy that announces the librarian's individuality and progressive estrangement from the group. In this way, she recalls the character Delfina in the novel *La ciudad de los prodigios*, whose relationship with the anarchists is similarly defined by affection and betrayal. In the series, apart from Teresa, Glòria is also contrasted with the frivolous Maria, who appears repeatedly in long shots, in a red dress, performing cabaret numbers. As a female subject, the lively good-natured girl from a working-class factory neighborhood is the opposite of Glòria: She lacks intellectual wherewithal and shares Karl's hedonism, which is risky for woman without the safety afforded by the architect's class position. The two women do, however, commune in the end: In the final scene, Glòria wears a vaporous blue dress while she watches María sing and dance on stage. Here, the main character emanates a serene and liberated beauty that results from a process of maturation symbolically attained in the previous sequence when she is shown in bed nude with Karl.

The experience of growth out of which individuals derive a sense of selfhood in society while preserving their independence is a key aspect of the plotline focused on the encounter between the anarchist female and the upper-class male. The process involves compromise and sacrifice and inevitably leads to a certain disillusionment with one's surroundings. Glòria learns to express herself in the first person, that is, to speak as an individual instead of a spokesperson for the political association to which she belongs, when the judge (Pep Antón Muñoz) offers to help her father in exchange for sexual favors. While she vacillates over how to respond, Karl finds himself caught up in a tangle of espionage as a result of his father's dealings in the flourishing arms trade. The manipulations to which both are subjected are projected on-screen through erotic encounters that are experienced differently by virtue of each character's class and gender positions. In two parallel scenes, Glòria stoically accepts the judge's proposition and Karl succumbs to the advances of the beautiful Portuguese spy (Soraia Chaves). The use of crosscutting highlights the contrast between submission and pleasure and counterpoints the tender love scene between Karl and Glòria at the end of the series. María's story offers a middle ground: While she appears to be independent outwardly, her fate nonetheless depends on men, and so she is likewise forced to learn from disillusionment. Her success on the Parallel is short-lived when she hooks up with a hustler (Felipe Duarte) and is raped by the cabaret owner (Nicolau Breyner). The theme of prostitution as a social ill suffered by women of the lower classes fits into the television audience's expectations for a story set in the context of early twentieth-century Barcelona. At the same time, it is also a staple theme of anarchist literature of the Restoration period.

In terms of narrative structure, *Barcelona, ciutat neutral* draws on another constant feature of libertarian fiction: The happy ending. Based on a constructive notion of art as means to imagine other possible worlds, anarchists, as opposed to Naturalist writers, reverted back to the model set by the Realists by ending their stories on an optimistic note (Litvak 1991, 341). In spite of attempting to avoid melodrama by using more sophisticated narrative conventions, the series ultimately cannot avoid implying that the union between Glòria and Karl is somehow dependent on the convergence of their ideological perspectives. The fiction opts to materialize the relationship in the intimate encounter between the two that only happens once Glòria takes conscious steps to pursue her individual interests against the demands of her group affiliation. In this instance, she also comes to recognize Karl's unwavering support as well as his unconditional love. For his part, when his father reprimands him for being seen in the company of anarchists and other unsavory characters, the young bohemian appears to be unaware of the gravity of the supposed infraction of propriety and also bemused by the accusation that the librarian is a radical agent.

In the end, Daniel is released thanks to Karl, who reaches an understanding with his father and then suddenly leaves Barcelona to fight on the side of Austria in the war. In the chain of resolutions, through which Karl comes to terms with the contradiction between his class position and his bohemian inclinations, he comes to foresee the unhappiness and certain failure of the marriage of convenience his father has arranged for him to ensure the family's power and position in the future. Through the undoing of the father's scheme, *Barcelona, ciutat neutral* introduces an important corrective to the plotline of Agustí's 1943 novel *Mariona Rebulla* adapted in *La saga de los Rius*, which is driven by the disastrous union between Mariona Rebull and Joaquín Rius designed to maintain the latter's social status.

Barcelona, ciutat neutral appears to close on a melancholy note when Glòria receives a letter from Karl announcing his departure for the front. However, in the last scenes, which function as a coda, the action flashes forward to 1918: Karl returns to Barcelona where he is reunited with Glòria at a theater event held to welcome home Catalan volunteers who fought on the side of France in the war. The ensemble of characters from the first scene of the series is brought together again: María entertains the crowds as Cinto, now acting as her agent, looks on with pride, and Catarina finds among the crowd of union members her beloved Sebastiá who also fought and was wounded in the war (Fig. 3.2). In the final sequence, the group of secondary characters are left behind in the theater as Karl and Glòria stroll out hand in hand, and then look at the camera,

Fig. 3.2 *Barcelona, ciutat neutral* (TV3, 2011): Episode 2—Karl and Glòria, reunited

smiling, and disappear. The closing image offers a utopic vision of a harmonious Catalan society, but with certain omissions. With the licenses allowed fictions in the pursuit of happy endings, *Barcelona, ciutat neutral* situates Catalonia in relation to European heritage by having two of the characters participate voluntarily in the Great War, but without delving into the issue that the two Catalan men, Karl and Sebastiá, fought on opposite sides of the conflict. The neutrality of Barcelona implied in the title thus becomes questionable when Spain is left out of the picture.

CONCLUSION

Even though *Barcelona, ciutat neutral* and *Ull per ull* were produced independently, the coincidence in format and dates suggests that the two series respond to a similar impulse to vindicate anarchism as part of a historically determined Catalan cultural identity. The Restoration, defined by economic development and political oppression, is key to understanding how the fate of Catalonia in the twentieth century is linked to both that of Europe and Spain. The two miniseries avoid historical events, although neither fits easily within the parameters of the costume drama genre that seeks only visual pleasure in the evocation of period and eschews deeper inquiry into the past. The accumulation of period references and allegorical allusions to the ideas and leading figures of anarchism define the movement as heritage both as a class identification and marker of Catalanness. The nostalgic preciosity of the mise-en-scène at times erodes the pretension to historical authenticity of both stories, although at the same time it also indicates, especially in the case of *Barcelona, ciutat neutral*, a degree of self-reflexivity about the role of the imagination in the process of historical recreation.

Through the museumization of anarchism as a factor in the development of Catalan society during the Restoration, the movement is presented as a model for direct political action and a repository of progressive ideological values. *Ull per ull* and *Barcelona, ciutat neutral* draw out both dimensions and, indeed, complement each other in a dialectic that contests a supposed hegemonic narrative of the past. Notwithstanding, the miniseries adopt a recognizable narrative format within the discourses of heritage in dialogue with a literary, cinematic, and televisual canon. The complementarity of Enric and Glòria derives from the figuration of the anarchist as a militant activist for social justice and advocate for gender equality. The tactic of entangling the anarchist in a love affair not only adds an affective dimension to the figure, but also serves to flesh out the professed antagonism with a bourgeoisie that adopts a more progressive social consciousness with each passing generation. In parallel with the roles each woman plays in her respective series, Eulalia and Glòria represent a feminization of the figure of the liberal intellectual as a product of the confluence between the spheres of bourgeois liberalism and anarchism. On the surface, Enric and Karl appear to be diametric opposites in terms of the manner each adopts for confronting the structures of bourgeois society. Yet, the terrorist and the bohemian overlap in presenting a revised model of masculinity based on sensitivity rather than strength, and the will to accept a liberated woman as a life partner.

The affective and physical unions depicted in the two TV3 series dramatize the sublimation of anarchism through the absorption of its essential humanism and individualism into a reformulated version of bourgeois liberalism. Even in light of the concessions made in the interests of arriving at a satisfactory denouement, whether happy or ambiguously pessimistic, both fictions clearly sketch out the symbiosis of the two ideological positions. Beyond this, the endings also coincide in two interlocking eventualities: The death sentence of an anarchist is commuted thanks to a negotiation within the family representing the economic and political elite, but at the expense of a potential sacrifice of the male protagonist who is sent off to fight in a "foreign" war. Ultimately, the resulting unions take on a different tone: Whereas in *Barcelona, ciutat neutral,* participation in the First World War contributes to the prosperity and cosmopolitan aura of Barelona, in *Ull per ull* the obligation to serve in Africa subjugates the city to a decadent and doomed colonial cause. Barcelona as a museum space preserves the affluence that singularizes the city within the destiny of the nation (and the history of the Restoration). The miniseries bring to life the anarchist, whether tragic victim or survivor, commemorated on solemn plaques and monuments, in celebrated works of art, and in the names of streets and bars, and so contribute to curating an identity that is aesthetic and nostalgic in its wistful combination of two apparent opposites.

NOTES

1. Agustí's *Mariona Rebull*, published in 1942, was previously adapted in 1949 by Luis Saínz de Heredia; the 1944 novel *El viudo Rius* is the first of five that comprise the pentalogy *La ceniza fue árbol*, source material for *La saga de los Rius*.

2. The miniseries, *Tarancón. El quinto mandamiento* (TVE, Radiotelevisión Valenciana, 2011) y *El asesinato de Carrero Blanco* (TVE, Euskal Telebista, 2011) have been broadcast various times, while others have been suspended indefinitely, such as *El precio de la libertad* (TVE, Euskal Telebista, 2012), *Tornarem* (*Volveremos*; TVE, TV3, 2012) or *La conspiración* (TVE, Euskal Telebista, 2012); likewise the second season of *14 de abril. La República* (TVE, 2011), studied in this volume, has yet to air, even though TVE successfully screened other historical series like *Isabel* (TVE, Diagonal TV, 2012–2014) and *Carlos, Rey emperador* (TVE, Diagonal TV, 2015–2016).

3. Homar had recently portrayed King Juan Carlos I in another TVE-TV3 coproduction, *23-F: El día más difícil del rey* (2009).

4. A similar scene appears in Mario Camus's adaptation of *Fortunata y Jacinta*, where the scene is transferred to the repression of student revolts in 1868 (see George 2009, 63).

5. The article in *La Vanguardia* that informs of this exhibition describes the painting's "compleja operación de traslado" (complex relocation operation), under "vigilancia policial" (police surveillance), that inevitably recalls the exhibition of *Guernica* in Madrid just one year prior (see Canals 1982).

6. In 2001, a committee of neighbors took the initiative of restoring the deteriorated plaque.

7. Martínez Anido, born in El Ferrol like Francisco Franco, did not agree with the repressive policies engaged by the future dictator during the Civil War; he died in mysterious circumstances in 1938 (see Romero 2014).

8. Ferrer Guardia was implicated in the events of the Tragic Week and executed at Montjuic in 1909; he was also accused of instigating the attempted assassination of Alfonso XIII during his visit to Barcelona in 1906.

BIBLIOGRAPHY

Álvarez Junco, José. 1991. *La ideología política del anarquismo español (1868–1910)*. Madrid: Siglo XXI.

Canals, Enric. 1982. "El cuadro 'La carga', del pintor modernista Ramón Casas, se expone en Barcelona." *El País*, December 9.

De Groot, Jerome. 2016. *Historians and Heritage in Contemporary Popular Culture*. London: Routledge.

De Luna, Manuel. 2017. "Las 'líneas rojas' de Televisión Española." *El Periódico*, June 18.

Díez, Xavier. 2013. *L'anarquisme, fet diferencial català. Influència i llegat de l'anarquisme en la història i la societat catalana contemporània*. Barcelona: Virus.

Epps, Brad. 2005. "Seeing the Death: Manual and Mechanical Spectrors in Modern Spain (1893–1939)." In *Visualizing Spanish Modernity*, edited by Susan Larson and Eva Wood, 112–141. Oxford: Berg.

Espigado Tocino, Gloria. 2002. "Las mujeres en el anarquismo español (1869–1939)." *Ayer* 45: 39–72.

Esteban, Paco. 2013. "Xavier Díez: 'El anarquismo catalán es una corriente telúrica y subterránea, una constante en la historia del país.'" *Rojo i negro*, June 5. http://www.rojoynegro.info/articulo/ideas/xavier-d%C3%ADez-el-anarquismo-catal%C3%A1n-es-una-corriente-tel%C3%BArica-subterr%C3%A1nea-una-constante.

Geli, Carles. 2017. "Barcelona s'explica sempre des de l'òptica burgesa." *El País*, January 7.

George, David R., Jr. 2009. "Restauración y Transición en la *Fortunata y Jacinta* de Mario Camus." In *Historias de la pequeña pantalla: Representaciones históricas en la televisión de la España democrática*, edited by Francisca López, Elena Cueto Asín, and David R. George, Jr., 53–71. Frankfurt: Iberoamericana.

Hite, Katherine. 2013. *Politics and the Art of Commemoration: Memorials to Struggle in Latin America and Spain*. London: Routledge.

Huyssen, Andreas. 1995. *Twilight Memories*. New York: Routledge.

Johston, William. 1991. *Celebration: The Cult of Anniversaries in Europe and the United States Today*. New Brunswick: Transaction.

Koek, Richard. 2013. *Cine/Scapes: Cinematic Spaces in Architecture and Cities*. London: Routledge.

Litvak, Lily. 1991. *España 1900. Modernismo, anarquismo y fin de siglo*. Barcelona: Anthropos.

Monegal, Ferran. 2011. "La Barcelona que nunca existió." *El Peródico*, November 30.

Morales Muñoz, Manuel, and Pere Gabriel. 2002. *Cultura e ideología en el anarquismo español, 1870–1910*. Málaga: Centro de Ediciones de Diputación Provincial de Málaga. http://books.google.com/books?id=h6baAAAAMAAJ.

Nash, Mary. 2010. "Libertarias y anarquismo". In *Tierra y libertad. Cien años de anarquismo en España*, edited by Julian Casanova, 139–165. Barcelona: Crítica.

Oswald, Kalen R. 2006. "Anticipating Transformations: The Urbanization Consciousness of Eduardo Mendoza's *La verdad sobre el caso Savolta* and *La ciudad de los prodigios*." *Letras Hispanas* 3 (2): 41–61.

Pierre, Nora. 1972. "Lévénement monstre." *Communications* 18: 162–172.

Romero, Santiago. 2014. "El general coruñés cuya familia salvó al padre de Suárez se enfrentó a Franco por la repression." *La opinión. A Coruña*, March 6. http://www.laopinioncoruna.es/espana/2014/04/06/general-corunes-cuya-familia-salvo/828823.html.

RTVE. 2010. "Charla de los internautas con el 'patriarca' de la miniserie 'Ojo por ojo' de TVE y RTVE.es." http://encuentrosdigitales.rtve.es/2010/lluis_homar.html. Accessed February 20, 2018.

PART II

Imagining Technologies

New Technologies and Transmedia Storytelling in *Víctor Ros*: Captivating Audiences at the Turn of the Century

Mónica Barrientos Bueno and Ángeles Martínez García

Víctor Ros, the eponymous hero of the 2015 Televisión Española (TVE) series,[1] is adventurous and intuitive, but also guided by logical, deductive reasoning. His character undeniably echoes the archetypal detective par excellence, Sherlock Holmes. Rescued from a life of juvenile delinquency by a policeman, Ros becomes the most brilliant officer in the fictional Metropolitan Brigade in Madrid, where he does not hesitate to apply techniques akin to those used in Scotland Yard. Premiering on January 12, 2015 on channel one of Spain's public broadcasting network,[2] the series achieved in its first season an audience of 2,342,000 viewers and a share of 11.7% of the market, 2.2 points above TVE's average quota during the period in which the show was broadcast. The second season was produced a year later without the participation of its original creator

M. Barrientos Bueno (✉) · Á. Martínez García
Universidad de Sevilla, Seville, Spain
e-mail: mbarrientos@us.es

Á. Martínez García
e-mail: angelesmartinez@us.edu

© The Author(s) 2018
D. R. George, Jr. and W. S. Tang (eds.),
Televising Restoration Spain,
https://doi.org/10.1007/978-3-319-96196-5_4

Javier Olivares, and its broadcast had less impact: The audience was 1,491,750 viewers on average, with a quota of 9.25% of the market share for the eight episodes broadcast in November and December of 2016.

The fourteen-episode series transports the viewer back to the last decade of the nineteenth century, a key period in Spanish history in which the foundations were laid for many aspects of contemporary Spanish culture, politics, and society. The setting in 1895, as the Restoration system faced social and political crises at home and abroad, and Spanish society struggled to adapt to technological modernity, imbues *Víctor Ros* with a pedagogical function to instruct viewers about the past as well as to entertain them. This chapter explores how the Restoration period (1874–1931) is represented in the universe of Víctor Ros, particularly through the use of transmedia. The series depicts a brief period, from 1895 to 1898, but includes numerous references to different historical events and characters outside of this time frame. The use of transmedia storytelling, and its associated technologies, to expand the narrative universe of *Víctor Ros* is especially notable in facilitating a connection with contemporary audiences. Several different storytelling platforms are used to bring the viewer into closer contact with aspects of the Restoration as they allow the user a deeper immersion in this sociohistorical context. Transmedia likewise plays an active role in facilitating a closer identification of the spectator with the characters, especially Víctor Ros. This analysis centers on the techniques that connect the past depicted on-screen to present-day viewers throughout the series' two-season run, with an eye on the progression of the media strategy and resources used between the first and second seasons. Initial efforts focused on developing and updating the main character's personal Twitter account, which built up his backstory within an established historical period and allowed Ros to personally answer his followers. In contrast, the second season saw a notable expansion of the transmedia strategy, with elements of gamification and interactivity soliciting the spectator to take part in the story, and thereby Restoration history, in one way or another. It is notable that in both seasons audiovisual materials from the Restoration and fictional recreations are mixed in order to connect the series with current audiences. These materials must be considered in examining the series as a portrait of this historical period.

VÍCTOR ROS AND THE RESTORATION

The end of the TVE monopoly closes the first broad golden age of historical series featured on Spanish television, which extends from the middle of the 1970s to the end of the 1980s. Its rebirth occurs in the twenty-first century with the success of the series *Águila Roja* (Globomedia, 2009–2016), which was followed by more than 70 productions that approximate and reproduce different moments of the Spanish past (Rueda Laffond and Coronado Ruiz 2016, 90). Within this context of renewed interest in historical period dramas, *Víctor Ros*, based on the detective stories by Jerónimo Tristante, depicts Spain at the turn of the nineteenth century. To date, Tristante has published five novels in which Victor Ros appears as the protagonist: *El misterio de la casa Aranda, El caso de la viuda negra* (both in 2008), *El enigma de la calle Calabria* (2010), *La última noche de Víctor Ros* (2013), and *Víctor Ros y el gran robo del oro español* (2015). The novels and the series' original script situate the action in the middle of the nineteenth century rather than its end; the change in setting to the period of the Restoration was motivated to a certain point by the desire to reproduce the look of Madrid at the end of the century, which required the consultation of abundant photographic documentation to achieve visual and historical fidelity (De la Fuente et al. 2016, 34). Showrunner Javier Olivares thought that the end of nineteenth century would be a more attractive period to portray on-screen, not to mention that the development of Madrid as the modern capital of Spain was carried out in this period. The changes that Spain experienced during the Restoration are represented in a metaphorical and visual sense through Madrid's physical and symbolic transformation into a modern European capital.

As previously stated, Víctor Ros is an inspector with the Metropolitan Brigade, a fictional special police force that uses the scientific methods of Scotland Yard to solve the most difficult crimes, which makes them pioneers in Spain. The first season takes place in Madrid and the second begins in Madrid, but in the following episodes Víctor Ros moves to Linares, a real town in Andalusia, in the south of Spain. During the protagonist's investigations, several historical characters appear, while social and political aspects of the Restoration period are also represented, such as delinquents linked to anarchism, and the first forays into criminal investigation and forensic medicine. Real historical cases are also introduced, such as the werewolf of Allariz (1841) and the vampire of Raval (1912),[3] altering their chronology in order to include them in the temporal frame of the script (Gutiérrez 2015, 34–35). Furthermore, the reality of the times is reflected through situations and characters such as Clara, Víctor's love interest, who is a suffragist and very conscious of the power of education as a motor for social progress.

Generally speaking, the series presents the Restoration period in terms of the clichéd antinomy between what José Ortega y Gasset identified as an "España real" (real Spain) and an "España official" (official Spain) (De Miguel 1972, 281). In this sense, three key oppositions can be identified in the portrayal of Spanish history on the show: Madrid versus Andalusia, the Metropolitan Brigade versus the Civil Guard, and rationality versus irrationality. In the first case, North—Madrid and South—Andalusia (exemplified in Linares) are an example of the contrast between turn-of-the-century cosmopolitan and provincial environments. Though it remains much smaller than Madrid, Linares becomes one of the most dynamic Andalusian cities of the late-nineteenth century given its important mining industry, intense journalistic activity and the presence of diplomatic delegations from several European countries. For these reasons, the character of Madame Suberwick, a female novelist of French origin living in Linares, is plausible in the context of the series. Similarly, the Bank of Spain opens an important branch office there; this is connected with the narrative axis of the second season of the series. Another prominent dichotomy is established between the Metropolitan Brigade and the Civil Guard. The former represents the origins of the scientific police, personified in Víctor Ros and his companions in the series. In contrast, the Civil Guard represents the authority in the countryside, working with less rigorous research methods, as is shown in the series. Finally, the series portrays a clash between the rational and the irrational. The former is clearly represented by the main character, and the latter by his sidekick Leon Cavestany, especially in the second season. During the Restoration, there was a very high rate of illiteracy in Spain: 63.78% of the population was illiterate and 2.66% was semiliterate (De Gabriel 1997, 202), which could explain why some people were largely motivated by the passions instead of by rational thinking in this period. This is reflected in the series through the inclusion of supernatural elements such as magic potions or spiritism.

The series also deploys stereotypes as a means to represent Spain in light of the contrast between Madrid and Andalusia. Partaking of the Romantic vision of the country, which persists into the present, Madrid is represented through a set of elements that build a traditionalist view of the capital: the *verbena* (a traditional outdoor dance party) and *chulapos* (men in the typical dress of Madrid), among others. Likewise, the south of Spain is focalized through the character of Madame Suberwick as the embodiment of the Romantic nineteenth-century traveler. At the same time, there are also connections between Víctor Ros and Bizet's 1875 opera *Carmen* based on Prosper Mérimée's 1847 Romantic novel. The opera's male protagonist Don José is clearly reflected in the characterization of Víctor Ros. Both men are agents of authority who fall in love with a rebellious, outlaw woman: Carmen in the opera and Juana/Elena in the series.

Given the reliance of the series on stereotypical tropes and figures, and the lack of adherence to a historical chronology of events, we can define *Víctor Ros* as a period series in which history works as a pretext. According to Salvador's classification, this televisual category includes:

> dramaturgias televisivas en las que la Historia actúa como simple trasfondo de la trama, independientemente de que se haga referencia a hechos y personajes reales ...; los conflictos y las relaciones entre los personajes se abordan desde la óptica característica del contexto histórico en el que han sido realizadas y no de la época en la que transcurre la ficción.
>
> (2016, 157–158; televised dramas in which history acts simply as background to the plot, independently of whether it refers to real people and facts ...; the conflicts and the relationships between the characters are tackled from the characteristic optic of the historical context in which they have been made and not of the epoch in which the fiction takes place).

Notably, *Víctor Ros* was created by Javier Olivares, who is also behind the biographical series *Isabel* (TVE, 2012–2014) and sci-fi time-travel drama *El Ministerio del Tiempo* (TVE, 2015–2017). While all these shows are marked by the trademarks of the Olivares brothers in their "representational strategies," they differ in their treatment of history. *Isabel*, for instance, "was created as a period drama with a sense of documentary rigor. For *Víctor Ros* ...it was essential to integrate history with fiction" (Rueda Laffond and Coronado Ruiz 2016, 91).

Historical Connection Through Transmedia

What allows audiences of the twenty-first century to connect with the fiction of *Víctor Ros*, which is anchored in a very specific moment of the Restoration, is largely the development of the transmedia of the series. In 1991, Marsha Kinder coined the phrase 'transmedia intertextuality' to refer to works of fiction in which the characters appear across various platforms.[4] Henry Jenkins joined the dialogue with his concept of the transmedia narrative, which is defined as "the development of content across multiple channels" (2001, 93). Further studies have suggested that transmedia engages audiences in novel ways: "<Transmedia story­telling> is telling a story across multiple media and preferably, although it doesn't always happen, with a degree of audience participation, interaction or collaboration" (Pratten 2015, 1). This occurs in a context of participative culture in which "consumers are active, socially connected participants within the changing media environment. New technologies become tools within a multimedia sandbox, empowering 'typical' consumers to become creators, artists, and visionaries" (Smith 2009, 17–18). Notably, transmedia storytelling covers the entire media panorama, from journalism to documentaries, to fiction and even advertising.

In *Victor Ros*, the concept of transmedia storytelling is applied to fiction. Thus, the story is extended from one medium to another and the aim is for the fans to participate actively in this expansion (Scolari 2014, 73). As a result, it is very difficult to know where a transmedia storytelling world ends. At its most basic level, transmedia storytelling needs to include two basic characteristics: offer the viewer different points of entry into a story, and facilitate audience collaboration, especially in stories told on the small screen. As Edwards explains, "For television specifically, companies have moved to incorporate new media developments, creating elements for their TV shows such as fan-centered websites, mobile phone applications, online games, and even music albums and tours, all imagined as features that help further the content" (2012, 2).

Recently, the transmedia storytelling in Spanish television series has expanded to increasing platforms and media, making it an indispensable part of the panorama of national televised fiction. Currently, the most representative example, for its range, ambition, and representation, is *El Ministerio del Tiempo*, whose transmedia universe "ha experimentado un desarrollo en el aspecto tecnológico, que ha conllevado también mayor profundidad en la trama argumental y en el crecimiento de los personajes" (Cascajosa and Molina 2017, 134; has experienced improvement in the technological aspect that has allowed for greater depth in the plot and in character development). Two more historical fiction series that stand out for their transmedia usage are the aforementioned *Isabel* and *Carlos, Rey Emperador* (2015–2016), both of which, like *Víctor Ros*, were produced by TVE. These series are exemplary in the expansion of transmedia to allow audiences to approach the different historical contexts and elements in an interaction that is more authentic than ever before. They are proof of TVE's commitment to maximizing the immersive experience of the spectator in the historical series, which is likewise seen in *Victor Ros*.

Notably, the transmedia maps of the first and second season of *Víctor Ros* differ as to the number of media and platforms that were deployed. To prepare for the launching of the broadcast in January of 2015, TVE developed a plan of complementary online activities and documentary productions for the series, which aired after each one of the episodes in the first season, under the title *La España de Víctor Ros* (*The Spain of Víctor Ros*). In consultation with Jerónimo Tristante, the author of the Víctor Ros novels, they introduced various aspects related to the historical context of the show, some of which were not even alluded to in the episode, but which nevertheless complemented the knowledge of the period and helped to make some of the show's content more comprehensible. Cast members from the series as well as specialists on the fictional and historical material collaborated on the project. On the Internet, the transmedia strategy focused on the webpage of the series on TVE's site, with on-demand access to the episodes and *La España de Víctor Ros*, along with selected scenes, photography, and other extras. As for social media, profiles for the show were created on Facebook and Twitter, with differing activity. Facebook was used essentially as a platform for promoting the series, with the specific purpose of publicizing what was happening on Twitter, the show's prevalent social media outlet.

The first season introduced the personal Twitter account of the protagonist, who communicated directly with followers as a relatively novel element central to the online transmedia strategy.[5] The television and social networking team from TVE, with the support of the show's producer, developed a complete script for Víctor Ros which they posted in 478 tweets throughout the month before the show's premiere. On Facebook, banners promoted the beginning of the story on Twitter, emphasizing Victor Ros's personality and the possibility to interact with him. For the development of this aspect of the storytelling, Jerónimo Tristante advised TVE's interactive media department (Álvarez 2015). Generally speaking, the decision to use a particular kind of social media strategy is not left to chance, but aims to attract young audiences, who are not the majority among TVE spectators. Given the popularity of Twitter among Spanish youth, @VictorRos_TVE was the focus of the transmedia strategy of the first season.

On Twitter, Víctor Ros communicates in the first person, in a kind of epistolary writing or diary that narrates a case that occurred before his arrival in Madrid, which opens the series. The choice of a first-person narration allows for more exposure to the character, still unknown to a large part of the social audience at this point, and it strengthens the affective ties to his followers, while simultaneously allowing them to become acquainted with his personality prior to the series. The choice of the Oviedo mission is not coincidental: It is alluded to in the fourth novel (*La última noche de Víctor Ros*), which serves as the main source for the televised Ros's personality. The protagonist's personal profile is employed strategically so that Víctor Ros can reveal his deepest feelings, such as falling in love for the first time. At times, strict narration is set aside in favor of reflection.

However, the Twitter activity does not remain a monologue; on the contrary, as Cortés, Martínez, and de la Fuente observe, the use of Víctor Ros's account and the hashtag #VictorRos evolves from this point onward to polyphony, with new content generated by audience interventions (2016, 166). Once the show premiered, Twitter usage evolved into a conversation between the character and his followers that is maintained even during the broadcast of each of the episodes, which results in a participative culture made possible by the characteristics of the social medium itself, "una interactividad social, virtual y colectiva que se basa en sus propios lenguajes y los usos que los individuos hacen de ellos" (Cortés et al. 2016, 157; a social, virtual and collective interactivity that is based on its own languages and the uses that individuals make of them). The result is the integration of the series' Twitter followers and the world of Víctor Ros.

On the other hand, in the same way that "la realidad histórica y documentación a través de la prensa de la época" (De la Fuente et al. 2016, 37; historical reality and documentation through the press of the era) nourishes the show's plots and sets, it likewise feeds the series' Twitter narration, which is especially visible in the introduction of historical facts about late nineteenth-century Spain. These are complemented with visual elements such as photographs of Oviedo at the end of the nineteenth century, pages from newspapers, and GIFs created from other images of the time, which expose users to the historical setting of the narration, although some of the photographs have been digitally retouched to include the figure or the face of Víctor to lend credibility to the story. All these photographs create a background that mixes fiction and reality, so that the visual universe of the series is credible for the spectator because it is supported by real photographs taken at the end of nineteenth century. The inclusion of Víctor Ros in the images is not invasive, as he is not the main subject in any of them. These photographs are analogous to the matte paintings in the series used to recreate turn-of-the-century Madrid in many shoots.[6] The appearance of authenticity in Ros's fictional world is also supported by the timing of publication of the Twitter content, which coincides with what is broadcast on TV (e.g., the nocturnal revelations that Víctor Ros makes after midnight) and the particular schedule of the main character. This coincidence is particularly important to bridge the gap between Víctor's story unfolding in 1894–1895 and his followers in 2014 and 2015.

Twitter is just one of many media platforms that accompany season two of *Víctor Ros*. The slogan "Descubre el nuevo universo transmedia de Víctor Ros" (discover the new transmedia universe of Víctor Ros) reveals the principle strategy that TVE follows during the show's second season. The official website features three star products: "El videoblog de Cavestany" (Cavestany's videoblog), "Los interrogatorios de Víctor Ros" (Víctor Ros's interrogations), and "Contenido exclusivo de la Caja de Oro" (Exclusive content from the Box of Gold). Additionally, the second season notably takes a very active role in social media networks like Twitter, Facebook, and Instagram. Furthermore, video meetings in which fans can pose questions to the show's actors in real time through platforms like Facebook Live are launched.

Working within a broader transmedia map than that of the first season, three media blocks can be distinguished in the transmedia strategy of season two; games (such as "Los interrogatorios de Víctor Ros"), where interactivity with the users is sought; behind-the-scenes reporting and promotional albums (like "El videoblog de Cavestany"), which increase the visibility of the series and uncover hidden details in order to grow its fan base; and historical materials (often found in "la Caja de Oro"), whereby the historical moment in which the plot develops gains special importance for the consumer of the series. Each of these blocks mixes history and fiction to draw users further into the world of Restoration Spain.

Whereas the games and behind-the-scenes materials featured online work to engage the user with the series and particularly its characters,[7] the category of historical materials includes the transmedia content that most explicitly connects the present-day viewer of the series to the historical background against which the plot unfolds. In this sense, the section "Caja de Oro" (Box of Gold) is perhaps the most relevant. This is accessed only by obtaining a satisfactory score in the games of "Interrogatorios interactivos," and its contents include previews, interviews, and other show extras. "Material extra" includes "Documento: la nueva identidad de Juana" (Document: Juana's New Identity) in which the user gets an exclusive look at the document elaborated by Cavestany to help the bandit elude her pursuers and start a new life. This is another a link between history, fiction, and present-day reality because, although it is a fictional document, it imitates the format of a real identification card of the period, drawing viewers into the minutiae of life in Restoration Spain.

In a second example, hashtag "#enigmavíctorros" includes four very brief videos which were apparently recorded by Víctor Ros in a more proactive role: "Víctor te acepta en el equipo, pero vas a sufrir" (Víctor accepts you to the team, but you will suffer) is the personal greeting from Ros, implying that the user has become part of the Metropolitan Brigade. The use of a handheld camera and the breaking of the fourth wall in the videos help the user to feel more deeply immersed in the historical context. In "Víctor nos cuenta quién es realmente León Cavestany" (Víctor tells us who León Cavestany really is), the main character defines the personality of the street trader, while in "Cuidado con los bandidos" (Beware of the bandits) and in "Víctor te anima a descifrar el enigma" (Víctor encourages you to decipher an enigma) he encourages the user to embark on online adventures. Bandits and street traders are an important connection between the series and the historical moment depicted, as they were characteristic of the final decade of the nineteenth century. Furthermore, bandits were the most romanticized figures of this period. In these videos, more information is shown about the way these characters acted in real life.

In addition to these features, the TV series *Víctor Ros* and related transmedia materials further reflect upon curious events that took place in the historical moment in which the protagonist lived, leading viewers to do the same. For instance, in the second season, the anarchist organization Mano Negra (Black Hand) becomes the *leitmotiv* of the series.[8] With roots in Andalusia, the group supposedly operated in the early 1880s, although its existence has never been proven. Evidently, *Víctor Ros* altered the timing of some historical events in the interest of fiction, in the same way that it altered historical photographs to include

Víctor's face in Twitter activity. The enigma surrounding the existence of Mano Negra continues to this day, and so it figures in the transmedia storytelling as an independent section in the "Caja de Oro" under the title "El misterio de la Mano Negra. La Mano Negra, ¿realidad o ficción?" (The Mystery of the Mano Negra. The Mano Negra, reality or fiction?). It consists of an article written by Leticia Romero, in which distinct, and sometimes contradictory, academic theories on the topic are analyzed.[9] Some relevant sections include: "¿Qué es la Mano Negra?" (What is the Mano Negra?), "¿A quiénes interesaba su existencia?" (In whose interest did they exist?"), "¿Fue el hambre la causa de sus acciones?" (Was hunger the cause of their actions?), and "El Reglamento de la Mano Negra, ¿verdadero o falso?" (The Mano Negra's Rule Book, true or false?). Here, the written text is complemented by a short TVE documentary on the supposed organization. In another section of the "Caja de Oro" called "Documentos," the user has access to a recreation of the *Rules and Statutes of the Mano Negra*.[10] Ultimately, it is up to the user to decide whether or not Mano Negra was a myth or a real clandestine organization formed by the Regional Spanish Federation (FRE). The material related to La Mano Negra is highly relevant for the development of the plot in *Víctor Ros* and its representation of the series' historical context. After all, anarchism gained traction as a political ideology in the late nineteenth century.[11] During this period, anarchists often turned to violence as a political tool, at times carrying out bomb attacks connected to the working-class struggle.[12] All this is portrayed on *Víctor Ros*, and the series' transmedia platforms ask users to actively participate in evaluating the historical truth behind the *Mano Negra*.

In addition to "La Caja de Oro," there is another feature that plays with the historicity of *Víctor Ros* titled "La Cámara Acorazada, en claves. ¿Es posible asaltar la Cámara de Oro del Banco de España?" (The Vault, in code. Would it be possible to steal the gold from the vault at the Bank of Spain?). "El gran robo del oro español" (Spain's Great Gold Heist) is the subtitle of the second season of *Víctor Ros*. The heist serves as the catalyst for the characters to be transferred to Linares so that they can solve the crime that could spell doom for the country on the verge of war, a situation which seems unthinkable today. In order to help audiences understand this precarious situation, and to relate to the historical moment depicted, "La Cámara Acorazada, en claves" presents an article with real information about the Bank of Spain and its gold reserves. The section called "¿Por qué se roba el oro español en *Víctor Ros*?" (why

would one steal Spanish gold in *Víctor Ros*?) is one of the most important to understand the difficult situation that Spain was going through
during the period of the Restoration. As in previous cases, there are several parts of this section in which real data are combined with fictional
material, which ultimately drives user interest in both the show and its
historical setting.

Lastly, the section "Víctor Ros bajo la lupa" (Víctor Ros under the
magnifying glass) makes a particularly compelling effort to bring today's
viewer closer to the late-nineteenth-century society depicted in the series.
Here the fictional liberal, independent, and progressive newspaper *La
Atlántida* is found. It consists of eight pages created specifically for the
development of the show. All of the pages are perfectly laid out in the
style of the era, and the user can navigate through the different sections.
On the front page, we find the lead story: the robbery at the Bank of
Spain. On page 2, there is a likeness of Víctor Ros and on the following page, a report about the sinking of the Maine, a real event from the
period in which the series is set that precipitated the Spanish American
War and eventual loss of Spain's remaining colonies in the Americas
and the Pacific. This fictional framing of a factual event highlights the
period of the Restoration as the context of the series by giving relevance
to a fact that was decisive in Spanish international relationships as well
as its own internal issues. Pages 4 and 5 of *La Atlántida*, under the
title "Linares, encrucijada y motor de Andalucía" (Linares, crossroads
and motor of Andalusia), introduce this real up-and-coming city at the
end of the nineteenth century. It also includes a column by the fictional
French writer Madame Suberwick, one of the secondary characters created for the series, which relates, in the style of the Romantic travelers of
the nineteenth century, hidden details in the life of Linares. "Los mejores
productos y servicios" (The best products and services) compiles real
period advertisements for soaps, pomades, shoes, and surgeons, and even
mixes in the story of the fictional León Cavestany. The last page, titled
"La Brigada Metropolitana" (The Metropolitan Brigade), is effectively a
print ad for the show itself, with a black and white photograph of Ros
and his colleagues, and a list of the actors and producers involved in the
series.

In summary, a mix between fiction and reality can be found in this
fake periodical, as in most of the transmedia materials. It is important
to highlight how fictional elements such as León Cavestany, the French
writer Madame Suberwick, and the Metropolitan Brigade serve as a

"hook" for the user fan. In this way, some kind of "History class" is presented to the user as a game, introduced by familiar characters. Through these materials, the viewer–user learns about the city of Linares and its important role at the end of the nineteenth century. Users can also find authentic period products through their advertisements in this newspaper. Finally, historical events, which appear in the series only as background because there is no place to deal with them more extensively, are shown as news. The pedagogical value of this section is undoubtedly high.

CONCLUSION

Víctor Ros is a Restoration period TV series in which history and fiction are interconnected. Audiovisual materials from the Restoration and fictional recreations are mixed in order to engage current audiences both with the series and its historical setting. For *Víctor Ros*, transmedia storytelling is particularly relevant in allowing the modern spectator or netizen to become submerged in the specific historical period of the Spanish Restoration, or at least a stereotypical vision of the period. The universe of transmedia presents "ficción y realidad, unidos por un medio y una actividad" (Cortés et al. 2016, 172; fiction and reality, united through a medium and an activity), integrating followers of the series into the world of Víctor Ros, and transforming them from spectators into participants. But they are not only participants of the show, but also of the nineteenth century, as they are called to be policemen by Víctor Ros, and gather new information about relevant historical events. Spectators are also invited to decide whether alleged clandestine organizations existed or not. Growing exponentially between the first and second seasons, the transmedia experience of *Víctor Ros* becomes a perfect example of enhanced TV, with a focus on interactivity and putting additional, alternative, and exclusive content into the hands of series followers. All the supplementary contents, whether it be a story told in first person through serial tweets or a newspaper imitating the font and style of the era, make the consumer feel closer to the real and contextual events of the Spanish Restoration from the anarchist machinations of Mano Negra to the beginning of the Spanish–American War in 1898 and the appearance of cities like Oviedo at the end of the century, ultimately arriving at a deeper understanding of the daily life, as well as the social, political, and economic conditions of the age.

NOTES

1. Television Española is the national general-interest public broadcasting network.
2. Víctor Ros was the first series that premiered in prime time on TVE since 2012.
3. The vampire of Raval likewise appears in episode 18 of the TVE series *El Ministerio del Tiempo (The Ministry of Time)*, attesting to the figure's popularity with Spanish audiences.
4. The term platform used here refers to different media such as TV, Internet, and podcasts.
5. In the USA, there was already a precedent of a fictional television character tweeting daily from his "reality": Don Draper of *Mad Men* (Costa and Piñeiro 2012, 122), which was co-produced by Lionsgate Television, Weiner Bros., and AMC, and broadcast from 2007–2015.
6. Matte painting: A painted (natural or digital) set or location used by filmmakers to create the illusion of an environment that is not present at the filming location. Nowadays matte paintings are treated digitally.
7. In the games section, and sharing the format of a multiple-choice quiz, "¿Quién dijo qué?" (Who said what?) and the "Interrogatorio interactivo" (Interactive interrogation) stand out among the online content for the second season of Víctor Ros. With regard to promotional behind-the-scenes materials, it is worth mentioning the videoblog "Las aventuras de Víctor Ros según León Cavestany" (The Adventures of Víctor Ros, according to Leon Cavestany), which was uploaded before the broadcast of each episode of the season. Through the character of Cavestany, commentary on previous shows and previews of the next show are presented.
8. Interestingly, Mano Negra is also a theme in Diagonal TV's *Bandolera*; Francisca López's contribution to this volume discusses this series.
9. Leticia Romero is the journalist in charge of the development of most of the sections on the *Víctor Ros* webpage at www.rtve.es.
10. The document consists of 12 independent manuscript pages that can be enlarged by using a magnifying glass icon on the page.
11. Elena Cueto Asín's contribution to the present volume deals specifically with the anarchist tradition in Restoration Barcelona.
12. The most famous bomb attack took place at King Alfonso XIII´s wedding in 1906.

BIBLIOGRAPHY

Álvarez, José. 2015. "Las redes sociales como sistema de comunicación en *Víctor Ros.*" *Bupler.* http://bluper.elespanol.com/bluper/noticias/redes-sociales-sistema-comunicacion-serie-victor-ros. Accessed January 19, 2018.

Cascajosa, Concepción, and Juan Pedro Molina. 2017. "Narrativas expandidas entre la tradición y la innovación: construyendo el universo transmedial de *El Ministerio del Tiempo.*" *Tropelías. Revista de Teoría de la Literatura Comparada* 27: 120–135. https://papiro.unizar.es/ojs/index.php/tropelias/article/view/1544.

Cortés, Sara, Rut Martínez, and Julián De la Fuente. 2016. "Contribución de las redes sociales a la creación de narrativas transmedia de las series de ficción en televisión." *Comunicación y Hombre* 12: 153–176. http://www.redalyc.org/articulo.oa?id=129446703008.

Costa, Carmen, and Teresa Piñeiro. 2012. "Nuevas narrativas audiovisuales: multimedia, crossmedia y transmedia. El caso de *Águila Roja* (TVE)." *Icono 14. Revista de Comunicación y Tecnologías Emergentes* 10, no. 2: 102–125. http://dx.doi.org/10.7195/ri14.v10i2.156.

De Gabriel, Narciso. 1997. "Alfabetización, semialfabetización y analfabetismo en España (1860–1991)." *Revista Complutense de Educación* 8, no. 1: 199–231.

De la Fuente, Julián, Sara Cortés, and Rut Martínez. 2016. "El inicio de la televisión transmedia en España: TVE y *Víctor Ros.*" *Revista de la Asociación española de Investigación de la Comunicación* 3, no. 6: 28–42. http://www.revistaeic.eu/index.php/raeic/article/view/64/60.

De Miguel, Armando. 1972. *España, marca registrada.* Barcelona: Editorial Kairós.

Edwards, Leigh H. 2012. "Transmedia Storytelling, Corporate Synergy, and Audience Expression." *Global Media Journal* 11, no. 20: 1–12. http://www.globalmediajournal.com/open-access/transmedia-storytelling-corporate-synergy-and-audience-expression.pdf.

Gutiérrez, Angélica. 2015. "Archivo de ficción. *Víctor Ros.*" *Quadernos de criminología: revista de criminología y ciencias forenses* 30: 28–35. http://dialnet.unirioja.es/descarga/articulo/5444496.pdf.

Jenkins, Henry. 2001. "Convergence. I Diverge." *Technology Review* (June): 93.

Olivares, Javier. 2015–2016. *Víctor Ros.* New Atlantis, Telefónica Studios, TVE.

Pratten, Robert. 2015. *Getting Started with Transmedia Storytelling.* Createspace Independent Publishing Platform.

Rueda Laffond, José Carlos, and Carlota Coronado Ruiz. 2016. "Historical Science Fiction: From Television Memory to Transmedia Memory in *El Ministerio del Tiempo.*" *Journal of Spanish Cultural Studies* 17, no. 1: 87–101. http://dx.doi.org/10.1080/14636204.2015.1135601.

Salvador, Lucía. 2016. "Historia y ficción televisiva. La representación del pasado en *Isabel*." *Index Comunicación* 6, no. 2: 151–171. http://journals.sfu.ca/indexcomunicacion/index.php/indexcomunicacion/article/view/231/207.

Scolari, Carlos. 2014. "Narrativas transmedia: nuevas formas de comunicar en la era digital." In *Anuario AC/E de Cultura Digital:Uso de las nuevas tecnologías en las artes escénicas*, 71–81. Madrid: Acción Cultural Española.

Smith, Aaron Michael. 2009. "Transmedia Storytelling in Television 2.0. Strategies for Developing Television Narratives Across Media Platforms." Doctoral Thesis, Middlebury College.

CHAPTER 5

From Photography to Forensics: Technology, Modernity, and the Internationalization of Spanish History in *Gran Hotel*

Wan Sonya Tang

In June of 2016, the popular Egyptian channel Capital Broadcast Center (CBC) premiered a new television series titled *Grand Hotel* (Beelink Productions, Eagle Films, 2016). Following the trials and tribulations faced by the owners and employees of a lavish hotel in 1950s Egypt, the series aired during "super-prime time" Ramadan, when Arabic channels typically broadcast their best programming to capitalize on the particularly large viewership (VideoAge 2016). With high production values, an acclaimed cast, and an action-packed plot, the show quickly became an "obvious winner" of the 2016 Ramadan season (El Goarany 2016). Yet the Arabic series, which "rings truly Egyptian" in the words of film and television critic Soha Hesham, is not an original Egyptian concept, but rather a remake of the Spanish hit *Gran Hotel*, which originally aired on privately

W. S. Tang (✉)
Boston College, Boston, MA, USA
e-mail: Wan.tang@bc.edu

© The Author(s) 2018
D. R. George, Jr. and W. S. Tang (eds.),
Televising Restoration Spain,
https://doi.org/10.1007/978-3-319-96196-5_5

owned Spanish network Antena 3 from 2011 to 2013 (Hesham 2016).[1] Egypt's *Grand Hotel* is not the first international adaptation of the Spanish series, nor is it likely to be the last. Italy's state-owned RAI premiered their remake, miniseries *Grand Hotel*, in September of 2015, and Mexico's media conglomerate Televisa transformed the Spanish original into the *telenovela El hotel de los secretos*, which aired from January to May of 2016.[2] Argentine and Chinese adaptations may soon go into production, according to Spanish website formulatv.com (FormulaTV 2016), and in the United States, ABC is rumored to be developing its own version set in Miami Beach, with actress and producer Eva Longoria at the helm (Elidrissi 2017).

The global appeal of *Gran Hotel* is undeniable, and not only as source material for local, nation-specific remakes. Set in the 1905–1907 period, the Spanish series has enjoyed an overwhelming reception abroad since its national premiere on October 4, 2011; as of May of 2016, German distributer Beta Film had successfully sold the drama in roughly 70 countries worldwide,[3] ranging from Afghanistan to New Zealand, not to mention the show's enormous popularity on online streaming platforms such as *Netflix* and *Hulu* (FormulaTV 2016).[4] No Spanish television series has ever had such a successful international run, to the surprise of the show's own creators (FormulaTV 2016).[5] This remarkable popularity abroad leads us to question how a costume drama set in the Spanish countryside of the early 1900s captivates such diverse, multicultural audiences. If, as Iris Kleinecke-Bates posits in *Victorians on Screen*, viewers of historical fictions seek "authenticity, fidelity, and immediacy" in on-screen material (2014, 11), how do audiences with limited or no knowledge of the Spanish Restoration (1874–1931) evaluate the merits of *Gran Hotel* as a period series?

The answer is complex and involves myriad factors relating to the show's production, marketing, and content. In "Estrategias narrativas y género policíaco en la ficción televisiva de *Gran Hotel*," Pablo Sánchez Blasco argues that the show's appeal is due in large part to the hybridity of its genre, a novel mix of historical drama and thriller (2015). Paul Julian Smith further notes Antena 3's calculated use of social media in marketing *Gran Hotel* to "attract a younger and more upmarket audience than is customary for costume drama in Spain" (2017, 354). In terms of production, the creative team assembled by Bambú Producciones left no element of the show to chance. The series was created, written, and executive produced by the dream team of Ramón Campos, Gema R. Neira, and Teresa Fernández-Valdés, who had previously collaborated on the successful period piece *Gran Reserva* (Bambú, 2010–2013), and would go on to bring audiences such hit costume dramas as *Velvet* (Bambú, 2013–2016) and *Las chicas del cable* (*Cable Girls*; Netflix, Bambú, 2017–). Both subsequent series would find international success, although not to the same degree as *Gran Hotel*. Under the direction of Carlos Sedes and Silvia Quer, among others, *Gran Hotel* featured popular young actors Amaia Salamanca and Yon González as star-crossed lovers Alicia and Julio, as well as veteran actress Adriana Ozores as hotel owner Doña Teresa, and longtime fan-favorite Concha Velasco as head of hotel staff Doña Ángela.[6] As an added distinction, the series enjoyed a television score by award-winning composer Lucio Godoy and, most importantly for a visual medium, featured breathtaking locations, sets, and costumes.[7] This emphasis on the spectacular is essential, given that local and global audiences primed by Merchant Ivory's model for on-screen historical recreation, popularized in the 1980s and 1990s, have come to assess the quality of a period piece on the basis of its production values, such that the designation of "quality" television often depends on "how much money was invested in a production" (Oliete-Aldea 2015, 184). For international audiences who are unfamiliar with the Spanish cast, elements of mise-en scène acquire even greater significance in evaluating the series.

Given the expectation for visual splendor, a major element of *Gran Hotel's* appeal lies in its highly aestheticized recreation of an early twentieth-century seaside luxury hotel.[8] This comes as no surprise, considering that the series premiered just one year after British mega-hit *Downton Abbey* (Carnival Film & Television, Masterpiece, 2010–2015), which honed worldwide audience tastes for glamorous period settings. In the case of *Gran Hotel*, often marketed as "the Spanish Downton Abbey" (Beta Film, 2012), audiences expecting a visual feast are not disappointed. On-screen, the landscape is lush, interiors are lavish, costumes are sumptuous, and everywhere we see primitive iterations of modern technology, from early automobiles to the first Edison light bulbs. Nor is the presence of technology on the show limited to material devices; new developments in the social and physical sciences are likewise highlighted throughout the series. It is worth nothing here that *Gran Hotel* is one of only two Bambú productions that hired a historical consultant, Juan Luna, who was head curator of the Museo del Prado at the time of broadcast (Ruiz and Calvo 2011). Beyond a merely ornamental purpose, then, the carefully approved artefacts and techniques featured in the series function to present a calculated vision of Restoration Spain that ultimately contributes to the show's international appeal.

In this chapter, I examine the strategic on-screen placement and use of technology in *Gran Hotel*, particularly during the show's first season, arguing that the inclusion of period-specific devices and practices serves three interrelated purposes: firstly, to situate viewers within the sociohistorical context of early twentieth-century Spain, conceived of as a cosmopolitan milieu with modernizing impulses, but largely devoid of markers of national character; secondly, to heighten narrative intrigue by driving the plot forward, building character arcs, and highlighting thematic concerns, particularly in relation to class conflict as a *leitmotif* of the Restoration; and finally, to provide a point of connection with tech-savvy audiences in the twenty-first century, many of whom are consuming the series via non-traditional, streaming methods. All three functions of technology as represented in *Gran Hotel* conspicuously package Spanish history in an unchallenging and aesthetically-pleasing manner that transforms a local, national narrative of modernization and social change into a familiar, globally intelligible narrative, thereby engaging both Spanish and international viewers.

Setting the Scene in Restoration Spain

On the English-language website for Bambú Producciones, the synopsis of *Gran Hotel* reads:

> 1905. A young man [Julio Olmedo (Yon González)] arrives at the Grand Hotel, an idyllic place in the middle of the countryside to investigate the disappearance of his sister [Cristina (Paula Prendes)]. What he does not know is that his greatest love is about to cross his way: the beautiful daughter [Alicia Alarcón (Amaia Salamanca)] of the owner of the hotel [Doña Teresa Aldecoa (Adriana Ozores)] and the fiancée of its director [Diego Murquía (Pedro Alonso)]. Between them, although they come from opposite social classes, an uncontrollable and impossible love: A dangerous romance that will intertwine with all the mysteries and secrets hidden among the walls of the Grand Hotel. (Bambú Producciones, n.d.)

Just as the synopsis begins by unequivocally establishing the historical moment, the series immediately invites viewers into the setting of Cantaloa, a fictional small town along Spain's Cantabrian coast, at the start of the twentieth century. The title sequence, which establishes the tone for the entire show, makes it evident that audiences are traveling back in time. The opening credits are displayed against a series of what appear to be real sepia-toned photographs from the early 1900s that ends on a snapshot of the Palacio de la Magdalena in Santander, which serves as the fictional Gran Hotel within the series.[9] The decision to begin each episode with this selection of photographs is clearly a strategic move. As Joel Snyder recognizes in "Picturing Vision," "Photographs make a special claim upon our attention because they are supposed not only to look realistic ... but also to derive from or be caused by the objects they represent. This 'natural connection' has been taken as a reinforcement and even a guarantee of realistic depiction" (1980, 504). In other words, viewers instinctually ascribe an objective truth value to photographs, particularly those rendered in monochrome. This faith in the documentary quality of the photograph is often dramatized on the show itself, as in episode six of the first season, when Alicia frantically searches through old newspapers in the hope that photographs from the Gran Hotel's electrification party will corroborate her fiancé's alibi and prove that he was not involved in maid Cristina Olmedo's supposed murder. In terms of the series' title sequence, the apparent authenticity of the images featured behind the credits primes audiences to accept what follows—both the final image of the supposed Gran Hotel and the show's fictional content—as historical fact, that is, as if the preceding photographs were surviving documentation of the action that we will now witness on-screen. The animation of particular parts of the photographs—the moving dumbwaiter, flickering lightbulbs, curling cigarette smoke, and passing clouds—in otherwise static frames further add to the idea that *Gran Hotel* brings history to life.

Given the priming role of the title sequence, it is no coincidence that some of the animated elements draw the viewer's attention to technological innovations of the late 1800s, such as the mechanical dumbwaiter, invented in 1887, or the electric lamp, first installed in Cantabria in 1881 (Ibeas Cubillo 2011, 2), since turn-of-the-century technology, particularly the light bulb, will play an important role throughout the series. In the first season alone, comprised of just nine episodes, characters are frequently shown traveling by train and automobile, sending and receiving telegraphs, and making (and tracing) calls on antique telephones with the help of an operator. Additionally, a phonograph is repeatedly featured on-screen,[10] and we witness the installation of electricity, advancements in photography and cinematography, and the inception of forensic science. These and other period-specific technologies situate viewers in the early twentieth century without the need to explicitly reference the date, which is, in fact, never mentioned in the premiere episode.

Like historical costuming, technological artefacts provide easily recognizable visual cues of a bygone era, "stand[ing] in for period accuracy" (Kleinecke Bates 2014, 178). As a result, attention to technological innovation is a commonplace of period pieces.[11] What sets *Gran Hotel* apart is not only the degree to which technology figures both in the series' staging and plotlines, but also the fact that the technology featured across all three seasons of *Gran Hotel* is markedly international in nature. In the series premiere, while guests delightedly await the inauguration of electric lighting in the titular hotel, Doña Teresa, the hotel owner and matriarch of the wealthy Alarcón family, announces that 4500 imported Edison lightbulbs have made the technological advance possible (Fig. 5.1). As the episode unfolds, several interspersed close-ups of wooden crates stamped with the Edison logo drive this point home, and this acknowledgement of foreign innovation is noticeably repeated throughout the entire series. In season two, for instance, a new maître d' arrives astride a vintage Harley Davidson, whose logo is prominently featured on-screen (episode 10), while subsequent episodes feature close-ups of various imported automobiles: an Italian Fiat that

Fig. 5.1   *Gran Hotel* (Bambú, Antena 3, 2011–2013): Episode 1—hotel maids install Edison light bulbs

Doña Teresa's playboy son Javier (Eloy Azarín) covets (episode 12), and a French Delage that Julio and Alicia "borrow" from the hotel for their investigations (episode 13).[12] In other instances, the acknowledgement is oral and not visual, as in season one, when Detective Ayala (Pep Antón Muñoz) credits his dear friend Argentine Juan Vucetich with the fingerprinting powder he uses while solving a murder committed in the hotel (episode 9).[13] Similarly, in season three, a heavily-accented German doctor diagnoses Doña Teresa's traumatized eldest daughter Sofía with hysteria, and then employs hypnosis-based psychotherapy to cure her (episode 26).[14] As seen in these examples, foreign technological innovation is an on-screen constant across *Gran Hotel*'s three seasons.

The inclusion of such recognizable innovations and brands, many of which remain in circulation today, aids in situating the viewers of *Gran Hotel* in a familiar televisual landscape. Audiences who may have little knowledge of Spanish history but participate in globalized viewing practices can recognize many of the featured technologies from popular British period pieces, such as the aforementioned Merchant Ivory productions, and arrive at a basic understanding of Restoration Spain based on inferences drawn from the frequently televised settings of Victorian or Edwardian England. This is true not only for foreign viewers, but also for Spaniards with little awareness of the national past. Thus, the period technology, often of foreign origin, portrayed on-screen in *Gran Hotel* establishes what television scholar John Caughie describes as "commonalities of shared experience and communities of memory" in audiences across countries and cultures, regardless of their previous knowledge of life in Restoration Spain (2000, 13).

Furthermore, the inclusion of imported knowledge and machinery in *Gran Hotel*'s story lines hold an additional appeal for Spanish audiences by projecting a positive image of national past. As Vicente Rodríguez Ortega reminds us, "The historical film [and by extension, the historical television series] is thus most usefully understood as a multi-generic template that ... mobilizes a variety of generic registers in order to typically offer an understandable, linear, and ideologically skewed rereading of the past" (2013, 241). Any period piece conveys a particular interpretation of history, rather than an objective recreation of it. In the case of *Gran Hotel*, the continual inclusion of novel technologies underscores the Spanish desire for progress in the early twentieth century, even as certain archaic customs like the duel (featured in episode six of season one) lingered. For some viewers, the multiple nods to foreign advances in science and technology might communicate a kind of Spanish inferiority; after all, there are no references to Spanish innovation in *Gran Hotel*. However, in light of the scope of countries of origin represented in the various technological advances featured on-screen (we see contributions from Europe, North, and South America), we might instead view their inclusion in *Gran Hotel* as an attempt to dispel the myth of twentieth-century Spain as a European backwater. The Spain of *Gran Hotel* is a cosmopolitan place, where even the small town of Cantaloa can access the newest gadgets and most up-to-date knowledge.

This is, of course, an over-simplification, and the series is careful not to idealize Restoration Spain as a uniformly progressive place. After all, it is not truly the town of Cantaloa that embodies the modernizing impulse, but the Gran Hotel itself, notably a playground reserved for the affluent. Although the hotel attracts guests from all over the world, from Indian diplomats to South American entrepreneurs, these visitors represent only the elite classes of their respective nations. Access to an automobile or a film projector remains the privilege of the wealthy, as I will elaborate later in this chapter. Outside of the hotel, modernization is likewise occurring, but not without a struggle. In particular, *Gran Hotel* acknowledges the great divide between urban and rural Spain at the start of the twentieth century in the humorous contrast between the sophisticated Detective Ayala—who hails from the capital and is well-versed in the study of forensics—and the lovably incompetent local police inspector Hernando (Antonio Reyes). In his meticulous methodology and reliance on logic and science, Ayala recalls popular fictional detectives Sherlock Holmes and Hercule Poirot, both of whom have inspired countless film and television adaptations.[15] The condescension with which Ayala initially addresses Hernando in season one renders evident the divide and perceived hierarchy between the distinct worlds that the two characters represent, and it is not by chance that the duo's first clashes concern proper protocol for new forensic techniques. These differences in awareness of technological innovation and its usage paint a picture of the uneven modernity that characterized Restoration Spain, constituting the greatest political statement that the series offers in terms of twentieth-century Spanish history.

In contrast with a series like *Downton Abbey*, which is set during the World War I era and explores notable events of British history (Shattuck and Mandeville 2016), *Gran Hotel* is largely devoid of concrete references to national history. The final (and longest) season of the Spanish series is perhaps the most historically-engaged of the three. An early plotline concerning Doña Teresa's wayward son Javier incorporates some discussion of the Spanish military actions in Morocco (episodes 25 and 26), although there is no reflection on the recent *Desastre* (Disaster) of 1898 and the resultant loss of Spain's imperial status in the Americas and the Pacific, which exacerbated the nation's identity crisis well beyond 1905. Later, in episode 30, the young king Alfonso XIII (Guillermo Barrientos) graces the halls of the Gran Hotel as the only Spanish historical figure to appear in the series, but he does so only to carry out an extramarital affair, making no reference to matters of the State.[16] The monarch's story line serves largely as comic relief, since his presence causes Alfredo (Fele Martínez), Doña Teresa's son-in-law and ex-Marquis of Vergara, to act the fool in an effort to win back his aristocratic title. Finally, the series concludes with an outbreak of cholera at the hotel, which alludes to the devastating epidemic that struck the nation in 1885 without explicitly referencing the event. Evidently, life in the Gran Hotel is only tangentially affected by contemporary events and politics.

This lack of engagement with political history is not exceptional for a television period piece. After all, "the predominance of costume dramas, usually associated with female spectators, has centered on the micro-history of the 'private' or 'domestic sphere'," that which Miguel de Unamuno deemed *intrahistoria*, rather than major events of national significance (Oliete-Aldea 2015, 179). Generic conventions aside, this domestic focus is understandable in the case of *Gran Hotel*, since the Restoration in general, and particularly the 1905–1907 period that series creators Campos and Neira chose to portray, is relatively uneventful in terms of Spanish history. Consequently, it is both easy and logical for familial intrigue and interpersonal conflict to overshadow any drama unfolding on the national stage.

That is not to say that *Gran Hotel* invites no reflection on Restoration society. Beyond the struggles of individual characters, viewers observe the dynamics of class conflict as represented in the tensions between the hotel owners and their guests, on the one hand, and the staff on the other. Characters like the aforementioned Alfredo, the disgraced Marquis of Vergara, who is anachronistically obsessed with preserving the family's honor, and even king Alfonso XIII himself, in his comedic cameo, invite viewers to contemplate the nobility as a useless and perhaps even obsolete social stratum in the twentieth century. The series' use of period technology further highlights the tension between classes, as we will later see. The changing role of women is likewise a recurrent theme in *Gran Hotel*. For all intents and purposes, the hotel is run by two matri-archs: Doña Teresa, the hotel's owner, upstairs, and Ángela, the head housekeeper, downstairs. Although they represent different social strata, the two nevertheless share similar exacting standards and a desire for order and control. Similarly, Doña Teresa's two daughters, Sofía (Luz Valdenebro) and Alicia, are both intelligent and independent women, although their mother ironically underestimates them time and again. Season three introduces additional recurring characters Laura (Marta Hazas) and Maite (Megan Montaner), the first an heiress moonlighting as a nurse and the second, one of Spain's first female lawyers.[17] In terms of both class and gender relations at the start of the twentieth century, *Gran Hotel* offers plenty of food for thought.

Nevertheless, these same conflicts and considerations could be explored in nearly any early twentieth-century Western society, just as Edison light bulbs and Harley Davidsons might play a role in any European or American costume drama portraying the early 1900s. Indeed, the juxtaposition of upper- and lower-class lives has long been a staple of these period series, with obvious examples in the recent *Downton Abbey* and the classic *Upstairs, Downstairs* (London Weekend Television, 1971–1975), recently revived as *Upstairs Downstairs* (BBC Cymru Wales, Masterpiece Theater, 2010–2012). Similarly, the plight of women at the start of the twentieth century is a central theme of many television dramas set in this period, in which strong female fig-ures abound. As Katherine Byrne, author of *Edwardians on Screen*, notes "most of [these series] are as progressive about gender concerns as they are reactionary about privilege and social hierarchies" (2015, 12). In light of these thematic similarities to foreign productions, the considered inclusion of international technology in *Gran Hotel* appears to be part of a deliberate focus on a generalized European social his-tory rather than specific events of national significance, thereby remov-ing the "Spanishness" from the historical period depicted. In "Places of Memory in the New Millennium: British Influence on Spanish Transnational Heritage Cinema and Television," Elena Oliete-Aldea concludes that Spain's "heritage" series allow "otherwise 'fragmented imagined communities' to share an emotional revision of the local past through 'global' generic conventions" (2015, 190). However, in *Gran Hotel*, the local past, with its imported technology, is presented as decid-edly devoid of local color.

This revisionist history is further sustained by the series' wardrobe department. In an interview with entertainment news site *Vanitatis*, costume designer Helena Sanchís describes the selection of clothing for *Gran Hotel* as based in rigorous historical research, but with a conscious effort to glamorize historical Spanish dress based on foreign models: "Hemos utilizado sobre todo referentes de la alta sociedad española, inglesa y francesa de aquellos años, intentando quitarle el lado rancio de algunas tendencias que había en nuestro país, más de zarzuela y con menos clase" (in Ballano 2012; We have used above all examples from Spanish, English, and French high society from those years [1905–1907], trying to remove the stale element of certain tendencies that existed in our country, more fitting for *zarzuela* and less classy). Thus, between the foreign technology that shapes the lives of the characters and their internationally-inspired costumes, both the show's narrative and its mise-en-scène turn to outside influences to represent Restoration Spain as chic and modern. As a result, the internationalized image of the country in the early twentieth-century that *Gran Hotel* projects on-screen looks familiar to contemporary audiences across national borders.

HEIGHTENING DRAMA AND HIGHLIGHTING CLASS CONFLICTS

Perhaps because of the creative liberties taken in reimagining Restoration Spain on *Gran Hotel*, Bambú categorizes the series as an "investigation thriller" rather than as a historical drama or as a "historical thriller," the descriptor attached to *Imperium* (2012), another of the company's productions (Bambú, n.d.). The simple categorization as "thriller" erases the series' historical element, implying that the meticulous staging is merely decorative rather than central to the plot. However, this idea undersells the role of the period-appropriate technology depicted on the show. From the photograph to forensic science, each piece of technology visually featured or explicitly referenced in *Gran Hotel* plays some role in the series' plot, character or thematic development, foregrounding particularly the rigid class divisions at the hotel. Although this is true across the show's three seasons, I will focus particularly on season one for the sake of brevity.

In a first example, the phonograph serves a largely symbolic function within the series. Appearing expressly in episodes 5 and 7 of the first season, the phonograph's placement in the office of the hotel director designates the apparatus as a status symbol. This is particularly evident in episode 7, when Diego, whose has been ousted as director of the Gran Hotel by Doña Teresa, enters his old office, now occupied by Teresa's son Javier and son-in-law Alfredo, the hotel's new director and subdirector, respectively. In these newly acquired positions, the two men are obviously in over their heads, which is visually communicated through Alfredo's clueless fiddling with the phonograph. In a stark contrast of body language, Diego strides purposefully over to the device as a startled Alfredo backs away, and he turns on the apparatus in a practiced motion, using only one hand. The power differential between the two men is clear. "Hay veces que las cosas no funcionan, Alfredo" (There are times when things aren't working, Alfredo), Diego remarks over the music played by the phonograph, "lo importante es saber qué es lo que hay que hacer para arreglarlas" (the important thing is to know what one must do in order to fix them). There is no mistaking the dual meaning of his words; just as Alfredo, ever representative of a bygone era, cannot understand the workings of new technology, he is likewise helpless before Diego's machinations. In this scene, the phonograph denotes power, and that power is most effectively wielded not by an antiquated nobleman, but by an ambitious, self-made social climber, whose return to the director's office is inevitable. Although it plays a relatively minor role in the first season, the phonograph serves both to highlight the differences of temperament between Diego and Alfredo, and to comment upon the changing state of Spanish society.[18]

In a second example, the telephone appears frequently throughout the first season of *Gran Hotel*, and its usage similarly advances the plot while providing implicit social commentary. Like the phonograph, the hotel's main telephone is located in the director's office, but whereas the former is placed off to one side, the telephone occupies a prime location on the director's desk. As with the musical device, the telephone likewise denotes status, or at the very least, wealth. As of 1905, there were only 16,400 telephones in all of Spain (Calvo Calvo 1998, 64), and within the fiction of the series, two of them reside in Doña Teresa's hotel: one reserved for the director, and the other for guest usage. The presence of this guest phone as an available amenity speaks to the social class of the hotel guests, who are accustomed to a life of modern comforts.

Unlike the phonograph, the telephone appears in almost every episode of season one. Notably, almost all the calls made during the season are related to power struggles between the characters. The telephone is never used for purely informational purposes within the world of *Gran*

Hotel. Instead, it serves to blackmail, extort, and call in reinforcements. Not surprisingly, the majority of calls in the first season originate in the hotel. In light of the mounting body count in Cantaloa and specifically on hotel grounds, Doña Teresa repeatedly calls local authority Judge Barreda to obstruct or manipulate the outcome of Detective Ayala's investigations. When Judge Barreda's hands are finally tied by an executive order from Madrid, Doña Teresa encourages son-in-law Alfredo to call the civil governor, using his aristocratic title and family ties to garner the support of the highest political authority in the province (episode 9). Together, these calls establish the phone as a medium of privilege; more often than not, it is used to secure a pact of allegiance between individuals of the socially prestigious classes, who are furthermore portrayed as entitled and corrupt. Working-class characters, too, use the telephone with villainous intentions, but their plans tend to end in tragedy. Pascual (Alejandro Cano), the hotel's receptionist, calls Diego from the guest phone as part of an elaborate blackmailing scheme, but unbeknownst to him, his call is traced back to the hotel, and once Pascual is identified as the blackmailer, Diego personally shoots and kills him.[19] Similarly, Cristina, Julio's sister and former hotel maid, calls Doña Teresa to set up a meeting at which she intends to trap and kill her adversary, but ironically it is she who ends up dead on the hotel's kitchen floor. It would seem that, in season one of *Gran Hotel*, technology serves as an ally to the privileged classes only.

Passing usage of technological devices such as the phonograph and telephone reveal the character of *Gran Hotel*'s various personages and simultaneously call into question early twentieth-century class relations, but electricity is the true technological centerpiece of the series' first season. The action of season one begins with the hotel's grand inauguration of electric lighting, and ends with the electrocution of Julio's best friend and fellow hotel employee Andrés (Llorenç González), who also happens to be Doña Teresa's deceased husband's illegitimate son and the rightful owner of the Gran Hotel. In episode one, the electrification of the hotel defines the establishment and, to a certain extent, Spain as modern and cosmopolitan spaces with profitable international connections.[20] Not only has the event required the importation of 4500 Edison lightbulbs, but numerous guests from the Americas have made the same trans-Atlantic journey to be present at the momentous occasion.

Beyond establishing a sense of Spain's international relations and global commerce, the electrification of the hotel generates narrative intrigue at several key moments. This is made clear in the premiere episode, when the hotel lighting party provides the perfect distraction for Cristina to escape from the hotel, where she had just been threatened by Doña Teresa. Cristina's flight across the property matches the pace with which the grounds are electrified, such that garden lights flicker on exactly as she passes each section of the property. This synchronization provides the ominous sensation that she is being watched, which indeed she is, by a knife-wielding assailant, whose point of view is momentarily adopted by the camera. Cristina's fate, however, remains unclear until the second half of the season. Her disappearance following the lighting festivities brings protagonist Julio to the Gran Hotel, setting in motion the series' narrative arc as he seeks to unravel the mystery of his sister's whereabouts. Although the hotel's electrification does not directly lead to Cristina's disappearance, it allows her the opportunity to slip away unnoticed, and the incorporation of electric lighting into the scene of her attempted escape is orchestrated to heighten the drama of the spectacle.

Similarly, in the first season's finale (episode 9), electricity plays a pivotal role in the closing minutes. On the day of Alicia's wedding to reinstated hotel director Diego, an arranged marriage of convenience that is an inherently tense affair, Andrés is tasked with replacing all the lightbulbs in the hotel dining room in anticipation of the wedding reception. Considering that the lightbulbs have only recently debuted at the Gran Hotel, their replacement is a completely gratuitous display of the Alarcón family's wealth. It furthermore serves as another plot device by prompting the season's shocking closing scene. In the last sequence, three cross-cut scenes unfold concurrently: a uniformed Andrés on a ladder, swapping out lightbulbs in the dining room's magnificent chandelier, Alicia and Diego getting married in the church, and Julio provoking a fight and getting pummeled in Cantaloa's disreputable tavern. As each scene unfolds, the dramatic tension mounts, which is augmented by the increasing pace of the cross-cutting. Andrés's situation is particularly suspenseful, as several close-ups linger on a live wire tucked in the chandelier, and the audience watches helplessly as each bulb Andrés screws in brings him closer to electrocution. A few excruciating minutes later, Andrés's wife Belén (Marta Laralde) finds him lying unconscious on the dining room table. The camera zooms in on his lifeless face, blood streaming from his ears and mouth. We then cut to Alicia pronouncing a joyless "I do," closing credits roll, and viewers are left to wait for the next season to see if Andrés has survived.

Once again, technology plays a multifunctional role in *Gran Hotel*. Much like in the season opener, the depiction of electric lighting at the season's end functions to engage audiences by both ramping up the show's drama and inviting reflection on the social divide pervading the Gran Hotel: The rich flaunt their fortunes, and the poor can't seem to escape certain doom. From a marxist perspective, Andrés's potentially fatal electrocution might even suggest that, at the titular hotel, workers are quite literally sacrificed in order to satisfy the demands of the leisure class. At this point, it is important to note that this chapter examines the representation of period technology in season one of *Gran Hotel* only. In later seasons, as Detective Ayala discovers the truth behind Don Carlos's death, and the narrative arc progresses toward a happy resolution rife with poetic justice, technology turns in favor of the oppressed,[21] affirming that "technology brings change in society and undermines convention" (Alfred P. Sloan Foundation 1999, 19).

The fact that technology mediates the experiences of and interactions between the working class and the wealthy throughout *Gran Hotel*'s run is not surprising. As Richard Rhodes makes clear in his introduction to *Visions of Technology*, "science and technology are demonstrably objective and effective; but they're unquestionably bound up with power relations as social systems" (1999, 14). New inventions inevitably bring up questions of production and ownership (By whom is it created? And for whom?), not to mention access and usage (Who can obtain the new technology? Who operates it? And whom does it serve?), and these questions are particularly pertinent in the Restoration period, which is marked by a new sense of class consciousness. Although the idea of the middle class as we understand it today dates to the early nineteenth century in Spain, the term "burgués" (bourgeois) only appears in the last third of the century, around the time of the Restoration (Cruz 2011, 8). Similarly, it is "between 1875 and 1914" that "new mass parties ... displaced parties composed of old monarchist nobles" (Jacobson and Moreno Luzón 2000, 109). By representing class conflict and its reflection in local politics on-screen, *Gran Hotel* accurately paints Restoration society as socially stratified. Moreover, the exploration of class dynamics, particularly as embodied in a forbidden romance across class lines (between Julio and Alicia) is an age-old, universal trope of literary, filmic, and television fiction. Consequently, in drawing attention to class differences and power struggles, the technology featured in *Gran Hotel* further contributes to the series' attractiveness both at home and abroad by drawing viewers into a familiar discourse of social inequality that remains at the forefront of much present-day political debate worldwide.

LINKING PAST TO PRESENT

As a means of situating viewers in the proper sociohistorical context and engaging them in the drama unfolding on-screen, the technology depicted on *Gran Hotel*, particularly in the first season, foregrounds universally-relatable interpersonal and class struggles instead of delving into the intricacies of Spanish political history. Setting the series in the Restoration, a period that witnessed incredible technological advances, particularly in urban centers, is strategic in this regard. This resultant portrait of the Spanish past casts the nation as analogous to England and other European models, challenging persistent myths of Spanish inferiority and attracting broader international viewership. To this end, the pervasive role of early twentieth-century technology in *Gran Hotel* aids in appealing to a wide range of contemporary viewers, whose own lives and dramas often revolve around gadgets and screens. The materiality of on-screen technology transcends linguistic and cultural boundaries, and featured devices like early models of the telephone or automobile further provoke viewer interest both for their datedness and for their familiarity.

On the one hand, the historicity of the devices and techniques portrayed confers upon them an aura of prestige that appeals to contemporary audiences. A ten-year-old model is simply unfashionable, but one that is over a hundred years old automatically acquires distinction as an antique. We have only to look to long-running British series *Antiques Roadshow* (BBC, 1979–), and its numerous European, North American, and even Australian versions, to confirm an abiding audience interest in the conferred value of dated artefacts. In fact, shows "predicated upon the public value of [dated] objects" like "*Flog It!* (BBC2), *Cash in the Attic* (BBC1), *Car Booty* (BBC1) and *Bargain Hunt* (BBC1) were, together with *Antiques Roadshow*, the top performing history-related programmes [in the UK in] 2005–2006" (De Groot 2009, 69). To pique our interest, however, these antiques must still remain recognizable to current viewers, as is the case with the technology portrayed in *Gran Hotel*. Commenting on the British documentary series *What the Victorians Did for Us* (BBC, 2001), Kleinecke-Bates posits that the viewer's "personal relationship with the past ... depends on our ability to recognize the inventions and innovations discussed in the programme as part of our own everyday experience of life or as still a recognizable part of contemporary society" (2014, 154). That we still recognize the early phones and cars handled by the Gran Hotel's guests and staff establishes a sense of material continuity that allows us to identify with the society depicted on-screen. Moreover, although modern-day technology has evolved far beyond the innovations featured in the series, the same impulses to travel, communicate, and assert dominance or flaunt social status through new and sophisticated devices continue to color our current usage. Ironic as it may seem, the on-screen presence of technology emphasizes the shared humanity of its users, however flawed it may be.

Beyond the physical objects themselves, the presentation of technology in *Gran Hotel* likewise translates easily to the twenty-first-century televisual experience. The plethora of foreign brands on parade in the Spanish series differs little from the typical product placement found in much modern-day commercial television programming, thereby linking the televised past to the viewer's present. As reported in the *Hollywood Reporter*, "In such countries as Spain ..., which have long allowed in-program plugs, product placement is one of the fastest-growing forms of advertising" (Roxborough and Kemp 2010). Looking backward from the era of globalization, Spanish and foreign audiences alike may find the mix of imported products in 1905 Cantaloa to be familiar, and even natural. Moreover, in the original Antena 3 broadcast context, viewers might sense the similarity between the familiar brands of the past featured in the series and those of the present advertised during commercial breaks, thus establishing a certain continuity in past and present material realities. Similarly, Detective Ayala's skillful application of forensic science to examine cadavers and murder weapons raises eyebrows within his fictional community, but for today's viewers, it simply recalls the BBC's recent smash hit *Sherlock* (2010–) or the hugely successful *CSI* franchise, which established forensic science as a convention in the global collective imagination.[22] In contextualizing a period series, we must recognize that today's viewers are shaped not only by the political and social history of their respective nations, but also by their televisual practices, and the globalized media and products that they consume. In this regard, *Gran Hotel*'s success stems partially from its ability to convey "authenticity, fidelity, and immediacy" to international audiences through the presentation of period technology that is not only historically accurate, but also dialogues with the contemporary television landscape (Kleinecke-Bates 2014, 11).

One of the commonplaces of British heritage film and television, largely Victorian in nature, is that it allows viewers to return to the birthplace of English modernity (Kleinecke-Bates 2014, 5). Although a certain escapist impulse may well be involved, historical productions require viewers to relate on some level to the supposedly antiquated society shown on-screen. In the context of the heritage genre, this connection between past and present applies at the national level above all. In the case of *Gran Hotel*, where the "Spanishness" of the past is underplayed in favor of a vaguely European vision of the early 1900s peppered with authentic period technology, the goal seems not to offer an exploration of the roots of Spain's current sociopolitical reality, but rather an understanding of the start of our worldwide dependence on and fascination with new technologies and the social relations that they shape, a subject that will continue to resonate with new, untapped audiences as the *Gran Hotel* franchise continues its conquest of global markets.

NOTES

1. The degree to which the Egyptian *Grand Hotel* acknowledged its origin in the Spanish series is unclear. According to *Daily News Egypt*, screenwriter Tamer Habib was "massively criticized" in online postings by Egyptian audiences familiar with the Spanish original for not acknowledging the Spanish series in the show's credits (Yasser 2016). Habib then took to social media to publicly recognize his debt to the Spanish original, whose influence he claimed was self-evident in the Egyptian production (Yasser 2016).
2. For a thoughtful comparison of the Spanish and Mexican series, see Smith (2017).
3. Beta Film likewise handles the show's international adaptations.
4. As just one example, *Gran Hotel* was the most watched series on *Netflix* in Argentina as of May of 2017 (Estéviz 2017).
5. Creators Ramón Campos and Gema R. Neira express genuine surprise over the staggering international popularity of *Gran Hotel* in an interview with FormulaTV found on Youtube (2014).
6. Salamanca had previously starred in the hugely popular *Sin tetas no hay paraíso* (Grundy Producciones, 2008–2009), a controversial Spanish

adaptation of a Colombian telenovela, and González was known for the teen-age fantasy/mystery series *El internado* (*The Boarding School*; Globomedia, 2007–2010). A veteran of theater, television, and film, Ozores had won a Goya Award for her supporting performance in the film *La hora de los valientes* (1998), and Velasco, whose illustrious career on stage and screen began in the 1950s, has long been a household name in Spain.

7. In an interview with Álvaro Onieva, series creator Ramón Campos was quick to acknowledge the collective talent involved in the staging and filming of *Gran Hotel*:

En la ambientación de Carlos Dorremochea logramos transmitir al espec-tador esa sensación de introducirse en un cuadro de Soroya [sic]. [...] En la fotografía el trabajo de Jacobo Martínez fue espectacular ya que tuvo que hacer que una serie en blancos y negros, casi sin color, resp-landiece [...], el vestuario de Helena Sanchís, la música de Lucio Godoy, la peluquería de Mara Collazo... una tras otra las piezas fueron encajando como nunca lo habían hecho. (Campos 2012; In Carlos Dorremochea's set design we successfully transmitted to the viewer the sensation of step-ping into a Sorolla painting. [...] In photography, Jacobo Martínez's work was spectacular given that he had to make a series in whites and blacks, almost without color, shimmer [...], Helena Sanchís's wardrobe, Lucio Godoy's music, the hair styles of Mara Collazo... one by one the pieces fit together as they never had before.)
All translations in this chapter are mine.

8. The setting of a high-end hotel logically lends itself to dramatic narra-tives, as the constant flow of guests allows for diversity of interactions and unending intrigue. The idea of a grand hotel in particular is a common-place in European and American narrative of the early twentieth century, as seen in works ranging from Ramón Gómez de la Serna's novel *El gran hotel* (1930) to Edmund Goulding's film *Grand Hotel* (1932).

9. In reality, the Palacio de la Magdalena was constructed between 1908 and 1912, a few years after the events depicted on *Gran Hotel*.

10. The phonograph will later play a key role in two secondary story lines in season two: It allows Doña Ángela's son Andrés to reconnect with his supposedly deceased father (episode 4) and records the confession of Julio's vengeful ex-lover Cecilia, who is intent on framing him for murder (episode 5).

11. The use of technology as a visual cue for modernization crops up in discus-sions of other Spanish series such as *As leis de Celavella* (Voz Audiovisual, TVG, 2003–2004), *Víctor Ros* (New Atlantis, TVE, 2012–2016), and *Las chicas del cable*, all of which are discussed in the present edited volume.

12. FIAT debuted its first model in 1899, and the first FIAT plant produced 24 automobiles in 1900 (Mossy FIAT, n.d.). The first Delage automobiles date to 1905 (Vack 2011), so its on-screen appearance on season two of

Gran Hotel, set in the same year, could serve to emphasize the absolute modernity of the hotel, at the forefront of adopting new technology. In contrast, while the first Harley Davidson was sold in 1903, the motorcycles were not mass produced until 1907 (Harley-Davidson Museum, Inc. 2018), such that the bike's appearance in 1905 Cantaloa is slightly anachronistic.

13. Argentine anthropologist and policeman Vucetich was the first to use fingerprinting technology to identify a killer in a homicide case in 1892.

14. French doctor Pierre Janet argued for the use of hypnosis in the investigation and treatment of hysteria in the late nineteenth century, influencing the work of Sigmund Freud, who published *Studies on Hysteria* in 1889 (Tasca et al. 2012).

15. Additionally, Ayala's physical appearance, particularly his carefully groomed mustache, echoes that of Poirot, whose creator Agatha Christie furthermore appears as a character in season two of *Gran Hotel* (episode 15).

16. Unsurprisingly, given *Gran Hotel*'s penchant for the inclusion of the foreign, two non-Spanish historical figures had previously appeared on the series: the aforementioned Agatha Christie and Harry Houdini in episode 19.

17. The character of Maite is slightly anachronistic, since it was not until 1922 that the first Spanish woman earned a law degree (De la Fuente 2008).

18. Regarding the phonograph's importance for season two of *Gran Hotel*, see note 11.

19. Pascual's call furthermore serves to heighten the drama on-screen by employing the familiar horror-film trope of the menacing call made from within the same house.

20. Doña Teresa does state that the Gran Hotel will be the first Spanish hotel to boast of electric lighting, which undermines the image of Spain as thoroughly modern.

21. Sánchez Blasco argues convincingly that "Ayala predice la aparición de las instituciones modernas como garantía para una sociedad democrática" (2015, 57; Ayala foretells the appearance of modern institutions as a guarantee of a democratic society).

22. Counting live viewing and online streaming, the third series of *Sherlock* was named the "most watched [BBC] drama series in over a decade" (*The Independent* 2014). Similarly, "at its height, CSI attracted 26 million American viewers and 63 million viewers worldwide," making it "the most watched show in the world" (McAloon 2015).

BIBLIOGRAPHY

Alfred P. Sloan Foundation. 1999. "Preface to the Sloan Technology Series." In *Visions of Technology: A Century of Vital Debate About Machines, Systems and the Human World*, edited by Richard Rhodes, 19–20. New York: Simon & Schuster.

Ballano, Elena R. 2012. "El arte de vestir a los personajes de Gran Hotel." *Vanitatis*, November 19. https://www.vanitatis.elconfidencial.com/estilo/2012-11-19/el-arte-de-vestir-a-los-personajes-de-gran-hotel_492666/. Accessed February 25, 2018.

Bambu Producciones. "*Grand Hotel*." Bambu Producciones. https://bambu-producciones.com/en/work/grand-hotel. Accessed January 20, 2018.

Beta Film. 2012. "British Media Praises *Grand Hotel* as 'Spanish *Downton Abbey*.'" http://betafilm.com/en/news/d/uid-ef94d46a-67e9-7327-e7ad-641a6afcaf02.html. Accessed January 27, 2018.

Byrne, Katherine. 2015. *Edwardians on Screen: from Downton Abbey to Parade's End*. New York: Palgrave Macmillan.

Calvo Calvo, Ángel. 1998. "El teléfono en España antes de Telefónica (1877–1924)." *Revista de Historia Industrial* 13: 59–81.

Campos, Ramón, Interviewed by Álvaro Onieva. 2012. *Espinof*, February 28. https://www.espinof.com/series-de-ficcion/si-pudiese-hacer-la-serie-que-me-apeteciese-llevaria-a-cabo-una-de-ciencia-ficcion-realista-entrevista-a-ramon-campos. Accessed January 21, 2018.

Campos, Ramón, and Gema R. Neira, Creators. 2011–2013. *Gran Hotel*. Bambú Producciones, Antena 3.

Campos, Ramón, and Gema R. Neira, Interview by FormulaTV. 2014. Video, 10:30, January 15. https://www.youtube.com/watch?v=qPHj8MOI3ng. Accessed February 4, 2018.

Caughie, John. 2000. *Television Drama*. Oxford: Oxford University Press.

Cruz, Jesús. 2011. *The Rise of Middle Class Culture in Nineteenth-Century Spain*. Baton Rouge: Louisiana State University Press.

De Groot, Jerome. 2009. *Consuming History: Historians and Heritage in Contemporary Popular Culture*. London: Routledge.

De la Fuente, Mercedes. 2008. "La primera abogada de España." *ABC*, June 14. http://www.abc.es/hemeroteca/historico-14-06-2008/abc/Valencia/la-primera-abogada-de-espa%C3%B1a_1641933196731.html. Accessed January 27, 2018.

El Goarany, Ahmed. 2016. "*Grand Hotel*: A Journey Through Time." *Daily News Egypt*, July 3. http://dailynewsegypt.com/2016/07/03/grand-hotel-journey-time/. Accessed May 30, 2017.

Elidrissi, Fátima. 2017. "*Gran Hotel* viaja a Miami de la mano de Eva Longoria." *El mundo*, November 21. http://www.elmundo.es/television/2017/11/21/5a146cd-f268e3ee6198b4577.html. Accessed February 4, 2018.

Estéviz, César. 2017. "Un estudio revela cuáles son las series más vistas de Netflix en cada país." *FormulaTV.com*, May 11. www.formulatv.com/noticias/67649/estudio-series-mas-vistas-netflix-cada-pais. Accessed May 30, 2017.

FormulaTV. 2016. "'Gran Hotel' abre sus puertas en Oriente con su adaptación en Egipto." *FormulaTV.com*, May 24. www.formulatv.com/noticias/56373/gran-hotel-adaptacion-egipto. Accessed May 30, 2017.

Harley-Davidson Museum, Inc. 2018. "Get the Rest of the Story." https://www.harley-davidson.com/us/en/museum.html. Accessed February 25, 2018.

Hesham, Soha. 2016. "Grand Hotel TV." *Al-Ahram Weekly*, June 30–July 13. http://weekly.ahram.org.eg/News/16776.aspx. Accessed May 30, 2017.

Ibeas Cubillo, Diego. 2011. "Review of the History of the Electric Supply in Spain from the Beginning Up to Now." *Universidad Carlos III de Madrid Repositorio Institucional e-Archivo*. http://hdl.handle.net/10016/13718. Accessed May 31, 2017.

The Independent. 2014. "Sherlock Series Three Named Most-Watched BBC Drama in a Decade." *The Independent*, January 22. https://www.independent.co.uk/arts-entertainment/tv/news/sherlock-series-three-named-most-watched-bbc-drama-in-a-decade-9077574.html. Accessed March 4, 2018.

Jacobson, Stephen, and Javier Moreno Luzón. 2000. "The Political System of the Restoration, 1875–1914." In *Spanish History Since 1808*, edited by José Álvarez Junco and Adrian Shubert, 94–109. London and New York: Arnold and Oxford University Press.

Kleinecke-Bates, Iris. 2014. *Victorians on Screen: The Nineteenth Century on British Television, 1994–2005*. New York: Palgrave Macmillan.

McAloon, Jonathan. 2015. "CSI Cancelled After 15 Years." *The Telegraph*, May 13. http://www.telegraph.co.uk/culture/tvandradio/11602967/CSI-cancelled-after-15-years.html. Accessed February 4, 2018.

Mossy FIAT. "History of FIAT." *Mossy FIAT*. https://www.mossyfiat.com/history-of-fiat.htm. Accessed February 25, 2018.

Oliete-Aldea, Elena. 2015. "Places of Memory in the New Millennium: British Influence on Spanish Transnational Heritage Cinema and Television." *Studies in Spanish & Latin American Cinemas* 12, no. 2: 175–195.

Rhodes, Richard. 1999. "Introduction." In *Visions of Technology: A Century of Vital Debate About Machines, Systems and the Human World*, edited by Richard Rhodes, 21–25. New York: Simon & Schuster.

Rodríguez Ortega, Vicente. 2013. "The Historical Film: Genre and Legibility." In *A Companion to Spanish Cinema*, edited by Jo Labanyi and Tatjana Pavlovic, 240–241. Oxford: Wiley-Blackwell.

Roxborough, Scott, and Stuart Kemp. 2010. "Product Placement Gains Foothold in Europe." *The Hollywood Reporter*, August 11. https://www.hollywoodreporter.com/news/product-placement-gains-foothold-europe-26581. Accessed February 3, 2018.

Ruiz, C., and S. Calvo. 2011. "'Gran Hotel' abre sus puertas en Antena 3." *La Razón*, October 3. https://www.larazon.es/historico/770-gran-hotel-abre-sus-puertas-en-antena-3-SLLA_RAZON_402105. Accessed February 28, 2018.

Sánchez Blasco, Pablo. 2015. "Estrategias narrativas y género policíaco en la ficción televisiva de *Gran Hotel* (2011–2013)." *Revista Comunicación* 13: 48–61.

Shattuck, Kathryn, and Hubert Mandeville. 2016. "'Downton Abbey' and History: A Look Back." *The New YorkTimes*, February 29. https://www.nytimes.com/interactive/2014/12/31/arts/television/12312015_DowntonAbbey-timeline.html#/#time357_10566. Accessed January 28, 2018.

Smith, Paul Julian. 2017. "Copycat Television?" *Gran Hotel/Grand Hotel* (2011–2013) and *El hotel de los secretos/The Hotel of Secrets* (2015–2016). *Studies in Spanish & Latin American Cinemas* 14, no. 3: 349–365.

Snyder, Joel. 1980. "Picturing Vision." *Critical Inquiry* 6, no. 3: 499–526.

Tasca, Cecilia, Mariangela Rapetti, Mauro G. Carta, and Bianca Fadda. 2012. "Women and Hysteria in the History of Mental Health." *Clinical Practice & Epidemiology in Mental Health* 8: 110–119. https://doi.org/10.2174/1745017901208010110. Accessed January 27, 2018.

Vack, Pete. 2011. "Delage, France's Finest Car. A Brief History Part 1." *Velocity Today*. http://www.velocetoday.com/delage-a-brief-history-part-1/. Accessed February 25, 2018.

VideoAge. 2016. "The Arabic Version of *Grand Hotel* Debuts During Ramadan." *VideoAge*, TV Trade Media, Inc., June 3. www.videoageinternational.net/2016/06/03/news/the-arabic-version-of-grand-hotel-debuts-during-ramadan. Accessed May 30, 2017.

Yasser, Nayera. 2016. "*Grand Hotel*: A Thriller Drama for Every Family." *Daily News Egypt*, June 21. https://dailynewsegypt.com/2016/06/21/grand-hotel-a-thriller-drama-for-every-family/. Accessed January 10, 2018.

PART III

Constructing Genders

Dresses, Cassocks, and Coats: Costuming Restoration Gender Fantasies in *La Señora*

Nicholas Wolters

The award-winning Spanish television series *La Señora* aired between March 2008 and January 2010 on channel 1 of the state-owned broadcaster Televisión Española (TVE).[1] Created and written by Virginia Yagüe, the show predates the globally successful British period drama *Downton Abbey* (2010–2015) by a few years and paved the way for other hit televisual dramas in Spain like *Gran Hotel* (2011–2013), just as broadcast funding for Spain's national television network was experiencing a transformative restructuring due in large part to the 2008 global financial crisis. *La Señora*'s airing also coincided with the collapse of Spain's housing market, sharp spikes in the national debt and unemployment rates, and the establishment of lasting and popular social activist movements like 15-M.[2] Whether or not *La Señora* resonated with its fans for its direct engagement with socioeconomic issues still relevant to them,

N. Wolters (✉)
Wake Forest University, Winston-Salem, NC, USA
e-mail: wolterna@wfu.edu

© The Author(s) 2018
D. R. George, Jr. and W. S. Tang (eds.),
Televising Restoration Spain,
https://doi.org/10.1007/978-3-319-96196-5_6

119

the show's creative team repeatedly draws attention to the historical and literary continuities that thread together nineteenth-, twentieth-, and twenty-first-century contexts.

For readers of Leopoldo Alas's *La Regenta* (The Judge's Wife, 1884–1885), or for viewers of Fernando Méndez-Leite's 1995 televised adaptation of the novel, the setting and mise-en-scène of *La Señora*—starring Adriana Ugarte, Rodolfo Sancho, and Roberto Enríquez—will seem remarkably familiar. Shot against the rocky and verdant backdrop of coastal Asturias and set during the final decade of the Bourbon Restoration (1874–1931), the serial dramatizes the coming of age of Victoria Márquez de la Vega (Ugarte), a young and intrepid woman who, together with her brother Pablo, inherits and manages her widower father's country estate and mining business.[3] Victoria's maturation during the second half of the Bourbon Restoration runs parallel to that of the show's other clear protagonist, Ángel González Ruiz (Sancho). Pressured to alleviate his working-class family's abject living conditions and to liberate his brother from an unjust imprisonment, Ángel eventually abandons his idealistic and transgressive relationship with Victoria to study in the seminary and become a socially engaged priest: a virtual saint to the sick and the poor, and a thorn in the side of the reactionary members of the village's ruling class. The series creatively echoes *La Regenta*'s paradigmatic love triangle as it seamlessly weaves together the lives and travails of the fashion-forward and strong-willed Victoria, the ruggedly handsome and conflicted young priest Ángel, and the coldhearted but seductively enigmatic Gonzalo, Marqués de Castro (Enríquez). Imbuing its stylish recreations of Ana Ozores and Fermín de Pas with a particularly strong ethical compass, the show's creators nimbly honor their literary precedents while similarly rendering homage to the "middle-brow" televisual adaptations of classic novels that popularized the period drama during Spain's transition to democracy in the 1970s and 1980s (Smith 2006, 54).

As evidenced by Yagüe's various statements on the show's intertexts, *La Señora*'s narrative dialogues explicitly with Clarín's masterpiece and Méndez-Leite's now classic televisual adaptation.[4] It similarly cites other Restoration-era literary predecessors—from Galdós's *Doña Perfecta* (1876) to *Celia en los infiernos* (1913). In the first episode of *La Señora*, for example, Victoria reads a passage from *Doña Perfecta* to the Márquez estate's kitchen staff and identifies "Don Benito" as a family friend. As David George remarks, the inclusion of such literary references in the series is far from gratuitous or superficial; on the contrary, it signals "una relación más compleja entre el argumento de esta ficción televisual seriada y la literatura de este período" (George 2009, 54; a more complex relationship between the plot of this televisual serial and the literature of the period). The show's contemporary reimagining of Restoration gender tropes such as the strong-willed female protagonist from the provinces or the enamored priest relies just as heavily on the deployment of a heterogeneous array of visual cultures inspired by fashions of the first third of the twentieth century: From Victoria's and Isabel de Viana's flashy, modern dresses that draw inspiration from fashion plates in the illustrated press, to Ángel's peasant's physique, scruffy countenance, prosthetic tonsure, and pristine, perfectly fitted cassocks that summon the topos of the brooding and virile "cura guapo." In the present study, I examine the mise-en-scène used to dress up *La Señora*'s protagonists and narrative, demonstrating the ways the TVE drama, in spite of its primarily non-literary content and source material, displays an unabashed interest in adapting the Restoration for the aesthetics and tastes of its twenty-first-century audience while nostalgically embracing its literary–visual precedents. Thus, the show adeptly brings into dialogue issues facing characters and viewers alike, highlighting instead of eschewing continuities between nineteenth-, twentieth-, and twenty-first-century contexts through its deliberately composite mise-en-scène.

COSTUMING ON THE SMALL SCREEN

Comprising integral elements of a production's mise-en-scène, wardrobe and cosmetics are responsible for visually reconstructing a given time period for contemporary audiences. According to data collected by Susana Rodríguez Marcos—the only scholar to have written at length about the serial—*La Señora*'s wardrobe is among the topics most discussed by fans of the show in online forums.[5] Here as elsewhere, wardrobe is one of the essential criteria used by viewers to appreciate and evaluate historical adaptations. Rodríguez Marcos posits that most televisual costume dramas relegate themselves to "la 'epidermis' del relato histórico: copian su *look* (las modas, las apariencias, sus elementos externos), pero no pretenden explicar sus causas internas" (Rodríguez Marcos 2015, 26; the 'epidermis' of the story: They copy a look [fashions, appearances, external elements], but they never try to explain their internal causes). Generally speaking, the thirty-nine episodes of *La Señora* corroborate Rodríguez Marcos's argument. The show introduces viewers to historical figures and events—such as the Primo de Rivera coup or the 1930 Jaca Uprising—but often does so with little or no explanation as to their significance beyond the immediate aesthetic and ethical impact on the sentimental plotlines. In this view, dress and fashion occupy more of a decorative–ornamental rather than substantive role in the series and others like it. In line with Paul Julian Smith's invitation to make "a return to aesthetics and close reading in both film and TV studies" (Smith 2015, 332), I suggest here that *La Señora*'s sartorial posturing produces meaning that far exceeds the more immediate or practical needs required to achieve a more or less proper sense of historical accuracy. Although there is a tendency for period dramas like *La Señora* to rely on mise-en-scène to convey ahistorical or only vaguely accurate or convincing portrayals of a given historical moment, a close examination of the sartorial conceits utilized in the TVE series helps to unveil how the show's production team relies on Restoration gender tropes at the same time that they package characters like the wealthy heiress and the enamored priest to be more palatable to twenty-first century tastes and interests.

Even if dress and fashion are only imperfectly reproduced in contemporary cinematic and televisual adaptations, they retain some capacity for allegorical readings and signification. In reference to Martin Scorsese's 1993 film adaptation of Edith Wharton's *The Age of Innocence*, for example, Christopher Breward writes that "the objects, interiors and dresses in his film were as actively involved in communicating the cultural and emotional concerns of late-nineteenth century New York society as his actors" (Breward 2003, 141n82). Beyond fulfilling a film or TV production team's desire or need to reconstruct the material realities of a given historical moment for the purposes of entertainment, while maintaining a more or less rigorous allegiance to the "look" of a given era, costumes and cosmetics are also used to affect the ways we interpret characters and their narrative circumstances. Whether an explicit component of a plotline or not, an actor's behavior and expressions in costume provide non-verbal cues about his or her character's desires and trajectories in ways that scripts and dialogues alone cannot. Indeed, fashion in fiction "is codified or endowed with meaning and a reader soon catches the writer's intent: a woman's downfall from silk to cottons, a young man's social rise through the cut of his coat, the slow stripping of clothing denoting a pecuniary decline or the startling makeover that carries a character from fledgling identity to full self-expression" (McNeil et al. 2009, 6). Costuming choices demonstrate how characters and their constructed environments dialogue with the historical periods they reimagine, and shed light on the priorities of the production, as well as contemporaneous aesthetics and tastes. By extension, costume drama as a genre, as Jerome de Groot puts it, "is never just a genre but always a site of contention about memory, national identity, and nostalgia. It is produced by a set of cultural institutions ... with their own agendas, by writers ... with particular biases, and for a set of markets ... with particular tastes and desires" (De Groot 2014, x–xi).

LA SEÑORA AND FASHION DURING THE 1920S

A particularly successful example of the costume genre in Spain, *La Señora* is set in a northern provincial town in the years encompassing Primo de Rivera's 1923 coup d'état, and just prior to the expulsion of Alfonso XIII after the declaration of the Second Republic in 1931. By the first decades of the twentieth century, both women's and men's fashion had already begun a process of democratization signaled by phenomena such as the popularization of cotton over more costly materials like silk, technological advances in the manufacture of textiles and periodicals, and increased affordability. Though social divisions along class lines persisted, it can at least be stated that more access to fashion meant greater potential for participation in the marketplace for men and women previously excluded from bourgeois cultures of consumption. As Isabel Vaquero Argüelles summarizes, "[e]n España ... , gracias a la difusión de la fotografía en revistas de moda y periódicos, el número de mujeres que pueden conocer las novedades impuestas por los grandes creadores crece notablemente" (Vaquero Argüelles 2007, 127; in Spain ... , thanks to the dissemination of photographs in fashion magazines and periodicals, the number of women that are aware of the novelties distributed by famous creators rises considerably). This type of mobility, or at least a desire for it, is reflected in several character arcs in *La Señora*. Conchita (Claudia Giráldez), for example, starts her upwardly mobile trajectory by working as a staff member in the Márquez household and ends up moving to Alicia's brothel before relocating to Paris to start a film career. Citing a desire to look like a fashionable "señorita"—like Victoria Márquez—Conchita's example showcases fashion's ability to announce, shape, or guarantee a consumer's social advancement. At one point,

Conchita is even scolded by Vicenta (Ana Wagener), the embodiment of tradition and etiquette in *La Señora*, for standing in front of the mirror while she tries on Victoria's dresses.

The fashion industry's process of democratization during the early 1900s, however, also coincided with the establishment of haute couture fashion houses across Western Europe's urban centers. In Spain, Cristóbal Balenciaga (San Sebastián, 1914; Madrid, 1920) and Pedro Rodríguez (Barcelona, 1919) responded to the demand for high-quality, original fashions that women had begun to associate with the Parisian brands of Paul Poiret and Coco Chanel. Then as now, such shops appealed primarily to clientele with enough disposable income or access to capital to imitate both artistic and highly conceptual fashion plates disseminated in magazines like *La Gazette du Bon Ton*. These socioeconomic realities are reflected in the final season of *La Señora* in Alicia's (Carmen Conesa) transformation of her brothel into an haute couture dress shop. While Alicia's success story whimsically, if somewhat unbelievably, imitates the rags-to-riches tales of historic fashion designers, her success hinges on the patronage of the town's wealthiest socialites, even those who were at first unwilling to overlook the designer's sordid past.

According to a promotional video on TVE's website, *La Señora*'s fashion designer Pepe Reyes and his team took particular inspiration from a variety of source materials: from Spanish and French fashion and lifestyle magazines to books and photographs dating to the first third of the twentieth century. As evidenced by character boards reproduced by Rodríguez Marcos, many of the looks of middle- and upper-class characters including Victoria and Isabel de Viana were based on fashion plates published in Restoration-era magazines such as *La Moda Práctica* and *La Gazette du Bon Ton*; the latter is explicitly referenced in the series by Hermosilla (Alberto Rubio) in a conversation with Isabel. Such journals were responsible for disseminating visual and textual paradigms of sartorial behavior that men and women were expected to follow lest they risk marginalization in or exclusion from polite society. In a typical illustration from the March 19, 1922 issue of *Blanco y Negro*, for example, the artist depicts a trio of fashionable women and a man in attendance at an aristocratic soirée. The man wears a snugly fitting tuxedo, hair slicked with pomade, and a thin mustache. By the early twentieth century, three-piece suits in black or neutral colors had become de rigueur for men, especially those wishing to penetrate the worlds of business or politics (McKinney 2012, 81). The two women in the foreground wear shortly coiffed hairstyles, dresses in rich fabrics with plunging necklines, and showy accessories. The ideal silhouette for women—on display here as elsewhere in other iconic magazines of the period—was marked by a significant loosening thanks in part to the gradual disappearance of the corset and crinolines that predominated in late-nineteenth-century and earlier *Belle Époque* styles depicted in flashbacks to Victoria's childhood. As is the case with men's apparel, the world of sport and energetic movement became fashionable and women's dress reflected similar interests. Generally speaking, hairstyles became shorter, and dresses flattened and narrowed the female body, thus epitomizing the *estilo garçon*: a waifish aesthetic that deemphasized curves and championed boyish hairstyles and svelte figures, all of which coincide with new freedoms for women in both public and private spheres. Photographs of Spain's first female participant in the 1924 Paris Olympic games—Lilí Álvarez—corroborate this necessarily nimble style of dress that Isabel de Viana adopts while playing tennis with Hermosilla (Cuesta 2017, 345-346n1). As Rodríguez Marcos asserts, "[l]os armarios de Victoria e Isabel de Viana debía[n] reproducir los cambios experimentados: desaparecen los corsés, los vestidos están menos estructurados, los largos suben hasta la rodilla, etc." (2015, 82; Victoria's and Isabel de Viana's wardrobes needed to reproduce these changes: corsets disappear, dresses are less structured, hemlines rise up to the knee, etc.)[6]

For working-class characters (e.g., Ángel before his ordination, Salvador, Encarna, Visitación), costume designers relied for the most part on photographic evidence, since the fashion magazines mentioned above were geared toward those who could afford to participate in Spain's burgeoning consumer culture in the first decades of the twentieth century. Even if fashion houses sprouted up throughout Spain and the rest of Europe during this period, only a small fraction of consumers could afford a dress designed and confectioned by the likes of Chanel or Balenciaga. For practical reasons, working-class styles were more austere and emphasized comfort and efficiency (Rodríguez Marcos 2015, 85). *La Señora*'s official website galvanizes these distinctions by organizing the show's characters according to their social classes. Working-class characters like Ángel's mother Amalia (Pepa López) and his brother Salvador (Raúl Prieto) are categorized as "humildes y rebeldes" (humble and rebellious), and the wardrobes of these characters reflect as much. Salvador, for example, frequently appears on-screen in worn-out shirtsleeves and suspenders and is often covered in dust or dirt from long

days in the mine. The timeless wardrobe of *La Señora*'s provincial pro-
letariat undoubtedly conjures earlier Restoration contexts and evokes
related historical topoi. While the show's male miners appear to only
just be initiating their fight for more representation, rights, shorter work
days, and wages, the coalfields of Asturias historically played host to miners' revolts in 1873, 1879, 1881, 1884, and 1887, and intensified during
the first third of the twentieth century (Shubert 1987, 105). *La Señora*'s
costume designers thus mine the nineteenth-century origins of Asturian
social conflict through the rustic wardrobes of the miners—a social type
described crudely and unsympathetically in *La Regenta* as "osos de la
cueva" (Alas 1981, 1: 504).

Below, I examine a few ways in which *La Señora*'s costuming and
mise-en-scène open dialogues with some of the gendered types and
circumstances from Alas's *La Regenta* and Méndez-Leite's 1995 adaptation. I then point out some of the ways in which *La Señora* reshapes
those circumstances to suit the more "liberated" 1920s time frame, with
the ultimate aim to appeal to contemporary viewers while nostalgically
reanimating Spain's social historical past.

Fashionable Femininity: From Ana and Obdulia to Victoria Márquez and Isabel de Viana

While *La Señora*'s plot is firmly anchored in 1920s Spain, the conflicts
faced by its female characters also trace roots to earlier Restoration discourses of femininity; Clarín's *La Regenta* is one such discursive terrain.
In *La Regenta*, the contrast between natural and artificial beauty—one
that is prioritized both narratively and visually in *La Señora*—is exemplified by the friendship of sorts between Ana Ozores and Obdulia Fandiño.
Ana is often described by Clarín's narrator as a paragon of natural
beauty in the eyes of Vetusta's denizens, and it is the same beauty that
compensates for her mother's ill repute and her general lack of financial
capital before her marriage to retired magistrate Víctor Quintanar. For
Obdulia, Ana is the only real beauty in the provincial town, and all other
womenare merely "maniquí[es] de colgar vestidos" (Alas 1981, 1: 335–336;
mannequins for displaying dresses). According to the novel's narrator, the
men see in Ana the timeless and beautiful product of a classical sculptor,
and the gossipy women of Vetusta consider her to be "una real moza;
un *bijou*" (Alas 1981, 1: 225; a real woman; a jewel). Obdulia, on the

other hand, is described frequently by the narrator and other characters as a *cursilona* or a bourgeois woman who exaggeratedly shows off borrowed and used fashions from a cousin in Madrid (Alas 1981, 1: 54). While Obdulia succeeds in attracting the attention of many men in Vetusta, the narrator rather critically draws attention to her overwrought look and physique. In Méndez-Leite's adaptation of Clarín's novel, Ana's role as ingénue is heightened by Aitana Sánchez-Gijón's performance; the Regenta's more demure character is thrown into sharp relief by the casting of Fiorella Faltoyano and Virginia Mataix as her friends Visita and Obdulia, respectively. These actresses' exaggeratedly haughty comportment and wardrobes contrast with the more restrained performance and luxurious but understated fashions of Sánchez-Gijón's Ana Ozores.

In Carmen de Burgos's *El arte de ser mujer* (1920), the author—known also by her pen name Colombine—articulates this binary that mobilizes early twentieth-century fantasies of fashionable femininity and features prominently in *La Señora*: namely, the divide between ineffable and effortless (i.e., natural) versus artificial beauty. Throughout the text, Burgos lingers on fashion as both a "fantasía pura" (pure fantasy) and a "noción práctica" (de Burgos 2014, 18–19; practical concept). On the one hand, feminine modishness is described by Burgos as an ineffable and natural quality emanating from women as a sign of their inherent *savoir-faire*. On the other hand, Burgos discusses fashion as a language that any woman has the ability to master through practice and repetition. The second half of her book, for example, includes practical fashion advice for women on a range of topics—from color coordination to fabric selection. Rita Felski identifies this binary in terms of "the fin-de-siècle association of femininity with nature and the primal forces of the unconscious," and the idea that women were also seen as a "surface without substance, a creature of style and artifice whose identity is created through the various costumes and masks that she assumes" (Felski 1995, 4). This nature–artifice divide, one that also preoccupied nineteenth-century authors from Théophile Gauthier to Charles Baudelaire, is made visible in the on-screen sartorial characterizations of Victoria Márquez and her bourgeois foil, Isabel de Viana. Through the use of both narrative and visual formal devices, Victoria embodies fashionable femininity as something inherent to her character—a woman "avanzada a su tiempo" (Rodríguez Marcos 2015, 64; ahead of her time)—whereas in characterizing Isabel, *La Señora*'s designers make visible the mechanics required in materially maintaining the feminine ideal. Though Victoria is sometimes shown seated at her toilette, her "natural" embodiment of feminine ideals reinforces her saintly altruism and benevolence toward the miners who work for her, and for whose financial well-being she sacrifices herself symbolically in the series' denouement.

In line with Victoria's natural beauty and benevolent character, often emphasized and fetishized by the men that surround her, her personal experience serendipitously gives shape to what is considered to be fashionable at any given moment in the course of the narrative. In other words, Victoria's sartorial shifts naturally set the trends for the other young women to follow in the Asturian village. Even Victoria's surname (Márquez) appears to inscribe her with a sort of natural nobility that elevates her above her bourgeois peers, making the title of *Marquesa* she eventually acquires upon her marriage to Gonzalo a perfect fit.[7]

Examples of Victoria's natural embodiment of feminine beauty ideals of the 1920s abound. In the pilot of *La Señora*, the eponymous heroine descends the staircase bedecked in the sartorial signs of fashionable femininity of the period: Her low-waistline dress glitters as she draws the attention of everyone there to celebrate her entry into high society. Later in the series, in an act of defiance against the Marqués—part of her personal protests against him after she discovers his hand in the death of her father—Victoria shears her already short hair and refuses to eat, resulting in some weight loss. During a visit to Gonzalo's palatial home, Vicenta— the *ama de llaves* of the Márquez estate and Victoria's surrogate mother figure—displays concern while remarking upon Victoria's waifishness and exaggeratedly thin figure. Isabel de Viana, unconcerned by Victoria's precarious emotional state or political protest, misreads the heiress' situation; indeed, Isabel envies her rival's "fashion-forward" physical transformations, even though Victoria's concerns are for all intents and purposes unrelated to fashion. Critical of a standard of beauty that would require bodily harm in its practitioners, Colombine harps negatively on this habit of comportment in her manual, but in so doing alludes to its hegemony among fashionable women during the 1920s: "La mujer moderna quiere estar delgada, y no falta quien diga a su doctor: 'envenenadme; pero hacedme adelgazar.' Con este exceso se han ido perdiendo los placeres de la mesa" (de Burgos 2014, 70; Modern women want to be thin, and there is never a shortage of those who say to their doctor: "go ahead and poison me, but make me thin." Embracing this excess, women have started losing the pleasures of the table). Colombine's assertion provides necessary context for Isabel de Viana's rather cruel brand of envy, as Victoria's self-proclaimed rival embodies the stereotype of the woman who is desperate to maintain a fashionable figure at any cost. Thus, Victoria's bodily transformation accurately if ironically glosses ideals of femininity published and consumed in fashion manuals and magazines of the period: They make of Victoria a paragon of fashionability in the provincial Asturian town and thus seamlessly weave together her senti-mental plotline with aesthetic and social changes affecting women in the 1920s. Victoria's convalescence is not unlike that of Ana Ozores—who constantly suffers from bouts of hysteria—and represents yet another indication of the inescapability of nostalgic nineteenth-century tropes of feminine comportment that pervade throughout the series. Furthermore, Victoria's ailments appear to communicate an underlying problem in the options available to women—even a business-oriented one like Victoria during the 1920s: The heiress' only mode of protest is through her own body, just as Ana Ozores' hysteria is a physical manifestation of the repressive environment in which she has been raised and lives.

Ugarte's Victoria Márquez effortlessly, if at times unintentionally, embodies early twentieth-century feminine ideals, thus providing the illusion of an abiding, natural beauty that corresponds to an inner good-ness and sense of purpose in *La Señora*. In this way, her character is like Ana Ozores before her moral and spiritual downfall, or even more so the angelical, altruistic heiress of Galdós's *Celia en los infiernos*, in whom "[e]l capitalismo, seco y egoísta comúnmente, en [ella] se trueca en virtud sublime" (Pérez Galdós 1913, 222; capitalism, normally dry and egotistical, becomes in her a sublime virtue). On the other hand, Lapausa's Isabel de Viana showcases the stereotypical mechanisms thought to be necessary in order to maintain such a polished sartorial veneer. In *La Señora*'s second season, Isabel proactively models herself after the examples of *La Gazette du Bon Ton* and *La Moda Práctica* as she takes instruction from her homosexual confidant Hermosilla. However, it takes Isabel some time to arrive at her fashionable apogee, and vari-ous narrative and cinematographic elements in *La Señora* emphasize the steps of her journey. At the start of the second season, Isabel is accused by her husband of dressing like a "provinciana," which seems to be an excuse for him not to be seen in public with her. She is made to feel unworthy of her recently promoted husband Hugo (heir to his father's shipbuilding business and now a delegate of the army) for her traditional patina. In the same episode, a cruel Hugo embarrasses Isabel in front of his father, Álvaro, over her stagnant look: "¿con esta pinta quieres salir?"; "¿has visto una mujer con un vestuario más provinciano que la mía?" (You want to go out looking like that?; Have you seen a wife with a more provincial wardrobe than mine?). When Isabel attempts to correct this perception by consulting Victoria for fashion advice, it does not come as a surprise when the Márquez heiress demonstrates an ignorance of the subject: She does not subscribe to or read fashion magazines. In accordance with her moral compass, however, she of course happily shares her dresses with the critical and envious Isabel.

From this moment forward, De Viana ends up going through a gauntlet of aesthetic and behavioral changes that are reflected in her constantly shifting wardrobe—with most of these changes being directed by her homosexual friend-made-fashionable Pygmalion, Hermosilla. According to Burgos, men expected this attention to appearances of their female counterparts (de Burgos 2014, 27–28). To conform to socially prescribed rules of comportment, middle- and upper-class women were encouraged to immerse themselves in the consumption of cosmetics and Parisian luxury goods, from perfumes to lingerie, in order to broadcast and edify their sense of modern femininity. In *La Señora*, Isabel is constantly shown ordering dresses, receiving and opening boxes that arrive to the household, and discussing fashion with Hermosilla. However, Isabel's consumption of fashion is not depicted as morally reprehensible, as in the case of Clarín's Obdulia, Flaubert's Emma Bovary, and Galdós's Rosalía de Bringas. Instead, shopping for clothes provides Isabel with an escape valve for her stifled desire, as her consumption of fashion coincides with a love affair she maintains with her husband's friend Fernando Alcázar (Víctor Clavijo).

At the end of *La Señora*'s third season, when Victoria's love affair with Ángel is made known, Isabel realizes that there is little differentiating her from Victoria. Similarly, when the nature of Ana Ozores's relationship with Don Álvaro is made public in Clarín's *La Regenta*, Obdulia parades through the streets holding her head high as she comes to the realization that Ana is just like all the other *demimondaines* of Vetusta: "'¿Ven ustedes? –decían las miradas triunfantes de la Fandiño—. Todos somos iguales'" (Alas 1981, 2: 525; You see?—said the triumphant looks of Fandiño. We are all the same). Isabel's satisfaction parallels that of Obdulia when she, too, comes to the realization that Victoria is a woman just like the rest of those in the unnamed Asturian village despite her supposedly natural embodiment of the signs and symbols associated with ideals of femininity during the Bourbon Restoration: "En el fondo, Victoria" (Deep down, Victoria), Isabel says to herself, "somos iguales" (we are the same). Exploiting a heterogeneously composed 1920s wardrobe, its

Fig. 6.1 *La Señora* (Diagonal, TVE, 2008–2010): Season 2, Episode 14—
Isabel de Viana consults Victoria for fashion advice

patchwork history and the comportment of its actresses, *La Señora*'s creative team imaginatively visualizes their subject matter while consciously
or unconsciously highlighting continuity between the nineteenth- and
twentieth-century contexts with which the show engages dialogically. The
visual and narrative characterization of Victoria Márquez and Isabel de
Viana simultaneously communicates the persistence of traditional moral
standards for women, even as their fashion-forward styles of dress reflect
positive social change and gender mobility (Fig. 6.1).

MEN OF THE CLOTH: FROM FERMÍN DE PAS TO ÁNGEL RUIZ

Like its female characters, *La Señora*'s male characters and the masculinity they embody trace roots to a common literary historical predeces-
sor, *La Regenta*, along with its popular televisual adaptation. Spectators
of Méndez-Leite's 1995 adaptation of *La Regenta* are first introduced
to Fermín de Pas—played by actor Carmelo Gómez—in the religious
paraphernalia shop which he operates with his mother Doña Paula.[8] In
medias res, he delivers a sermon he has prepared on papal infallibility
plucked by the miniseries's writers from Chapter 11 of the first volume

of Clarín's novel. Rather appropriately, Fermín pontificates to the audience of his mother Doña Paula, who tends to the shops registers, and Teresina, the family's servant who wipes dust off of the religious statuettes for sale. As the gaze of the camera and viewer settles on Fermín, the first word the priest utters is "La infalibilidad." Glossing the novel, Carmelo's Fermín is immediately aligned with the powerful preacher whose observance of papal infallibility, proclaimed doctrine by Pius IX in 1870, is emblematic of the importance he devotes to matters of dogma and his own power to exercise it on behalf of Vetusta's humble bishop.

In the scene that follows, Fermín leaves the shop for the cathedral. As he exits, clad in his new cassock prepared for him at the end of the previous scene by Teresina, he enacts the textual Fermín who glides peacock-like through the streets and the nave of the cathedral to a musical motif that Linda Willem has described as evocative of his grandeur (2011). Upon his entrance into the cathedral, Fermín marches with sharp glances and armed in his long black cloaks with purple trim. Carmelo Gómez brilliantly adapts Fermín's exhibitionistic and pompous attitudes in Méndez-Leite's miniseries, riffing on the dandyish and performative elements that are manifest in the novelistic character. On a surface level, La Señora's Ángel deploys a very similar aesthetic: formidable in the floor-length cassock, Sancho's brooding glances and "cara de sufrido" (sufferer's face) round out his resemblance to Fermín de Pas as he is described in the novel and as he is performed by Carmelo Gómez. La Señora's representation of both lay and priestly attire through its protagonist Ángel Ruiz serves to accurately represent the presence of the Church in provincial Spain during the final decade of the Bourbon Restoration. It simultaneously stylizes the historical period according to the tastes of contemporary audiences and provides commentary on matters of gender and social class. Unlike his literary precedent in La Regenta, however, La Señora's enamored priest is altruistic and actively engaged in caring for the sick, taking advantage of—not exploiting—his privileged position. He does this first as a respected town priest and finally as a papal legate to fight for workers' rights, even though his attractive, visual characterization through wardrobe and cosmetics summons classic images of the egotistical Fermín de Pas.

Audiences witness Victoria's first encounter with Ángel in a flashback to 1915. In the scene, the young, scruffy man from a humble, working-class family is dressed in plain, neutral green and brown garments with sleeves rolled up while he assists in removing the skin of a recently caught rabbit along the Asturian coastline. Ángel's rustic look and practical activity stand in stark contrast to those of Victoria and her brother Pablo, whose clothing has a more polished and infantilizing effect while the siblings run to and fro with a kite. Victoria, for example, wears a frilly, mauve dress trimmed with ribbons, and her hair is wavy and long, all of which distance her from the cropped, modern, and more mature look she shows off after her return from Madrid in the party scene that opens the episode. After a series of events—Ángel rescues the fallen kite, and Victoria later mends a wound Ángel endures as a result of a hunting accident—a romance develops between the two and ultimately sets in motion one of the principal plotlines that will drive the entire series; but unlike *Pepita Jiménez*'s seminarian Luis de Vargas, Ángel does not abandon the cassock to pursue his love interest. Ricardo Márquez, Victoria's father, eventually discovers the relationship between the two and to avoid a scandal sends his daughter to the Institución de Libre Enseñanza in Madrid, while Ángel—at the recommendation of his spiritual and biological father Padre Enrique (Pedro Miguel Martínez)—is destined for the seminary and the deaconate. Sending him away allows him to avoid the harsher lifestyle facing his brother and other men from his class in the mine, while also allowing him to capitalize on his gentle soul and capacity for learning. Still, to the chagrin of his superiors, Ángel constantly challenges the status quo in his defense of miners's rights and labor unions, recalling the social protests that date back to the 1860s in Asturias.

Consonant with Victoria's maturation and social transformation from innocent, provincial girl to the modish and modern socialite she evokes upon returning, Ángel's new vocation is marked visually by his adoption of the floor-length cassock. Still worn today, the cassock is an item of clerical daily wear that increased in popularity during the papacy of traditionalist Pius IX. After his sentimentally charged ordination in the sixth episode, Ángel wears the sartorial signs of a man of the cloth: He sports a tightly fitted cassock in the streets, opulent liturgical garments when saying mass, and a tonsure or shorn patch atop his head symbolizing humility. Prior to Vatican II, it was common for priests to adopt this hairstyle to formalize their commitment to God and the Church and to distance them from laymen. In several TV interviews from 2010, Sancho reveals that his character's tonsure was necessarily prosthetic, given his other commitments at the time and the gauche and anachronistic look of it—the show's creative team could hardly have expected the actor to walk around with a bald patch that is not de rigueur for present-day

Catholic priests. Despite a clear desire to signal Ángel's change in station post-ordination, Sancho's Ruiz maintains the actor's signature "scruff," which contributes to the virile image of the priest and the erotic potential of the priesthood as a metaphor for masculine sexual energy restrained, stifled, or kept in check.

A great degree of attention was paid to ensuring that twenty-first-century audiences recognized Ángel as a sex symbol. As Rodríguez Marcos reminds viewers, *La Señora*'s creative team needed Ángel to embody "la imagen del galán, del héroe, del príncipe" (Rodríguez Marcos 2015, 91; the image of the gallant, the hero, the prince). With his perpetual five-o-clock shadow, "así [Ángel] se ajustaba más a los parámetros actuales de belleza masculina ('daba mejor en cámara')" (Rodríguez Marcos 2015, 91; as such [Ángel] measured up to present-day parameters of masculine beauty ('it looked better on camera')). The priest's physical attractiveness is further enhanced by the casting of Rodolfo Sancho, who has played a similar "sex symbol" in the long-running soap opera *Amar en tiempos revueltos* (Love in Difficult Times; Diagonal TV, 2005–2017), for which Yagüe is also a writer. If Sancho's popularity on the show's official forums is any indication, the strategy worked: The thread "Loc@s por Rodolfo" continues to be one of the most commented upon on the website with 819 comments as of the writing of this chapter. The first commenter justifies the creation of the thread, citing the "mayoría Angelista" ("'team Ángel' majority") that constitute the site's fan base. The erotic potential of the priest, otherwise shackled by his cassock, is underscored in the series in the many scenes that show Ángel shirtless in his bed, in front of a mirror, or knelt down castigating himself with a whip. Despite the fact that Sancho's facial hair speaks to contemporary paradigms of masculine beauty more so than the polished bourgeois norms of the latter half of the Bourbon Restoration, the image of the hardened and hard-bodied cleric from the provinces was one that was common in the nineteenth century. In one memorable scene from Clarín's *La Regenta*, for example, Fermín examines his hairy torso in the mirror of his toilette. He appears frustrated by the fact that his priestly persona has no apparent need for the formidable musculature cultivated in his youthful years in the Asturian countryside. In a similar scene toward the end of the novel, Fermín contemplates himself again in the mirror and wonders whether or not he should wear his cassock or his huntsman's outfit to the countryside while he admires the way the fabric lays over his shapely figure. In recreating this common narrative trope of nineteenth- and

Fig. 6.2 *La Señora* (Diagonal, TVE, 2008–2010): Season 1, Episode 6—Ángel kneels in his room while chastising himself

early twentieth-century Spanish literature, while adjusting it to the tastes of contemporary TV audiences, *La Señora*'s Ángel functions as a kind of priestly palimpsest that like his feminine counterparts blends historical and literary gendered tropes with ideals of social justice in the creation of an altogether unique character that ultimately appeals to twenty-first-century fans of the show (Fig. 6.2).

Conclusion

To be sure, *La Señora*'s heterogeneous mise-en-scène sustains a more or less unique story line about a bourgeois heiress and an enamored priest. However, it also demonstrates a nostalgic allegiance to the literary and visual cultural products of the Bourbon Restoration. In *La Señora*, this becomes particularly apparent as the expository references to Galdós's *Doña Perfecta* are summoned several times in the episodes leading up to the finale—even though these references are absent throughout the bulk of the series. As Victoria dies from wounds inflicted from the explosion in the mine—an event that was foreshadowed in the earlier explosion in the Márquez household during her symbolic coming of age—both she and Ángel whisper to each other the idealistic and romantic phrase Rosario utters to Pepe Rey in *Doña Perfecta*: "te quiero desde antes de conocerte" (I've loved you since before having met you). This is the third time this phrase is repeated in the episode and marks a narrative return to the show's pilot in which Victoria is shown reading this passage of *Doña Perfecta* to the kitchen staff. *La Señora* inventively refashions the past, even as its attractive *bricolage* of mise-en-scène and narrative intertextuality with works by Clarín or Galdós demonstrate nostalgic attachments to the show's literary-historical predecessors, which ultimately confer cultural legitimacy upon the series. Stylishly dressing up the nineteenth- and twentieth-century pasts that it stages with an eye to satisfying its twenty-first-century audiences, *La Señora* effectively mines its kaleidoscopic array of sources in its reanimation and interpretation of the Spanish past and its abiding or transforming gender roles.

NOTES

1. *La Señora*'s actors won in five categories at the XIX Unión de Actores (Actors' Union) awards ceremony, including awards for best actor and best actress in a leading role (Ugarte and Enríquez). I capitalize "*Señora*," since the title is used as a nickname, and the show's producers do the same in promotional publications. All translations are by the author unless otherwise noted.
2. 15-M is now a globally influential social movement, born out of Madrid-based protests, which strives to end socioeconomic inequalities through the reconceptualization and implementation of alternative, anti-capitalist pathways to democratic politics.
3. Though it is established early on in the show that iron is the metal extracted from the mines, the final episode shows workers reverently placing a few pieces of coal on Victoria's casket. On both historical and symbolic levels, coal is much more representative of Asturias than any other mined object, and its extraction played a decisive role in shaping the region's social history (Shubert 1987, 25–27).
4. Yagüe defended her artistic license and the universality of her subject matter against charges of plagiarism that were eventually proven to be unfounded: "[t]endría más sentido que [les] denunciaran los del *Pájaro espino,* serie que también contaba el amor de una mujer con un cura. ¿Y qué pasa entonces con *La Regenta*?" (It would make more sense if the creators of *The Thorn Birds*—a series that also tells the love story between a woman and a priest—were to bring them to court. And what about

La Regenta?) (Grande 2010). *The Thorn Birds* (1977) is an Australian novel by Colleen McCullough. It was better known in Spain by the homonymous 1983 miniseries starring Richard Chamberlain in the role of an enamored priest.

5. Rodríguez Marcos reports that most of these viewers identify as female: of 360 users, only 15, or around 4%, identify as male (Rodríguez Marcos 2015, 287).

6. The "mujer emancipada" (emancipated woman) aesthetic coexists in the series alongside other types of turn-of-the-century femininity. These include, to borrow Rodríguez Marcos's terminology, the "mujer vampiresa" (vampire woman) or *femme fatale* embodied by characters like Alicia—the madam and owner of the town's brothel—and Bianca (Ana Alonso), an Italian fascist who serves as a love interest for Victoria's brother Pablo (Rodríguez Marcos 2015, 83–84).

7. Gonzalo is only a marquis because of his previous marriage to Irene de Castro. After the death of Irene, and before his marriage to Victoria, Gonzalo purchases the title of marquis from his brother-in-law so that he may claim the title in his own right. At the end of the series, Gonzalo—not entirely unlike *La Regenta*'s Álvaro—is forced to flee from the village.

8. Carmelo Gómez also plays a version of Fermín de Pas in Gonzalo Suárez's 2007 parody of *La Regenta* titled *Oviedo Express*.

BIBLIOGRAPHY

Alas, Leopoldo. 1981. *La Regenta*. Edited by Gonzalo Sobejano. Madrid: Castalia.

Breward, Christopher. 2003. *Fashion*. Oxford: Cambridge University Press.

Cuesta, Luis F. 2017. "Sports-Themed Kiosk Novelettes and the Silver Age Debate on Tradition and Modernity." In *Kiosk Literature of Silver Age Spain: Modernity and Mass Culture*, edited by Jeffrey Zamostny and Susan Larson, 329–352. Chicago: Intellect.

de Burgos, Carmen. 2014. *El arte de ser mujer*. Edited by Pedro Gómez Carrizo. Barcelona: Biblok.

De Groot, Jerome. 2014. "Foreword." In *Upstairs and Downstairs: British Costume Drama Television from The Forsyte Saga to Downton Abbey*, edited by James Leggott and Julie Taddeo, ix–xii. Lanham, MD: Rowman & Littlefield.

Felski, Rita. 1995. *The Gender of Modernity*. Cambridge, MA: University of Harvard Press.

George, David R. 2009. "Restauración y transición en la *Fortunata y Jacinta* de Mario Camus." In *Historias de la pequeña pantalla: representaciones históricas en la televisión de la España democrática*, edited by Francisca López, Elena Cueto Asín, and David R. George, 53–71. Frankfurt: Iberoamericana.

Grande, Ricardo. 2010. "La productora de la serie La señora desmiente el pla-gio." *El País*, March 25. https://elpais.com/diario/2010/03/25/radi-otv/1269471603_850215.html.

McKinney, Collin. 2012. "Men in Black: Fashioning Masculinity in Nineteenth-Century Spain." *Letras Hispanas* 8 (2): 78–93.

McNeil, Peter, Vicki Karaminas, and Catherine Cole. 2009. "Introduction." In *Fashion in Fiction: Text and Clothing in Literature, Film, and Television*, edited by Peter McNeil, Vicki Karaminas, and Catherine Cole, 1–8. Oxford: Berg.

Pérez Galdós, Benito. 1913. *Celia en los infiernos*. Madrid: Librería de los Sucesores de Hernando.

Rodríguez Marcos, Susana. 2015. "*La Señora*: entre el drama y la historia." Doctoral diss., Universidad Complutense de Madrid.

Shubert, Adrian. 1987. *The Road to Revolution in Spain: The Coal Miners of Asturias, 1860–1934*. Urbana and Chicago: University of Illinois Press.

Smith, Paul Julian. 2006. *Television in Spain: From Franco to Almodóvar*. London: Tamesis.

———. 2015. "Notes on the Future (and Past) of Spanish and Latin American Media Studies." *Bulletin of Spanish Studies* 92, no. 3: 331–340.

Vaquero Argüelles, Isabel. 2007. "El reinado de la Alta Costura: la moda de la primera mitad del siglo XX." *Indumenta. Revista del Museo del Traje*, 123–134.

Willem, Linda M. 2011. "High Fidelity: Scoring the Text in TV's *La Regenta*." In *Studies in Honor of Vernon Chamberlin*, edited by Mark A. Harpring, 277–292. Newark: Juan de la Cuesta.

Yagüe, Virginia. 2008–2010. *La Señora*. Diagonal TV, Antena 3.

CHAPTER 7

"Las normas son para romperlas": Emilia Pardo Bazán, Carmen de Burgos, and the Unruly Women of *Seis Hermanas*

Linda M. Willem

Seis hermanas (Six Sisters) is an afternoon series consisting of 490 episodes televised on TVE1 from April 22, 2015 through April 21, 2017.[1] The story takes place in Madrid from 1913 to 1917. The six protagonists are young upper-class women whose lives are dramatically changed when their father unexpectedly dies of a heart attack, leaving them without either parent alive. The initial premise of the series is founded on their fear that, as women without a male sibling, they will lose control of the family business. Consequently, they hide the truth from the public and secretly embark on career paths that develop their individual talents. The creators of *Seis hermanas*, Gema R. Neira and Ramón Campos, have stated that the series is "una historia de superación" (a story of overcoming) in which "el tema de la discriminación de la mujer" (the theme of discrimination against women) is explored as the sisters "desafían las convenciones sociales" (defy the social conventions) of their era (RTVE, n.d.).

L. M. Willem (✉)
Butler University, Indianapolis, IN, USA
e-mail: lwillem@butler.edu

© The Author(s) 2018
D. R. George, Jr. and W. S. Tang (eds.),
Televising Restoration Spain,
https://doi.org/10.1007/978-3-319-96196-5_7

139

In this essay, I will examine how the series draws on the lives and writings of two of the era's strongest proponents of women's rights—Emilia Pardo Bazán and Carmen de Burgos—to explore the social and legal situation of women in Restoration society and to raise such issues as gender and class barriers, spousal abuse, infidelity, divorce, and lesbianism. I will show how the writings (both cited and unacknowledged) of these authors inform the plots of the story, and how the presence of Carmen de Burgos as a recurring character serves as an alternative voice to the traditional views of the day. Although the series takes place during the Restoration, its social sensibilities are anchored in the twenty-first century. By highlighting the ideas of women writers who were ahead of their time, the series presents issues of injustice from a more progressive point of view than was generally accepted by the mainstream society in which the characters live. As such, the writings of Pardo Bazán and Burgos justify the transgressive actions of the sisters as they defy social and legal norms in pursuit of freedom and self-actualization. Furthermore, these women writers serve as a bridge to today's television viewer whose twenty-first-century perspective validates their ideas that were once considered radical but are now accepted.

During the promotional campaign leading up to the premiere of the series, its director, Antonio Hernández, emphasized how *Seis Hermanas* would differ from the soap operas that normally fill the 4:00 p.m. *sobremesa* (post-lunch) time slot, stating that the goal of the series was to "concederle a la tarde un puntito más de estética" (RTVE 2015c; to make the afternoon a bit more aesthetic). He specifically cited the high production values and cinematic quality of the series, its spectacular sets built to accurately represent the era, its cast of well-respected actors, and the research done by the scriptwriters to add to the authenticity of the story lines. As such *Seis Hermanas* shares many of the characteristics of the British-made heritage costume dramas that have been the hallmark of quality BBC programming and exportation since the late 1960s. Indeed, Campos stated that *Seis Hermanas* would remind viewers of "las grandes producciones históricas de países como Gran Bretaña, series como *Arriba y Abajo* (the great historical productions from countries like Great Britain, series like *Upstairs, Downstairs*)," and actress Marta Larralde further reinforced that association by indicating that the dress she wore for the premier episode originally came from the *Downton Abbey* series (RTVE 2015d).

Period dramas written specifically for television, such as *Upstairs, Downstairs,* and *Downton Abbey,* have an advantage over adaptations of classic novels because they do not need to be faithful to a single text. Rather, they can present "a more progressive representation of social politics" and can "draw on the conventions of different genres, particularly the soap opera" with its melodrama and sensational plot devices, but place these elements within the heritage costume drama formula (Chapman 2014, 138). Such is also the case with *Seis Hermanas.* According to Hernández, the visual aesthetics and social engagement of the series set it apart from the typical afternoon fare: "es como si fuera de otro género. Si la tarde de la televisión fuera un género, ésta sería una nueva apuesta" (RTVE 2015c; it's as if it were another genre. If afternoon television were a genre, this would be betting on something new).

Thus, through its advance publicity, *Seis Hermanas* positioned itself as an afternoon version of prestige television, and to attract the type of audience that would watch quality programming, RTVE televised the premiere episode in the evening, in Spain's 10:00 p.m. prime time slot, and not only on channel 1, where it would be regularly aired, but also on the more culturally oriented channel 2. Jane McCabe has observed that the premiere episode of prestige television programing often "acts as a showcase" and "establishes its own artistic worth as a distinct and highly original piece of TV art by creating a hyper-reality, with an authentic-looking and ornately beautiful period style" (2013, 188).

The special premiere episode of *Seis hermanas* clearly follows this pattern by presenting the elite lifestyle of the six Silva sisters: Adela, Blanca, Diana, Celia, Francisca, and Elisa. It is Blanca's betrothal celebration, and the cream of Madrid society fills the Casino's central patio. This building, constructed in 1910 and featuring a sumptuous *modernista* (Art Nouveau) style, was the emblematic venue for the aristocracy of wealth that arose during the Restauration to display its ability to rival the celebrations of the titled aristocracy it was emulating. Blanca is happily fulfilling her prescribed role as a woman of her class by marrying the eldest son of the prestigious Loygorri banking family. The opulence of the venue, the expensive automobiles of the guests, and the elegance of their clothing give the television viewer a glimpse of the "glamour" and "lujo" (luxury) of "la vida de la clase alta al principio del siglo" (the life of the upper class at the beginning of the century), which according to Campos, is "un tema que casi nunca se ha retratado en España" (RTVE 2015d; a subject that almost never has been portrayed in Spain).

The Silva sisters do indeed lead a life of privilege, but we soon see that theirs takes place within a proverbial gilded cage when their father refuses to accept any of their aspirations that do not conform to the traditional pattern of marriage, home, and motherhood. Whereas self-made men like Fernando Silva live active lives within the public sector, their wives and daughters are expected to be content within the private realm. Consequently, Fernando summarily dismisses both Francisca's hopes for a career as an opera singer and Celia's desire to study literature at the Sorbonne. But Celia challenges her father by saying that "las normas son para romperlas" (rules are made to be broken) and she threatens to go to Paris without his permission. These are her last words to him before his sudden death. The theme of breaking rules is next developed by Adela, the eldest sister who returned to her family home after being widowed. Having been left without an inheritance due to the machinations of her husband's family, she is determined not to be victimized again. Reminding her sisters that "nosotras somos mujeres. No tenemos derechos, solamente tenemos deberes" (we are women. We don't have rights, just duties), Adela informs them that earlier that evening she had heard their uncle, the co-owner of the Silva textile factory, threaten to take control of the business, and she warns them that their father's death could facilitate that process, thereby jeopardizing their financial security. Consequently, they make the joint decision to bury their father under a false name and pretend that he is traveling through America on a long business trip. The result of this lie is threefold: First, since their father supposedly is still alive, no male family member steps in to fill the role as head of the house, which transforms the structure of their family life from a hierarchical model to a democratic one, with each woman having an equal voice and voting on important decisions. Second, by pretending that their business decisions are dictated to them by their father, they exert a greater degree of control over the factory than women normally were allowed. Third, through their daily dealings with the factory workers, they form personal relationships that cross class boundaries.

The title of this opening episode, "Derechos y deberes" (Rights and Duties) references Adela's assertion that women of their time have none of the former and all too many of the latter, but Celia's declaration that rules are made to be broken expresses the defiant attitudes that were starting to formulate among women at this point in history. Hernández has stated that the early part of the twentieth century was chosen as the setting for the series because of its "aspecto revolucionario, que es ese cambio social que hace que las mujeres trabajen, que cambie la forma de ver la sexualidad y que conquiste nuevos derechos que antes no se contemplaban o incluso, estaban castigados" (RTVE 2015c; revolutionary aspect, which is the social change that allows women to work, to change their way of looking at sexuality, to conquer new rights that were not considered before, or even were punished). The clothing for the series reflects that transitional phase. According to Elena de Lorenzo, the costume designer, "en principio iba a ser 1920, pero luego decidimos que la época de 1913 era mucho más interesante por lo romántico del vestuario y porque es un período de cambio en el vestuario de la mujer, mantenía ese romanticismo de la época anterior y ya empezaba a vincular con la mujer moderna de los años veinte" (RTVE 2015a; at first it was going to take place in 1920, but then we decided that the 1913 era was much more interesting because of the romantic quality of the clothing and because it is a period of change in women's clothing, retaining the romanticism of the previous era but already beginning to make connections with the modern woman of the twenties). Indeed, this time period was "un momento muy potente" (a very powerful moment) for women because it marked the beginning of the feminist movement in Europe (RTVE 2015d).

In her book, *Women and the Law*, Anja Louis notes that "first wave feminism was preoccupied with legal rights" and "defined justice as consisting of gender neutrality and equality before the law" (2005, 2 and 22). *Seis Hermanas* echoes these concerns by placing the legal and social status of women at the center of its plotlines. The legal codes in force during this time were the *Código civil* (Civil Code) of 1889, the *Código penal* (Penal Code) of 1870, and the *Código de comercio* (Commercial Code) of 1885. As Geraldine Scanlon has observed, the legal position of single women differed markedly from that of their married counterparts. After the age of 25, an unmarried woman was allowed to move out of her parents' home without their permission. She could "enajenar y gravar sus bienes" (sell, transfer, and levy a tax on her property) and even "dirigir una banca, un comercio, una industria" (Scanlon 1986, 123; manage a bank, a business, an industry). Nevertheless, her ability to exercise these rights was severely curtailed by social conventions, which deemed it dishonorable for upper- and middle-class women to work. Financial security was largely achieved through marriage, which meant relinquishing their rights as adults to their husbands, who became their guardians, with control over not only their property, but also their movements and their bodies. As Scanlon has noted, "las presiones sociales y psicológicas ejercidas sobre la mujer para que cumpliese su destino matrimonial ... crearon la irónica situación de que un número enorme de mujeres se entregaron voluntaria e incluso entusiásticamente a la esclavitud legal" (1986, 126; the social and psychological pressures exerted over women to fulfill their matrimonial destiny ... created the ironic situation of an enormous number of women voluntarily and even enthusiastically giving themselves over to legal slavery). Indeed, Adela had freely chosen to marry, but her legal obligation to obey her husband under article 57 of the Civil Code soon subjected her to an unbearable level of stress.

In episode 21, Adela reveals to Blanca the dark side of her married life. In the beginning, she and her husband, Eusebio, were happy, as if on an extended honeymoon, but gradually he became jealous of her every move. He did not want her to socialize or do anything without him. Characterizing her daily life as "un infierno" (a Hell), Adela further says:

> Un día después de una discusión terrible Eusebio me dijo que se habían terminado nuestros problemas, que ya no habría más discusiones ni celos. Me enseñó un revólver y me dijo que yo era libre para hacer lo que quisiera, pero que si mi conducta era inapropiada, él sacaría el revólver. Yo no me atreví a contradecirle lo más mínimo. ¿Y sabes lo peor de todo? Que cuando me quedé viuda, busqué como una loca el revólver, y cuando lo encontré, el revólver no tenía balas. Me había estado sometiendo durante todos estos años con un revólver sin balas.

> (One day after a terrible fight Eusebio told me that our troubles are now over, that there will be no more arguments or jealousy. He showed me a revolver and told me that I was free to do whatever I wanted, but if my conduct was inappropriate, he would take out the revolver. I didn't dare contradict him in the least. And do you know what was the worst of all? When I was left a widow, I searched like a madwoman for the revolver, and when I found it, the revolver didn't have any bullets. I had been subjugated all those years by a revolver without bullets.)

Adela's words directly parallel the plot of Pardo Bazán's 1895 short story, "El revolver" (The Revolver). Unhappy marriages are often featured in Pardo Bazán's nearly 600 short stores, but each narrative provides a personalized portrait of a specific situation. Although "El revólver" is not credited as influencing this portion of the series, the matching details of the unique form of psychological abuse suffered by Adela clearly point to it as the source text. On the contrary, the novels of Carmen de Burgos give a more generalized view of marriage, with individual works documenting the numerous abuses typically experienced by wives of the time and employing the emotionalism of melodrama "to turn affect into moral sentiment" in favor of the "virtuous victim" being depicted (Louis 2005, 151). Of particular interest is *La malcasada* (The Unhappily Married Woman), which "is exemplary in its treatment of the injustices married women were subjected to and is Carmen de Burgos's finest example of a narrative illustrating the legal machinery women were entrapped in" (Louis 2005, 44). Dolores, its protagonist, must endure the gambling, drinking, and womanizing of her husband, who beats her when she disobeys him and tries to rape her when she rebuffs his sexual advances. At issue here is Dolores's "ownership of her own body" and her "right to freedom of the person," which are "inalienable natural rights and, as Burgos points out in her essays, these rights were incompatible with the positive codified law legislating categorically against those basic rights for married women" (Louis 2005, 44–45).

Dolores's social equal, Blanca Silva is similarly mistreated by Rodolfo, her fiancé, and eventual husband in the series. Blanca's suffering begins even before their marriage, when she learns of Rodolfo's affair with another woman. Rosalía, the family's beloved but traditionally minded housekeeper, immediately advises Blanca to forgive Rodolfo, thereby illustrating Burgos's observation that women themselves have impeded the advancement of feminism because "acostumbradas a la esclavitud, se asustaban de la libertad" (accustomed to slavery, they were afraid of freedom) so "deseaban contentar a sus dueños con la sumisión" (de Burgos 1927, 13; they wanted to content their masters with submission). Blanca addresses the issue of women's complicity in their victimization by asking Rosalía in episode 48 "por qué siempre las mujeres nos recomendamos las unas a las otras perdón, aguanta, y ten paciencia?" (why do we women always tell each other to forgive, endure, and be patient?). Blanca threatens to break her engagement, but she eventually does forgive Rodolfo under one condition: that her opinion will henceforth count as much as his, and more than his mother's. However, when Blanca begins to act on that condition by choosing not to attend functions with Rodolfo and refusing to obey his mother's orders, he asks her in episode 70 why she cannot be "una mujer normal" (a normal woman).

Blanca's growing independence clearly displeases Rodolfo, so he schemes to return her to the subservient position of a "normal" woman by pressuring her into proving her love for him by having sexual relations before the wedding. The day after she capitulates, she realizes that Rodolfo's real motive had nothing to do with love and everything to do with power. In episode 112, he tells her "Ayer te hice mía. Ahora me perteneces, del todo. Yo seré el único que te querrá. ¿O crees que alguien aceptaría a una mujer que no llega virgen al matrimonio? … Yo quiero casarme contigo; quiero que seas la madre de mis hijos; siempre y cuando te comportes como una mujer debe comportarse" (yesterday I made you mine. Now you belong to me, completely. I am the only man who will want you, or do you think that anyone else will accept a woman who doesn't come to her marriage as a virgin? … I want to marry you; I want you to be the mother of my children; provided that you behave as a woman should behave). This emotional blackmail reflects the era's sexual double standard, and Rodolfo's declaration that Blanca now belongs to him is solely based on social norms, but after they marry, his dominion over Blanca is upheld by law.

Although a wife's degree of freedom is determined by her husband, he is allowed to come and go as he likes without informing her of his whereabouts. Consequently, Rodolfo spends nights away from Blanca, gambling, drinking, and frequenting bordellos. In episode 135 when Blanca attempts leave the house to attend Francisca's wedding against Rodolfo's wishes, he says that he is going to show her "de una vez por todas que en esta casa y en este matrimonio se hace lo que yo digo" (once and for all that in this house and in this marriage things are done as I say), and he exercises his ultimate control over her selfhood and body by raping her on the desk in his office despite her pleads to stop. This scene visually conveys all of the melodramatic sensationalism of soap opera and the melodramatic emotionalism of Burgos's *La malcasada*. Furthermore, the fact that Blanca is dressed for a wedding reminds the viewer of the splendid public spectacle of her own betrothal party, which now contrasts sharply with this private spectacle of the reality of Restoration-era marriage. The next evening when Blanca tries to avoid Rodolfo's sexual advances, he says "ya sabes que hay dos maneras para hacerlo: como ayer o por las buenas. Así que tú eliges" (episode 136; you already know that there are two ways of doing this: like yesterday or on good terms. You choose). As Maryellen Bieder has observed, "the female body is the site of struggle in the marriage plots of Burgos's more overtly feminist fictions," and "Burgos describes marriage as ongoing physical consummation, something that most nineteenth-century novels– and novels by her male contemporaries–tend to address only covertly, if at all" (2001, 252–253). Burgos's *La malcasada* specifically focuses on the issue of nonconsensual sexual relations within marriage. In the chapter aptly entitled "La caricia insoportable"" (The Unbearable Caress), Dolores "no podía comprender que se le quisiera imponer la obligación de entregar su intimidad, sin amor, a un hombre que había llegado a repugnarle, como si ella hubiese abdicado de su libertad de espíritu. ... ¿Qué ley podía condenarla a besar?" (de Burgos 1923, 114; could not understand why anyone would want to place upon her the obligation to surrender herself intimately, without love, to a man who had become dis- gusting to her, as if she had abdicated her spiritual strength. ... What law could condemn her to kiss?). Like Dolores, Blanca has fallen out of love with her husband due to his mistreatment of her and she too is no longer willing to submit to him sexually. Articles 56 and 58 of the Civil Code required a wife to live with her husband, so when Blanca leaves Rodolfo to stay with her sisters after he contracts gonorrhea from a prostitute, Rodolfo has the police return her to him.

Just as the protagonist of *La malcasada* and the countless other unhappily married women in Burgos's novels and in real life, Blanca is trapped "in a marriage without any legal scope for escape" due to the existing divorce laws (Louis 2005, 44). Since marriage was considered to be indissoluble, divorce at the time was actually a legal separation, and the rules governing how it could be obtained differed by gender. Despite Rodolfo's numerous infidelities, Blanca could not divorce him because article 105 of the Civil Code states that a single instance of a wife's adul- tery was sufficient cause for a husband to divorce her, but she could only divorce him if his adulteries created a public scandal. Burgos advocated strongly for divorce law reform, not only to make legal separations more equitable for both parties, but also to create a means of legally dissolv- ing a marriage. As Louis has demonstrated, Burgos used her novels as case studies to illustrate her essays' arguments promoting the moderni- zation of divorce legislation. One such argument is that adultery occurs as a consequence of Spain's existing divorce laws: "Desde el momento en que la vida nos demuestra que no siempre el amor es eterno, no debe- mos obstinarnos en que el matrimonio sea indisoluble. Es la indisolub- ilidad del matrimonio la que da origen al adulterio" (de Burgos 1927, 161; from the moment when life shows us that love isn't always eternal, we should not obstinately insist that marriage is indissoluble. It is the indissolubility of marriage that is the source of adultery). In her novels, "Burgos tried to construct a moral position that makes the heroine's actions justifiable," so when a woman in an abusive marriage commits adultery, it is because she is expressing "her inalienable right to be with the man she chooses," which in turn is based on "the basic liberty of freedom of the person" (Louis 2005, 54 and 61). This same justification is made by Blanca when she enters into an affair with Rodolfo's brother, Cristóbal. Rodolfo could have divorced Blanca, but the resulting scandal would have hurt his political career, so he opts instead to not contest Blanca's petition for an annulment by the Catholic Church. This was an ecclesiastical loophole to the existing civil laws because a church annulment decreed there had been no marriage, leaving both parties free to marry others. Thus, although Blanca's infidelity was both socially and legally censurable, it did free her from Rodolfo's domination and thus represents another example of the Silva sisters achieving self-determination by breaking rules that unfairly control their lives.

Burgos not only addressed the legal inequalities of woman as wives, but also as mothers, and the *Seis Hermanas* series exemplifies this situation through Francisca's marriage of convenience to her piano teacher, Luís, which produces a son, Fernando, who is born in Italy while Francisca is undertaking voice training. According to article 154 of the Civil Code, the father holds complete control (*patria potestad*) over his minor children, with that right only transferring to the mother upon his death, but Francisca secretly entrusts the baby to the care of her sisters during her European opera tour to protect him from the physically abusive Luís, who had once nearly strangled her to death. When Luís discovers the truth, he removes his son from the Silva home. Entirely motivated by revenge, he arranges to have Fernando adopted by strangers. To prevent Luís from following through on this legal but morally reprehensible plan, Diana has the baby kidnapped and sent abroad to Francisca.

The stories of Adela's, Blanca's, and Francisca's marriages affirm Scanlon's characterization of marriage as legal slavery. However, Pardo Bazán's *Memorias de un solterón* (Memories of a Confirmed Bachelor) suggests that individual cases of marital equality can exist if the husband is willing to recognize the self-determination of his wife, and *Seis hermanas* exemplifies this in Diana and Salvador Montaner's relationship. Diana and Pardo Bazán's female protagonist, Feíta, have much in common. Both were brought up in families with numerous female siblings and headed by fathers with traditional views of a woman's role in society. Each becomes the main administrator of her family's affairs. Both declare that they never intend to marry because they want to keep their personal freedom. But both do marry, and each to a man transformed from a confirmed bachelor into a life partner who respects and celebrates his wife's individuality. Significantly, though, these two men are very different from each other.

Mauro Pareja, the bachelor of the novel's title, is an effeminate dandy who has chosen not to marry because it would alter his comfortable routine of enjoying cigars and fine food, paying meticulous attention to his attire, chastely courting women, and reading light fiction. Mauro's ambiguous gender identity has not escaped the attention of critics. Mark Harpring has examined how Mauro negotiates between his homosexual inclinations and the heterosexual model of bourgeois masculinity, and Akiko Tsuchiya has indicated that both Mauro and Feíta would have been considered deviant by their society because each defies the ideal of normative masculinity and femininity. Both critics agree that Pardo Bazán uses these non-traditional characters "to propose a revision of gender roles" (Harpring 2006, 208) and "to create new spaces of subjectivity for both men and women" (Tsuchiya 2011, 135). Mauro has been seen as Pardo Bazán's conception of "the new bourgeois man" (Harpring 2006, 208) and "the ideal mate" for a "companionate marriage" (Charnon-Deutsch 1994, 155). Furthermore, Beth Bauer considers this novel to be where Pardo Bazán "most clearly traces a blueprint for the modern woman and for enlightened marriage between equals" (1994, 23). However, Maryellen Bieder views Feíta's acceptance of Mauro's offer of equality within the limited realm of "la vida íntima, en la asociación constante del hogar" (private life, in the constant interaction of home) as a "capitulation" (1976, 101–108), and Zachary Erwin quarrels with the notion that the new ideal man "must be feminized in order to make men and women more equal" (2012, 549).

Seis hermanas builds on Pardo Bazán's premise but provides an alternate view of the new man, and of how his relationship with the new woman can function. Headstrong and independent, Diana finds her ideal mate in Salvador, who not only recognizes her as his equal, but also fights alongside her to publicly challenge the limitations society placed upon women both before and after marriage. Theirs is a love match with considerable sexual chemistry, and their shared care of their baby daughter not only shows Salvador redefining gender roles, but also exemplifies that motherhood is not incompatible with Diana succeeding in her career.

Salvador is introduced in the opening episode of the series as a bachelor who fully fits within his society's normative concept of masculinity. He is Rodolfo's friend from their school days who spends his time gambling, drinking, and above all, seducing women. A self-proclaimed "filántropo de amor" (philanthropist of love), he clearly indicates his aversion to the monogamy of marriage. In effect, he enjoys the typical freedom and pleasures of men of his age (mid-thirties) and social class (aristocratic), yet he differs from the vast majority of them in one important respect: He is attracted to strong-willed women who challenge him. Indeed, during his first encounter with Diana during Blanca's betrothal party, he tells her that "salvo yo, no sé de nadie aquí capaz de lidiar con un carácter tan impetuoso" (except for me, I don't know anyone here capable of sparring with such an impetuous strength of character), and then utters the phrase that he will repeat throughout the series to explain why he finds Diana so fascinating: "Me gustan las cosas complicadas" (I like complicated things). Unlike Rodolfo, who originally chose Blanca because she was the perfect embodiment of the submissive woman whose sole goal was to follow the dictates of society and her husband, Salvador does not want "una mujer normal" (a normal woman).

The Silva sisters contract Salvador to serve as director of the factory because their male clients refuse to do business with Diana, even when she operates under the guise of representing her father. In this position, he and Diana come in daily contact, with Salvador respecting her both as a person and an astute businesswoman. Gradually his feelings for her progress from attraction to love, and his goal changes from seduction to marriage. In episode 54 when he speaks the words "te quiero" (I love you) to her for the first time, he prefaces them by saying that she is "la mujer más valiente que he conocido en mi vida" (the bravest woman I have known in my life), and Diana eventually agrees to marry him because she realizes that her bravery is what he will continue to admire and nurture throughout their life together. As her husband, under articles 6 through 9 of the Commercial Code, Salvador had the legal right to forbid Diana from continuing to work, but on the contrary, he buys the factory from the sisters and formally appoints Diana as its director. He willingly abandons most of the pleasures of his bachelor life—turning down Rodolfo's invitations to accompany him to bordellos and preferring to return home early from social engagements rather than stay out all night drinking with his friends—but he does continue to indulge in his favorite pastime: gambling. Interestingly, this typical male voice is portrayed positively, with Salvador's skill at poker saving the factory from financial ruin both at the beginning and end of the series. Their marriage at times is stormy due to their strong personalities, but their conflicts are always resolved through mutual respect and love. Salvador and Diana provide a model for what marriage can be like when the husband does not measure his manhood by his degree of domination over his wife, and the woman can express her individuality both within her home and in the greater world.

In addition to the uncredited allusions to the writings and ideas of Pardo Bazán and Burgos mentioned above, direct references to these authors are also present in the series. It is not surprising that Celia, the intellectual of the family, becomes the vehicle for introducing them into the plotline. Since Pardo Bazán is her favorite author, Celia uses *Los Pazos de Ulloa* (The House of Ulloa), to teach Petra, a young factory worker, how to read. Petra's boyfriend, Miguel, is wary of the cross-class friendship that develops between Petra and Celia, but when his cousin, Joaquín, slaps Celia for rebuffing his sexual advances, Miguel defends Celia's honor by pummeling him. When Joaquín has Miguel arrested for assault, Celia testifies in Miguel's defense despite knowing it will cause a public scandal.

As a consequence, Celia receives a letter from a character portraying Carmen de Burgos asking to meet her. Although both Pardo Bazán and Burgos were well known during the early part of the twentieth century, Burgos never achieved the canonical status of Pardo Bazán, so the *Seis hermanas* series uses this fictional version of her to inform the television public of the life and concerns of the real Burgos. Calling Celia her "heroína" (heroine), Carmen praises her for denouncing the abuse of her attacker and for willingly risking her own social standing to help someone from the lower classes (episode 45). She goes on to tell Celia about how she reinvented herself by leaving her husband, coming to Madrid, passing qualifying examinations to teach, and taking advantage of travel grants. Through their conversion, it also is revealed that she is a journalist and war correspondent and that she is involved in an affair with Ramón Gómez de la Serna, twenty years her junior (Fig. 7.1).

In episode 46, Carmen tells Celia: "Usted, lo que tiene que hacer y pensar, y muy seriamente, es qué va a hacer con su vida. Debe tenerlo

Fig. 7.1 *Seis hermanas* (Bambú, TVE, 2015–2017): Episode 45—Carmen de Burgos and Celia Silva

claro, estar dispuesta a luchar por ello, o acabará infelizmente casada como tantas otras" (You, what you have to do and think about, and very seriously, is what you are going to do with your life. You need to have it very clear in your mind, to be willing to fight for it, or you will end up unhappily married like so many others). She also encourages Celia to use her interests and talents to write "sobre la problemática de las mujeres, sobre nuestro día en día, todas las presiones visibles o invisibles con las que hemos que vivir" (about the problems that face women, about our day to day existence, all the visible or invisible pressures we have to live with). In the next episode, Carmen tells Celia about Marcela Gracia and Elisa Sánchez, two Galician teachers who married each other by pretending that one was a man. When Celia seems shocked, Carmen concludes by saying that "el amor entre mujeres o entre hombres ha existido siempre" (love between women or between men has always existed).

Inspired by Carmen's example, Celia prepares for and passes the government examination to become a primary school teacher, and she focuses on her writing. She also starts to realize that her feelings for Petra are based on love and sexual attraction rather than just friendship, but when Celia acts on her feelings by kissing Petra, she is rejected, and in episode 90 Miguel publicly calls Celia "una depravada" (a degenerate). In keeping with the medical views of the day, Celia's attraction to Petra is considered an illness, so she is sent to Dr. Uribe, a psychiatrist with a record of successfully treating "desviaciones grotescas" (grotesque deviations) by using "terapia de conversión" (conversion therapy) based on the conditional reflex theories of Pavlov (episode 95).

During the latter part of the nineteenth century and into the early twentieth, female reading was strongly identified with sexual transgression, and health professionals warned about the "pernicious effects, especially of novel reading, on women, whose physiological system" supposedly was "more prone to nervous and sexual excitement than men's" (Tsuchiya 2011, 77). Consequently, in episode 97 Uribe has Celia show him her favorite books. The first three are by Pardo Bazán: her naturalistic masterpieces *Los Pazos de Ulloa* and *La Madre Naturaleza* (Mother Nature), and a minor work *El saludo de las brujas* (The Witches' Greeting), about a love, like Celia's for Petra, that crosses class lines. Uribe disapprovingly declares that Pardo Bazán writes "con los pantalones puestos, como un hombre" (with pants on, like a man) and he goes on to examine a book by Burgos, whom he calls "otra que tal" (another one just as bad) and books by Collette, George Sand, and Sappho. He calls these books dangerous influences because they are "llenos de libertinaje, de ideas absolutamente equivocadas sobre los roles del hombre y de la mujer" (filled with licentiousness, with completely erroneous ideas about the roles of men and women). He then begins their aversion therapy session, which consists of Celia ripping pages from Pardo Bazán's books while saying "este libro es basura y me da asco" (this book is garbage, and it disgusts me). But when this fails to alter Celia's admiration for Pardo Bazán, Uribe intensifies the therapy, having Celia kneel on floor and rip pages out of all the books, saying "abomino de Emilia Pardo Bazán" (I loathe Pardo Bazán) and continuing to name each author, while he beats Celia's back with a riding crop. This horrific scene combines melodramatic sensationalism and social critique to visually present a private spectacle of abuse and humiliation suffered by a woman literally at the hand of a male authority figure. Under Celia's high-necked, prim, and proper blouse is a non-conforming body that must be broken into submission. Celia's back is left covered with welts and her undershirt stained with blood, yet she subsequently must

undergo a series of electric shock treatments that Uribe says are necessary for a complete cure.

It is during one of these sessions the Celia meets Uribe's nurse,
Aurora, who tells her that Uribe's methods cannot cure her because she
is not sick. Aurora confides her own lesbianism to Celia and says that she
became a nurse to help women like them circumvent the medical establishment's insistence in labeling homosexuality as a disease. Together
Aurora and Celia devise a plan to have a male friend pose as Celia's new
boyfriend, thereby "proving" to Uribe the efficacy of his treatments.
The two women continue to see each other after Celia's supposed cure
releases her from further therapy, and they soon become lovers.

Aurora involves Celia in the women's suffrage movement, attending
clandestine meetings and speaking during public demonstrations. In episode 137 Celia recites aloud from a handbill they designed, which cites
Pardo Bazán's (1892) discourse *La educación del hombre y de la mujer*,
saying that "todas las mujeres conciben ideas, pero no todas conciben
hijos. El ser humano no es un árbol frutal que sólo se cultive por la cose-
cha" (Pardo Bazán 1976, 89; all women conceive ideas, but not all conceive children. A human being is not a fruit tree that only is cultivated
for its crop). It is important to note that Celia is wearing the same blouse
in this scene as the one she was wearing when Dr. Uribe had beaten
her. In this way, Celia's act of defiance in speaking in favor of women's
rights is visually contrasted with the suffering that society inflicts upon
those who do not conform to its norms of behavior. But Celia's cause is
not supported by Rosalía, who is against the idea of women voting and
fears that Celia will be arrested for distributing subversive material. In
response, Celia tells her that Pardo Bazán also said that "la educación
de la mujer no puede considerarse educación sino doma porque tiene
como fin la pasividad, la obediencia y la sumisión" (Pardo Bazán [1892]
1976, 92; the education of women cannot be considered education but
rather it is like taming a horse because it has passivity, obedience, and
submission as its goal). This analogy is further reminiscent of the scene
in Dr. Uribe's office because of the riding crop he had used, and it shows
Celia's determination not to submit any further to societal attempts to
dominate her will.

Celia and Aurora move to Arganzuela, an impoverished neighborhood in the far south of Madrid, where they both attend to the needs
of the poor: Celia with her teaching and Aurora through her nursing.
Their professions, which were becoming acceptable for educated women,

do not attract public attention, but their living arrangements do, and eventually the newspapers declare them "Las Safos de Arganzuela" (The Sapphos of Arganzuela) for sharing an apartment in "pervertido amancebamiento" (episode 391; perverted concubinage). The ensuing scandal provides the series the opportunity to inform the viewers more about Burgos's real life. Carmen commiserates with Celia, saying that she too was targeted by a newspaper smear campaign when she undertook a survey about divorce and was derisively called "La Divorciadora" (episode 393; The Divorcer). Carmen assures Celia that the public can be swayed as easily toward compassion as toward hate, so the important thing is to continue to fight for equality.

Celia does continue to advocate for women's rights throughout the remainder of the series, even taking up a cause that was strongly associated with Burgos: the repeal of article 438 of the Penal Code. Since Burgos' novella, *El artículo 438*, was written after the 1913–1917 time frame of the series, Celia does not mention it, but it serves as an implicit reference. As in Burgos's novella, Celia quotes from the text of the law in episode 422, but she adds a word for emphasis: "El marido que, sorprendiendo en adulterio a su mujer, matase en el acto a ésta o al adúltero o les causara algunas de las lesiones graves, será castigado *solamente* con la pena de destierro" (The husband who, surprising his wife in adultery, were to kill her or the adulterer in the act or were to seriously wound them, he will be punished *only* with banishment). In *El artículo 438*, Burgos points out the inherent inequality of this law because it does not allow "cualquiera de los dos esposos" (either of the two spouses) to kill the other if caught in adultery (1921, 55), and furthermore, the plot shows how a husband can manipulate the law to make premeditated murder appear to be a spontaneous crime of passion. This potentiality makes Celia's highlighting of the leniency of the punishment all the more significant because a man could be sentenced to as little as 6 months and one day of banishment for what should be classified as parricide, which carried the death penalty or life imprisonment (Louis 2005, 59; Rodríguez Núñez 1993–1994, 153).

Michael Ugarte has stated that Burgos "saw social change as a process of self empowerment" (1998, 61) and that is precisely the message that Celia conveys in the final episode when she recites aloud from the novel she has just begun to write:

A lo largo de su vida estas mujeres se preguntaron por qué se las juzgaba de manera distinta que los hombres, por qué la sociedad se empeña en recordarles que su lugar estaba escrito desde antes, y que no tenían derecho a cambiarlo. Todo el mundo tiene derecho a ser quien quiera, haya nacido hombre o mujer. Ellas han demostrado que aunque el camino esté lleno de obstáculos, siempre hay una razón para seguir adelante. Siempre hay una razón para seguir luchando, la de poder vivir en libertad. … Que su ejemplo sirva a otras generaciones que su lucha no se quede en la intimidad de la familia, que sus logros sean públicos para que otras mujeres sepan que se puede elegir, que se debe elegir.

(Episode 489; Throughout their lives these women asked themselves why they were judged differently than men, why society insists on reminding them that their place had been written beforehand, and they didn't have the right to change it. Everyone has the right to be who they want to be, whether born male or female. These women have shown that although the road is filled with obstacles, there always is a reason to keep moving ahead. There always is a reason to keep fighting. It is to be able to live in freedom. … Let their example serve other generations, let their battles not remain within the privacy of their home, let their accomplishments be public so that other women know that they can choose, that they should choose.)

These are the closing words of the series, and as such, they function as a summary of what the series has stood for as a whole. Celia's voice-over narration is heard over the images of a gala celebration of family and close friends in the Silva home. Although the sisters are dressed as elegantly as in the opening episode of the series, this is a private display of solidarity rather than a public spectacle of appearances. No longer fearful of what society may think of them, the sisters now allow Celia to write the story of their life under her own name, rather than the pseudonyms she had previously used. Her book, entitled *Seis Hermanas*, will be their public declaration of who they really are.

Celia's monologue contains two main points. The first concerns the bravery and determination it takes for women to overcome the limitations society places on them. According to Louis, the legal system during the Restoration "was used as a patriarchal instrument of social control" (2005, 9), but throughout the series Adela, Blanca, Francisca, Diana, and Celia undermine the power and authority of that mechanism by exposing its inequalities and refusing to follow rules that discriminate against them. The series uses these five women to show that justice can be achieved by breaking unjust rules and that challenging social and legal norms is valid when done in the service of a greater moral principle. But the series also uses Elisa, the sixth Silva sister, to show that rule-breaking should not be done for purely selfish reasons. Parties, fine clothes, and momentary pleasures fill Elisa's thoughts. She lies, steals, and manipulates others to indulge her frivolous and ever-changing whims, including betraying her best friend and her loving husband by having affairs simply out of boredom. Elisa is motivated entirely by self-interest, and as such, she serves as a negative example that throws into relief the principle of gender equality that motivates the transgressive behavior of her sisters, thereby justifying their actions in comparison with hers.

The monologue's second point is that the fight for women's rights is intergenerational, with its effects accruing over time, so women of today should look to those who came before them as they continue to strive for justice and equality. Campos has noted that Spain of 1913 seems to be "un mundo muy lejano" (a far-away world), but the theme of discrimination against women is "muy de la actualidad en nuesto país" (RTVE 2015b; is very timely in our country today). Although the writings of first-wave feminists such as Pardo Bazán and Burgos deal with the situation of Spanish women from a century ago, many of the issues they raise, such as workplace inequality and spousal abuse, still resonate now. The *Seis hermanas* series shows the modern-day viewer that the hard-won battles fought by Pardo Bazán, Burgos, and the women they inspired (both in fiction and in real-life) are the legacy upon which further progress can be achieved by those who are willing to "seguir luchando" (keep fighting).

NOTE

1. All translations are by the author unless otherwise noted.

BIBLIOGRAPHY

Bauer, Beth Wietelmann. 1994. "Narrative Cross-Dressing: Emilia Pardo Bazán in *Memorias de un solterón.*" *Hispania* 77 (1): 23–30.

Bieder, Maryellen. 1976. "Capitulation: Marriage, Not Freedom: A Study of Emilia Pardo Bazán's *Memorias de un solterón* and Galdós' *Tristana.*" *Symposium* 30 (2): 93–109.

————. 2001. "Carmen de Burgos: Modern Spanish Woman." In *Recovering Spain's Feminist Tradition*, edited by Lisa Vollendorf, 241–259. New York: MLA.

Campos, Ramón, and Gema R. Neira. 2015–2017. *Seis Hermanas*. Bambú Producciones, TVE.

Chapman, James. 2014. *"Downton Abbey*: Reinventing the British Costume Drama." In *British Television Drama: Past, Present and Future*, edited by Jonathan Bignell and Stephen Lacey, 131–142. Hampshire: Palgrave Macmillan.

Charnon-Deutsch, Lou. 1994. *Narratives of Desire: Nineteenth-Century Spanish Fiction by Women*. University Park: Pennsylvania State University Press.

de Burgos, Carmen. 1921. *El artículo 438. La novela semanal* 1 (15): 3–60.

————. 1923. *La malcasada*. Valencia: Sempere.

————. 1927. *La mujer moderna y sus derechos*. Valencia: Sempere.

Erwin, Zachary. 2012. "Fantasies of Masculinity in Emilia Pardo Bazán's *Memorias de un solterón*." *Revista de Estudios Hispánicos* 46 (3): 547–568.

Harpring, Mark. 2006. "Homoeroticism and Gender Role Confusion in Pardo Bazán's *Memorias de un solterón*." *Hispanic Research Journal* 7 (3): 195–210.

Louis, Anja. 2005. *Women and the Law: Carmen de Burgos, an Early Feminist*. Suffolk: Tamesis.

McCabe, Jane. 2013. "HBO Aesthetics, Quality Television and *Boardwalk Empire*." In *Television Aesthetics and Style*, edited by Steven Peacock and Jason Jacobs, 185–198. New York and London: Bloomsbury.

Pardo Bazán, Emilia. (1892) 1976. "La educación del hombre y la de la mujer." In *La mujer española*, edited by Leda Schiavo, 71–97. Madrid: Editora Nacional.

Radio Televisión Española (RTVE). 2015a. "Haciendo *Seis Hermanas*." Last Modified April 22, 2015. http://www.rtve.es/alacarta/videos/seis-hermanas/haciendo-seis-hermanas/3102318/.

————. 2015b. "Las mujeres toman la tarde de La 1." Last Modified April 22, 2015. http://www.rtve.es/alacarta/videos/seis-hermanas/seis-hermanas-mujeres-toman-tarde-1/3098325/.

————. 2015c. "Razones pare verla." Last Modified March 24, 2015. http://www.rtve.es/alacarta/videos/seis-hermanas/seis-hermanas-razones-para-verla/3051436/.

————. 2015d. "Una serie de principios del siglo XX." Last Modified March 24, 2015. http://www.rtve.es/television/seis-hermanas/extra/.

————. n.d. "La serie." http://www.rtve.es/television/seis-hermanas/la-serie/. Accessed December 18, 2016.

Rodríguez Núñez, Alicia. 1993–1994. "El parricidio en la legislación española." *Boletín de la Facultad de Derecho* 5: 145–171.

Scanlon, Geraldine M. 1986. *La polémica feminista en la España contemporánea 1868–1974.* Translated by Rafael Mazarrasa. Madrid: Akal.

Tsuchiya, Akiko. 2011. *Marginal Subjects: Gender and Deviance in Fin-de-Siècle Spain.* Toronto: University of Toronto Press.

Ugarte, Michael. 1998. "Carmen de Burgos ('Colombine'): Feminist *Avant la Lettre.*" In *Spanish Women Writers and the Essay: Gender, Politics, and the Self,* edited by Kathleen M. Glenn and Mercedes Mazquiarán de Rodríguez, 55–74. Columbia: University of Missouri Press.

PART IV

Restoring the *Telenovela*

CHAPTER 8

Bandolera: Limits and Possibilities of Period Telenovelas

Francisca López

Bandolera is a Diagonal TV production for Antena 3 that was on the air for two years, from October 1, 2011 to November 1, 2013. Except for its premiere, broadcast in prime time, it occupied the afternoon slot (horario de sobremesa), the most common for telenovelas in Spain. In this slot, the program earned an average share of 10.5% (Vertele) while competing on the national level with another period serial, Amar en tiempos revueltos (TVE), and a gossip show, Sálvame (Telecinco).

Set in Arazana, a fictitious Andalusian town in 1882–1887,[1] the series is a somewhat innovative hybrid product that draws from several genres. Mixing characteristics from period dramas, telenovelas and action shows, Bandolera tells the story of Sara Reeves, an English woman enamored of all things Andalusian who leaves her home and family in London to travel to Southern Spain hoping to bring some excitement into her life. Although perfectly integrated in her new home soon after her arrival (first as a reporter and, only a few months later, as a landowner and business woman), Sara does find excitement. She takes advantage of being

F. López (✉)
Bates College, Lewiston, ME, USA
e-mail: Flopez@bates.edu

© The Author(s) 2018
D. R. George, Jr. and W. S. Tang (eds.),
Televising Restoration Spain,
https://doi.org/10.1007/978-3-319-96196-5_8

kidnapped to develop a relationship with her *bandolero* (bandit) kidnappers and eventually joins them. Thus, she carries out parallel lives and, in contemporary superhero style, fights for justice and against evil both openly and secretly.

The series comprises 510 episodes arranged in two seasons of different lengths (168 and 342, respectively). The narrative arc, however, suggests three rather distinctive blocks, each one including a significant number of novel secondary characters as well as new plots and subplots. Block one wraps up in episode 177 with the resolution of the main story lines up to that point: Sara's band (el Espíritu de Carranza) defeats their fellow *bandolero* enemies (la banda del Navajas) and she and Miguel Romero, her first love interest in the show, makes plans to move to England and get married. Block two ends in chapter 319 when, after aborting several "terrorist" attempts against the liberal government of Práxedes Mateo Sagasta and King Alfonso XII, the members of El Espíritu de Carranza bury their weapons and Sara leaves for England with her son and her *protegeé*, Jimena. Finally, block three seems to be divided into two somewhat separate parts: The first one ends with the collaboration of the *bandoleros* and the *Guardia Civil* against a corrupt ex-officer-turned criminal and his henchmen (episode 383); the second concludes the series with the band's victory over their new enemy (La Garduña), a reburial of arms, and Sara and Raúl, her new romantic partner, walking away from the camera and ready to move to England with Sara's son. The impetus driving the narrative—centered around El Espíritu de Carranza's main enemy at any given time—changes from block to block, a change that alters in turn the type of conflicts they face, despite all three of them including parallel characters and situations.

Bandolera is best understood from the perspective of the new *telenovela* and the transformation that the genre has been undergoing in the last 20 years or so. Although it is fair to say that, as the narrative arc progresses, the story moves away from melodrama and closer to action/adventure, it is also true that this focus on action is something that the program shares with other contemporary *telenovelas*. Thus, I propose to analyze this series as such. In doing so, my objective is threefold. Firstly, I establish the connections between this Spanish production and the evolution of the genre since it began to enter the global market at the turn of the twenty-first century. Secondly, I look into the social and political ideologies driving the story. Thirdly, I explore a few parallels between the time period represented (1882–1887) and that of the show's emission (2011–2013). I hypothesize that, despite the fact that the period setting provides some material that is key for the creation and resolution of several story lines, the producers of *Bandolera* do not really engage the past in any significant way. Rather, they use it as little more than background for the representation of conflicts that draw large audiences in the present, thus securing the marketability of their product.

THE GENRE'S EVOLUTION: ADJUSTING TO NEW DEMANDS

Introduced in Spain in the late 1970s, *telenovelas* became truly popular in the 1980s. The titles broadcasted in this decade and in the early 1990s were all imported from different Latin American countries—especially Mexico, Colombia, and Venezuela—and, although country-specific trends did exist, they shared formal and thematic characteristics for the most part. The main plot, centering around the difficulties that a man and a woman in love must overcome before they become blissfully engaged or married, was only the leading story in a set of family relations that allowed for a number of related, interconnected stories, all of which were emotionally driven and developed throughout hundreds of episodes following the twists and turns typical of melodrama. From the early 1990s, however, the genre started to undergo significant changes.[2]

In his study of this evolution in México, Guillermo Orozco Gómez argues that the intended transnationalization of the new Mexican *telenovela* required both formal and thematic modifications. Formal changes include, but are not limited to, multiple plots, a faster pace, and an increase in outdoor scenes. More significant than these formal alterations, however, are their thematic, perhaps unintended, consequences. With the inclusion of subplots, for example, the main narrative often becomes so fragmented that it ends up being no more than a device to frame episodes as outlandish as they are disconnected from one another. Furthermore, the secondary stories usually reduce melodrama and emphasize spectacle, moving from seduction to excitement as the main mechanism to engage the audience. Seemingly seeking to achieve nothing beyond the promotion of their own consumption, contemporary *telenovelas* center around a *leitmotiv* intended to provoke the viewer's identification with and desire to buy the product, that is, to consume the *telenovela* itself, which often results in a hybrid audiovisual text. Orozco Gómez further notes the connection between the intended transnationalization of television products and the hybridization of fiction genres not only in Mexico but also in Latin America and beyond and concludes that the most important transformation affecting the production of *telenovelas* in the larger international arena is first and foremost commercial. Thus, he states that the ultimate goal of this industry since the early 2000s, in tune with the economic model of globalization, seems to be the creation of franchises (Orozco Gómez 2006, 30–32).

Orozco Gómez's arguments are reasonable, but it could be claimed that franchising need not always be the industry's first objective. I want to further suggest that new venues for broadcasting television products—from the specific corporation's website to platforms such as Netflix, Hulu, or Amazon—have also had an impact on the rapid transformation of the genre in the first decades of the twenty-first century, giving way to subgenres of sorts and hybrid televisual narratives. The use of humor and pseudo-feminist concerns to retell the basic plot of Cinderella in *Yo soy Betty, la fea* (Colombia 1999) was rather revolutionary at the time, initiating a trend that includes such titles as *Las Aparicio* (Mexico 2010), and seems to have culminated in parody with *Jane, the Virgin* (United States 2014). Likewise, titles like *Sin tetas no hay paraíso* (Colombia 2006) and *Rosario Tijeras* (Colombia 2010) introduced, besides a debatable "neo-realist truth" (Omar Rincón, quoted in Ramírez Murcia 2016, 60), elements of action/adventure that have been particularly exploited by USA productions such as *La Reina del Sur* (2011), *El Señor de los cielos* (2013), and *Camelia la Texana* (2014). Indeed, humor and action/adventure seem to have become somewhat frequent components of the genre, ready to be incorporated to a varying degree in a wide range of narratives. Seeking an ever-growing audience, the classic love plot of *telenovela* and its melodramatic presentation become almost—sometimes, truly—secondary, both getting diffused in stories that incorporate a bit of entertainment for everybody in the family.

These tendencies have coupled up in Spain with another cultural pattern prevalent in North Atlantic societies in the twenty-first century, a pervasive, quasi-obsessive interest in the national past. This is so much the case that one Spanish television scholar refers to two period *telenovelas* as emblematic of the 'Spanish- ization' of the genre (Chicharro Merayo 2009, 74; "emblemas de la 'españolización' del 'culebrón'").

Diagonal TV, a successful Spanish production company, can be considered responsible for this trend. They seem to have found the perfect formula for making products that attract a wide audience by combining melodrama and the growing obsession with the past characteristic of cultural production in Western Europe and the USA since the turn of the twenty-first century. Having produced more than a dozen period *telenovelas* for TV3 (Catalan public broadcaster Televisió de Catalunya), TVE (Spain's public broadcaster Televisión Española), and more recently for Antena 3 (a privately owned channel broadcasting nationally), Diagonal TV is indeed a perfect example of what Andreas Huyssen calls the "increasingly successful marketing of memory by the Western culture industry" (2000, 25). The company has used a diverse array of historical backgrounds for many of its serials, thus turning the use of the past into one of the genre's defining characteristics in Spain.

Bandolera is set in the 1880s, perhaps the only relatively uneventful historical period of nineteenth-century Spain. A *coup de état* led by General Pavía in 1874 brought about the beginning of the end of the first Spanish Republic and prepared the way for the Restoration of the monarchy under King Alfonso XII. Engineered by Antonio Cánovas del Castillo and supported by most of the economic and military establishments, the "Restoration" instituted a parliamentary monarchy that governed itself by a new constitution approved in 1876. This new constitution, along with the institution of the *turno pacífico*—an agreement between the two main political parties to alternate in power by manipulating elections—brought about a period of political stability that lasted until the proclamation of the Second Republic in 1931. Of this whole relatively stable period, the 1880s were without a doubt the years of least conflict. Choosing this time frame as the background against which *Bandolera* is set works well for several related reasons. First, this setting affords plausibility to the *Bandolero* narrative. Second, it provides historical elements that can easily be incorporated as key factors in a number of story lines, as I discuss below. Finally, and almost paradoxically, it facilitates the lack of real engagement with the past characteristic of the new period *telenovelas*. In fact, this title is perhaps Diagonal TV's best example of the genre in Spanish television: a highly episodic serial without a clear main plot, a narrative in which humor and action/adventure are at least as prevalent as melodrama, and one in which the past is engaged only insofar as it allows for the staging of present ideas and concerns.

The episodic nature of *Bandolera* relates to its main narrative impulse, the protagonist's determination to travel from Oxford, where she lives with her uncle, to Andalusia where she lived as child and where, we eventually learn, she was actually born of Spanish parents (episode 56). Her stated motives include: to understand her past, to become the master of her own destiny, and to write a novel about Andalusia (episode 1). Sara Reeves voices her plan to include the *bandoleros* as the main characters in her novel: "Pienso hacerles a todos protagonistas de mi novela" (episode 6; I plan to make them all characters in my novel), and she refers to specific scenes from her life (i.e., the series itself) in her diegetic writing (episode 40), such that the program could be viewed as the staging of that novel; a novel that, influenced by her readings of romantic stories of *bandoleros* in Andalusia, Sara sometimes foresees as one of adventures ("una novela de aventuras") and sometimes views as a "Realist" text ("que destile verdad") based on her lived experiences (episode 2).[3] This opens the narrative to the inclusion of multiple story lines of different natures that intersect one another in almost every episode: the *bandoleros* in their hideout, attacking coaches on the roads, saving the nation from an imminent *coup d'état*, making sure that powerful weapons do not reach the wrong hands (German), or undercover, interacting with the powerful in the bordello; the insignificant, often humorous, conversations among the townsfolk in the bar and the plaza; the discussions of peasants and laborers about their situation at the blacksmith's and in the fields, as well as the eventual staging of a popular revolt; and the twists and turns of love stories as they are affected by class differences, greed, jealousy and sexual desire, among other passions. Like the new *telenovela* in the era of globalization, *Bandolera* does not possess a main story, but rather a number of more- or less-developed subplots involving a revolving set of characters along with the protagonists.

Also in line with the new *telenovela*, *Bandolera* uses spectacle and excitement as mechanisms to engage the audience as often as it relies on melodrama and seduction. Spectacle and excitement are naturally afforded by the *bandolero* theme, but well beyond that, they are highly conspicuous strategies in the marketing of the series as well. In the presentation of the program found on antena3internacional.com, the word "aventura(s)" is used five times and the related "bandolero(s)" seven times, which seems a bit excessive in a text of 493 words. Likewise, the summary included in the company's viewing site succinctly comprises three sentences, of which the last one is: "La escritora Sara Reeves lidera la banda de Carranza e intenta hacer justicia en Arazana" (atresplayer. com; The writer Sara Reeves leads Carranza's band and tries to bring justice to Arazana). Furthermore, the promotional poster displays a close-up of Sara and Juan Caballero—one of the *bandoleros*, but not one of Sara's romantic partners—looking at the camera with a coy look, more suggestive of action and intrigue than of romance. Yet, despite this promotional display, action is only one of the basic components of *Bandolera*.

The summary quoted above also promises the impossible and passionate love stories and elements of period narratives ("elementos del relato de época y de las historias de amor imposibles y apasionadas") most commonly associated with *telenovelas* set in the past (atresplayer. com). Certainly, there are many love stories throughout the two seasons that follow some of the plot conventions associated with the genre in its most classic form. Among them, the marriage of convenience that must be annulled, estranged siblings attracted to each other who find out that they are in fact biologically unrelated, and lovers belonging to different social classes—including landowner/prostitute and master/maid—are worth noting. However, none of these love stories are either very passionate nor truly impossible, save the homosexual relationship between Pablo Garmendia and Captain Roca in the second season. Furthermore, the number of subplots and the highly episodic nature of the show make it almost impossible for the audience to actually empathize with the characters. This is also the case with regard to the protagonist, who engages in romantic interactions with four different partners, including two at the same time for a brief while (three if we take into account the *fiancé* left behind in England who also shows up at one point). Many of these relationships, nevertheless, do not sufficiently delay consummation and thus do not secure the audience's identification with the characters' growing desire; nor does the lovers' short-lived suffering garner the sympathy of viewers. In other words, melodrama is often minimized and at times even ridiculed or turned into satire.

Unlike historical dramas that tend to take themselves and their representations of the past rather seriously (Mujica 2007, 25), *Bandolera* uses humor liberally. It does so not only through the common device of funny secondary characters whose only role seems to be comic relief (Rafalín, Emilia Rivadesella, Carlota), but also by incorporating frequent comedic sketches featuring humorous conversations and interactions that are almost completely independent of both the main plot and the more serious subplots. This is the case of many of the scenes set in the town bar, especially those with Pepe—bar owner and eventually mayor—and his daughter, and those with Pepe and Damián, the town's priest. Other (intentionally) humorous subplots include older rich women asserting their sexual desire and agency with younger men.

In terms of genre, as I have argued here, *Bandolera* makes use of most strategies present in contemporary *telenovelas* around the world, a new type of hybrid product whose main objective seems to be the promotion of their own consumption by establishing a *leitmotiv* with which the audience can easily identify, which in this case seems to be superhero worship, that is, the reverence for an outwardly ordinary person who accomplishes grand feats in the guise of a more extraordinary masked persona.

PROGRESS AND THE ENEMIES OF THE MODERN STATE: GREED, AUTHORITARIANISM, CORRUPTION

Of the three blocks comprising the two seasons, the first (episodes 1 through 177) is the one that most clearly engages the past. Indeed, some relevant historical events of the 1880s are significantly referenced by certain characters, and others are directly incorporated into the narrative as key elements of a thematic line driving this part of the story. This theme, of changing times commonly associated with the flow of history, provides in turn the impetus for a number of unevenly developed plotlines. Social changes depicted on the show are related to the recent establishment of a modern democratic state in which rational exploitation of the land, individual rights, journalism, and freedom of speech seem to be highly valued; that is, the series portrays a social and political organization that resembles in important ways that of our present time. This resemblance lends a certain degree of verisimilitude to those present ideologies and concerns incorporated into the narrative that causes a sort of commingling—and confusion—of past and present.

Bandolera begins in 1882, and the constitution of 1876, the audience is often reminded, determines the current law.[4] The romanticized *bandoleros* that Sara hoped to meet in Andalusia are about to be eradicated with the help of a new law ("la ley de fugas") implemented by the relatively new institution of the *Guardia Civil* (episode 1).[5] In fact, Carranza, the last of these *bandoleros* and the hero for whom Sara's band is named, dies in the second half of the first season (episode 153), just

as the activity of the band picks up. The end of a premodern, romantic era mourned by the group (specially el Chato) is imminent; it affects
not only their world but also that of the old and stereotypical Andalusian
señorito (Germán Montoro), more interested in living the good life than
in growing his inherited capital. Like Carranza, Germán is a holdover of
a world about to be lost (that of classic *telenovelas*) and will also disappear by the end of the first season.

In contrast, modern landowners have different attitudes toward
change. The "black hats," represented by Álvaro Montoro first, and by
Eusebio Garmendia later, welcome development in the shape of new
inventions and machinery. They are businessmen interested in adopting new technologies that will reduce expenses and increase profits. As
such, they seek to turn their *cortijo* into industrial ventures by intensive
exploitation of the land, be it to grow agricultural produce or to raise
cattle. However, Álvaro and Eusebio also hold a premodern, highly hierarchical understanding of the world and see themselves as occupying
the top echelons of that hierarchy. Accordingly, they seem to think of
their workers more as imperfect machines than as real human beings and
expect the government and its institutions to work in their personal service: If building a train stop in Arazana is convenient for Álvaro, he will
negotiate it with the governor; if Eusebio needs all the water available in
town and the mayor does not allow him to take it, he will buy the elections and become mayor himself (episode 343), and if workers request
better conditions, the businessmen (with the help of a few corrupt
Guardia Civil officers) will blame an anarchist organization, La Mano
Negra, and hire their own private guards to fight both the laborers and
the *bandoleros*. That is, their view of development is exclusively related to
their economic gain; thus, it interferes with the political process and with
social progress. However, the "good landowners," represented by Sara,
Roberto Pérez, and Pablo Garmendia, readily embrace all of the changes
(supposedly) brought about by the new times—not just the technology
and economic development, but also the rules of democracy and new
social mores such as workers', women's, and gay's rights.[6]

These obviously anachronistic references to contemporary notions
of social justice and identity politics, along with the seemingly timeless
abuse of capital, are interesting because they relate to the very impulse
driving the new period *telenovelas*. Insofar as such attitudes reflect those
dominating the public sphere at the time of production, their representation in the historical story inspires a type of complicity with the audience

that is likely to win their loyalty. The impression that the show "tells it like it is" (even if in a metaphorical way) validates the viewers' opinions. At the same time, their expectation of a necessarily happy resolution, demanded by the very rules of the genre, offers a comforting feeling that (maybe in their real world as well) the "black hats" will be punished somehow.

Modern ideas in the form of labor politics are also embraced by peasant laborers who demand rights and stage several uprisings. This unrest is presented as rather reactive, however, always provoked by the greed of landowners.[7] Although discussions of Bakunin and of the revolts in Paris are incorporated into the story, the workers in Arazana only organize to resist their oppression. Neither their actions nor their goals are truly revolutionary. They seek no more than to improve their working conditions and, almost as a future dream, to be granted those rights that everyone is supposed to enjoy in any developed democratic society today: to establish "la reducción de jornada a ocho horas, la suspensión del destajo, del pago en especie ... prohibir que los menores de 14 años trabajen" (episode 38; an eight-hour work day, eliminate the practice of being paid on a job-by-job basis and payment in kind ... the prohibition of child labor). Initially claiming not to believe in God nor in authority and calling himself an anarchist (episode 2), their leader, Roberto Pérez, later opposes the Anarchist Union's demand to eliminate private property, stating defiantly: "Estamos dispuestos a luchar por lo que es justo, sí, pero no voy a colectivizar mis tierras" (episode 67; We are ready to fight for justice, yes, but I won't collectivize my land). He will eventually become a socialist politician and move to Madrid, invited there by Pablo Iglesias (episode 246).[8] That is, labor (Roberto) rejects revolutionary measures and—unlike most landowners—embraces politics to fight injustice and advance a social agenda.

Unfortunately, labor politics seem rather inefficient in the face of the power of capital. Despite the peasant workers' actions and in spite of inhabiting a modern democracy with a relatively progressive constitution, greed, authoritarian impulses, and corruption continue to undermine the political process in Arazana. This creates, in turn, a void for social harmony and justice that justifies the need for the new *bandoleros*. This is the impetus for the creation of El Espíritu de Carranza. The band starts acting in order to change the situation of "muchas familias que trabajan de sol a sol por dos perras y se están muriendo de hambre" (episode 54; many families who work from sunrise to sunset for pennies and yet starve to death). Drawing from her romantic notions of long-gone *bandoleros*, Sara proposes, and her men agree, to give part of their loot to those families. However, this is only the band's first objective. In fact, their actions alternate between helping others in need, helping themselves, and especially protecting themselves against the attacks of other bands or organizations (mainly La Banda del Navajas y La Garduña, and corrupt *guardias civiles* such as Olmedo, Roncero, and Ferrer), and protecting the recently restored Spanish monarchy. For example, they abort the plans for terrorist actions related to "un alzamiento militar promovido por la Banca Velasco" (episode 254; a *coup d'état* promoted by the Velasco Bank), including murder attempts on President Sagasta (episode 301) and on King Alfonso XII himself (314). They also engage in actions of international scope; these involve the presence of La Garduña in Arazana and consist of preventing this secret society from selling the Germans important new technology such as Isaac Peral's submarine blueprint and the new automatic machine gun, Maxine (episode 496). Once corruption has been eradicated—with the last cacique removed from the town hall by the free exercise of voting rights, and La Garduña defeated by the collaboration of El Espíritu de Carranza and the *Guardia Civil*—social harmony is restored and the *bandoleros*, in true superhero fashion, move on with their lives. In her farewell speech, Sara states: "Hoy no solo nos despedimos de una vida, también nos despedimos de una familia; una familia que ha luchado por un mundo mejor, más justo, por hacer las cosas bien en los tiempos difíciles" (episode 51; Today we say good-bye not only to a way of life but also to a family; a family that has fought for a better, fairer world and for doing the right thing in difficult times). The possibility of the band members facing charges for their illegal activities is not even mentioned, nor is their total integration in society ever questioned; even El Chato, who had always been the only one truly removed from the social structure, ends up announcing his plan to move to Galicia to farm the land and start a (real) family of his own.

The new Arazana is a happy place with no space for ridiculous attempts to install a military dictatorship or for outmoded caciques and a place with an incorruptible, efficient police force ready to defend the law of the land. It is not clear what happened to all those poor children who had to work in the fields from sunrise to sunset and to their abused and exploited parents. Nor is it clear what happened to labor unrest since this subplot was abruptly dropped at the beginning of the second season with Roberto's departure to Madrid to pursue a career in politics. This type of happy ending, characteristic of period *telenovelas*, combined with the thematic emphasis on the historical notion of the changing times, points to a comforting conception of history as progress. Although, as I will show below, the Restoration as portrayed in *Bandolera* is plagued by problems and injustices similar to those occurring in the audience's real world, which one might argue calls attention to a more disquieting notion of history, this is not actually the case. Rather, as I shall demonstrate, the superhero leitmotiv that carries the story forward obliterates the political relevance of all references to the present.

FOR WHOM ARE THE TIMES CHANGING?
GENDER AND SEXUALITY

The impact of the changing times on women's social position seems rather irrelevant in *Bandolera*. In the series, women operate almost exclusively within private spaces, drawing their relative power from their traditional roles as mediators. Both as mothers and as object of male sexual desire, they have a chance to influence specific events, albeit always only temporarily. The stockpile characters of classic *telenovelas* are fully used in the show: the domineering mother (Leonor), the good and wholesome prostitute (Lupe), the ambitious tramp (Martina), the innocent and virginal maiden (Inés, Julieta, Eugenia), the sexually insatiable widow (Emilia, Carlota), the patient, suffering wife (Elisa). Not many other, more "modern," types—which have been incorporated into the genre in the last decades—play relevant roles. Given the series' obvious presentism, treating Emilia and Carlota as self-assured, powerful characters instead of as laughingstock stereotypes might have been interesting, for example. Similarly, it would have been a bold choice to give some of the many females on the show a prominent public function. A few women hold jobs outside of the home, but always as maids, the school teacher, post office clerks, or in the family business. Comments in defense of women's rights are casually made throughout both seasons: "Yo no soy ninguna muñequita de porcelana" (episode 6; I'm not a little porcelain doll); "¿Por qué en España a las mujeres no se les permite entrar en una taberna?" (episode 8; why aren't women allowed to enter a bar in Spain?); "a mí no me controla nadie" (episode 198; no one controls me); "Yo no soy una de vuestras propiedades ni llevo el hierro de vuestra ganadería grabado en mi piel" (episode 393; I'm not one of your possessions, nor do I sport your cattle brand on my skin). However, there is often a disconnect between words and images when it comes down to female roles in the program.

Sara is the exception in this context. As a foreigner, she enjoys privileges not afforded to other women in town. Flor, her first female friend in Arazana and the town's teacher in the first season, immediately lets her know that "Aquí las mujeres lo tienen más difícil. Hay una escritora, Concepción Arenal.⁹ Pues se tuvo que vestir de hombre para entrar en la universidad" (episode 2; women have it more difficult here. There's this writer, Concepción Arenal. Well, she had to dress as a man to enter a university). It seems to be her status as an outsider that makes it possible for Sara to start working as a journalist at the printing house when Peralta, the reporter in charge, dies (this job disappears when she quits in order to invest more time into her own business). By the time we see Jimena, first, and later Adela attending customers there, the space has become a simple post office and no longer represents the power of journalism. And yet, despite having this privileged position in town, despite her role as a band leader in the mountains, and even despite flirting with two different men at the same time, Sara still wears a corset or the very sexy sash of the typical romantic *bandolero* outfit. Even more importantly, she takes a secondary role in her romantic relationships and never chooses a partner before having been chosen.

Several issues of importance to women—as much at the end of the nineteenth century as today—do become the subject matter of more or less developed subplots. The two most relevant ones concern the sexual abuse of minors within the family—Inés is repeatedly molested and impregnated by her mother's husband, Tobías—and domestic violence against women; Clara's husband beats and rapes her, literally asserting his property rights: "le pagué dos buenos bueyes a tu padre para que fueras mía" (episode 355; I paid your father two good oxen for you to be mine). Of these two subplots, the first is considerably more developed, appearing on the show for more than fifty episodes (177–235). The second, on the other hand, is quickly resolved in two episodes (354–356).

However, the (inexistent) right for women to walk away from an unsatisfactory marriage is reiterated with another subplot that develops roughly at the same time in the series and occupies significantly longer screen time, that of the wife who falls in love with another man because her gay husband is not interested in having sex with her: Elisa's and Pablo's story drags on for more than one hundred episodes, from about 325 to nearly the end of the series.

The theme of homosexual desire and gay rights indeed seems more interesting for the producers than that of gender concerns. It is introduced from the very beginning with Peralta, a Catalan reporter who, we eventually learn, arrived in Arazana as a result of having to flee Barcelona due to both his homosexuality and his militant anarchism. In his new home, it is also his (necessarily hidden) sexual preference that gives the corrupt Captain Olmedo ammunition to blackmail and force him to write the stories Olmedo wants from the perspective that he wants. Peralta dies in episode 16, but soon after (episode 32), another brief foray into the topic takes place when one of the girls working at "la Maña's Inn" makes a pass at and is rejected by Flor. It is in the second season that a rather long subplot dealing with this theme develops (episodes 325–505). Pablo Garmendia is a married gay man who is incapable of fulfilling his father's demand for an heir to prolong his lineage. Throughout the second part of the second season, the audience is enticed with a rather titillating presentation of this story that repeatedly includes intimate scenes showing Pablo's inability to perform in bed with his wife, his visible distress by the sight of attractive men (including a naked one), his proclamation of love to Captain Roca, steamy sex between the two men in the stables, and Pablo's advances on and rejection by another man, among others. This subplot, whether intended to attract and maintain a wider audience or not, affords the opportunity to comment on the negative and unjust consequences of an intolerant society. These include the suffering of a wife and husband trapped in an unhappy marriage, the physical attacks on gay men by those who feel the need to assert their own masculinity, and the fact that legal hurdles are not the only or even the most significant ones: "Ni en cien años la homosexualidad se tratará como algo normal; siempre seremos peor que leprosos" (episode 370; Not even in a hundred years will homosexuality be treated as normal; we'll always be worse off than lepers), states Roca in response to Pablo's momentary optimism.

Women's and gay rights are addressed in *Bandolera* rather ambiguously. While verbal comments point to a defense of those rights, and the camera often entices the audience by showing images that transgress the *status quo* and invite viewers to consider alternative behaviors, stories are repeatedly resolved in harmony with social expectations and that very *status quo*. This ambiguity in its anachronistic treatment of contemporary issues of concern set in the past is in line with a characteristic feature of the new period *telenovela* that seems to be at the center of its marketability and exportability. Presentism allows for the incorporation and intradiegetic discussion of topics of import in many modern societies around the globe as long as their treatment aligns with the type of non-controversial social values that are easily embraced by broad audiences everywhere.

Representing the Past/Engaging the Present

Generally speaking, historical references included in *Bandolera* are quite accurate. The 49 years since the death of José María el Tempranillo seems a long enough period for the historical figure to have developed into the internationally known legend that lures Sara to Andalusia in 1882. Likewise, Práxedes Mateo Sagasta's two first terms as president (1881–1883 and 1885–1890), the preliminary research and blueprints for Isaac Peral's submarine (1885–1887), the violence supposedly carried out by the anarchist organization La Mano Negra (1882–1833),[10] and the later years of Alfonso XII's reign (1857–1885) all fall within the time frame of the diegesis. The only events that can be considered anachronistic in the series are the actions of La Garduña, a purported secret society that, had it actually existed, would have been eradicated in 1822.[11]

However, despite this accuracy with regard to specific historical references, we would be hard-pressed to state that the producers intend to represent any type of official discourse about the national past, particularly regarding the Restoration period. The only understanding of a collective past (That of Spain? That of Andalusia?) included here refers to the romantic notions disseminated by the imagination of foreign travelers during the late eighteenth and early nineteenth centuries. Their writings are Sara's sources and *Bandolera* is Sara's story. In this sense, it is interesting that most specific literary references—despite the protagonist's degree in Hispanic literature—are to foreign writers, titles, and characters: *The Count of Monte-Cristo* (Alexandre Dumas), *Madame Bovary* (Gustave Flaubert), *Les Misérables* (Victor Hugo), and the character José María Tempranillo in some "literary gloss" by a non-specified, presumably English author. The fact that the only mention of a Spanish writer (Concepción Arenal) does not refer to her work but rather to a social issue—the status of women in Spain—and the conspicuous absence of Benito Pérez Galdós, whose *Doña Perfecta* could have inspired the character of Leonor and some of the subplots in the second part of the series, are also worth noting. Similarly worth mentioning is another even more conspicuous absence; that is, any reference to the historical figure El Barquero de Cantillana who inspired the most famous TV *bandolero* show of all time in Spain (*Curro Jiménez, TVE 1976-1979*), a show that at the very least seems to have inspired the makers of *Bandolera*. These references, or their lack thereof, along with the multiple mentions of how reality is often less plausible than fiction itself, point to an ambiguous attitude among the producers about whether or not to represent any kind of official discourse about the national past. In fact, the past in this *telenovela* has been "bracketed, and effaced altogether," to use Fredric Jameson's words (1991, 18). More simply put, despite the relative accuracy of historical references in the program, the time represented on-screen is actually more fluid than costumes, furniture, and props would have us believe.

By using the "look" of the past, *Bandolera* often works as an extended metaphor that engages the present. A cursory look at the main items in different news summaries (*Informe Semanal, EcoDiario*, and *Global Voices*) for the years 2011, 2012, and 2013 in Spain clearly shows this. Two salient themes appear across those three years: greed-related corruption among high-ranking politicians and public figures ("the Gürtel case," "the Noos case," and "the ERE case" are only some of the most relevant among the 28 open cases listed in the digital publication *República de ideas*),[12] and social unrest/grassroots organizing (particularly involving the Movimiento Indignados, Movimiento 25-S, and Plataforma Afectados por la Hipoteca). Also, repeatedly highlighted in the news from those years were cases of "violencia machista" (gender violence) and gay marriages, including the Supreme Court's rejection, in November of 2012, of the Popular Party's appeal against gay marriage on the grounds of unconstitutionality, presented seven years earlier (Cadena Ser). These issues making the national news (greed, corruption, social unrest, domestic violence, and gay rights) are also, as I have shown above, prominent topics both in the main plot and in many of the subplots of *Bandolera*.

Given these obvious connections between many thematic lines in the series and significant events taking place at the time of broadcast, it is important to ask: How are we to understand the way *Bandolera* engages the time represented (past) with that of representation (present)? On the one hand, by dramatizing similar issues to those that the audience reads about in the news day in and day out, the show seemingly promotes social awareness and a desire to fight corruption and intolerance. But on the other hand, by positing the *bandoleros* as the only ones who can solve economic, social, and political problems, the program seems to suggest a need for superheroes who can operate from without. This has several consequences. In terms of the past, it romanticizes the situation of agrarian societies in nineteenth-century Andalusia and minimizes both the exploitation of peasants and the political activism of agrarian anarchism in the region. In terms of the present, and especially considering the renewed presence of superheroes in popular culture over the last decade, it can be interpreted as promoting political passivity. After all, why should anyone go out into the streets and fight the fight if there are superheroes always prepared to take on that task for us? Neither the past (history) nor the present (politics) seems to be truly relevant in the series beyond the appeal that one and the other may have for a broad range of audiences: The first provides spectacle; that is, a visually attractive setting in which period clothing and furniture combine with outdoor shots of olive trees, creeks, and beautiful horses. The second contributes themes that resonate with and are of interest to contemporary viewers in multiple locales. In this, *Bandolera* is no different from other series of its type, like *Corazón salvaje* (Mexico, 2009) and *Los Pincheira* (Chile, 2004). Such are the limits and possibilities of period *telenovelas*.

NOTES

1. The starting year is clearly marked by a notice on the screen at the beginning of episode 1 as 1882. After that, there are not any other clear markers of time. Considering that Sara seems to have gotten pregnant with her son at least two years after arriving in Arazana (she has a previous pregnancy but loses the baby) and that the boy seems to be about two years old when the story wraps up, it makes sense to establish the narrative time as 1882–1887.

2. For a more detailed study of how this Latin American format was introduced and adapted in Spain, see Chicharro Merayo (2011).

3. All translations are by the author unless otherwise noted.

4. The Constitution of 1876 was, according to historian Raymond Carr, "un producto híbrido de la teoría política de los moderados de mediados de siglo y de las prácticas del parlamentarismo inglés" (Carr 1982, 338; a hybrid product of the political theory of the moderates at midcentury and practices of British parliamentarism).

5. The *Guardia Civil* was founded by the Duke of Ahumada in 1844, just after Queen Isabel II had reached the age of legal majority. The two main political parties at the time agreed by consensus on the need to found this institution as part of their project to create a modern liberal state in Spain. It was meant to end the growing corruption permitted—and aided—by the *Santa Hermandad*, to protect the new order brought about by land reform, and to keep the roads safe—especially in Andalusia where *bandoleros* were still very active in the mid-nineteenth century (Martínez Viqueira 2015, 124–125).

6. Roberto Pérez is the illegitimate son of Germán Montoro and his maid, Carmen. When Germán and Carmen decide to rekindle their lifelong secret romance and leave for Argentina, the patriarch leaves both of his sons (Álvaro and Roberto) in charge of his land. Before becoming landowner, Roberto had been the peasants' leader.

7. The violent acts that landowners and the *Guardia Civil* impute to the anarchist organization La Mano Negra are in fact their own doing and are meant both to justify detentions and torture and to push the liberal government to pass tougher legislation against workers' unrest (episode 86).

8. Pablo Iglesias founded the Partido Socialista Obrero Español (Spanish Workers Socialist Party), commonly known as PSOE, in 1879.

9. This sole reference to specific women activists in late nineteenth-century Spain is rather interesting. A TV movie titled *Concepción Arenal, la visitadora de cárceles*—co-produced by TVE, TVG (Galicia), Canal Sur (Andalusia) and TV3 (Catalonia)—aired in March 2014. Although this could be entirely coincidental, it could also be a case of television's tendency to self-referentiality, since plans for this show were likely at work a couple of years before its production.

10. The crimes allegedly committed by the secret organization La Mano Negra in 1883 were used by the government as an excuse to eradicate agrarian extremism in Southern Spain (Lida 1972, 23). See Barrientos Bueno and Martínez García's chapter in the present volume for more on La Mano Negra in the television series *Víctor Ros*.

11. According to the existing information, the last members of La Garduña were executed in Sevilla in 1822. In any case, the very existence of this organization is highly disputed since the only historical references to it are in a book by Víctor de Fereal that is most likely fiction (Arsenal and Sanchiz 2006, 326–335).

12. Gürtel case: A case of political corruption (bribery, money laundering, and tax evasion) implicating high ranking members of the Popular Party in Madrid and Valencia. Nóos case: Another case of corruption (diverting public funds to private companies) implicating the Nóos Institute and the royal family (Iñaki Urdangarín, Princess Cristina de Borbón's husband, and the Princess herself). ERE case: Illicit use of public funds implicating officials in the Andalusian government as well as the two major national unions, CCOO and UGT.

BIBLIOGRAPHY

Antena 3. 2017. "Bandolera: amor, aventura y venganza." August 23. http://www.antena3internacional.com/bandolera/bandolera_2016050300089.html.

Arsenal, León, and Hipólito Sanchiz. 2006. *Una historia de las sociedades secretas españolas (1500–1936)*. Barcelona: Planeta.

Cadena Ser. 2015. "Diez fechas clave del matrimonio homosexual en España." Last Modified June 28, 2015. http://cadenaser.com/ser/2015/06/28/sociedad/1435505015_522122.html.

Calero, Tirso. 2011–2013. *Bandolera*. Diagonal TV, Antena 3.

Carr, Raymond. 1982. *España 1808–1975*. Barcelona: Ariel.

Chicharro Merayo, María del Mar. 2009. "Información, ficción, telerrealidad y telenovela: algunas lecturas televisivas sobre la sociedad española y su historia." *Comunicación y sociedad. Nueva época* 11 (January–June): 73–98.

Chicharro Merayo, María del Mar. 2011. "Historia de la telenovela en España: aprendizaje, ensayo y apropiación de un género." *Communication and Society* 24 (1): 189–216.

EcoDiario.es. 2012. "Las 10 noticias más relevantes de 2012 en España." December 31. http://ecodiario.eleconomista.es/espana/noticias/4488819/12/12/Las-10-noticias-mas-relevantes-de-2012-en-Espana.html.

Global Voices. 2013. "España: El año 2013 resumido en 10 noticias y 10 fotos." December 26. https://es.globalvoices.org/2013/12/26/espana-el-ano-2013-resumido-en-10-noticias-y-diez-fotos/.

Huyssen, Andreas. 2000. "Present Pasts: Media, Politics, Amnesia." *Public Culture* 12 (1): 21–38.

Jameson, Fredric. 1991. *Postmodernism, or the Cultural Logic of Late Capitalism.* Durham: Duke University Press.

Lida, Clara E. 1972. *La Mano Negra: anarquismo agrario en Andalucía.* Madrid: ZYX.

Martínez Viqueira, Eduardo. 2015. "El servicio en la Guardia Civil de la época fundacional. Hacia una seguridad profesional." *Cuadernos de la Guardia Civil* 51: 124–148.

Mujica, Constanza. 2007. "La telenovela de época chilena: Entre la metáfora y el trauma." *Cuadernos de información* 21 (2): 20–33.

Orozco Gómez, Guillermo. 2006. "La telenovela en México: ¿de una expresión cultural a un simple producto para la mercadotecnia." *Comunicación y sociedad. Nueva época* 6 (July–December): 11–35.

Ramírez Murcia, Armando. 2016. "Telenovela y género en Colombia." *Nóesis. Revista de Ciencias Sociales y Humanidades* 25 (January–June): 45–64.

República de las ideas. 2013. "Los grandes casos de corrupción abiertos en España." March 22. https://www.republica.com/2013/03/22/los-grandes-casos-de-corrupcion-abiertos-en-espana/.

RTVE. 2011. "'Informe Semanal' resume los acontecimientos más importantes de 2011." December 17. http://www.rtve.es/noticias/20111215/informe-semanal-resume-acontecimientos-mas-importantes-2011/482196.shtml.

Vertele. 2012. "Adiós a 'Bandolera' en Antena 3 y hola a la segunda temporada de 'Isabel' en la 1." November 6. http://vertele.eldiario.es/verteletv/actualidad/Adios-Bandolera-Antena-temporada-Isabel_0_1407759221.html.

CHAPTER 9

Creating Locally for a Global Audience: *Seis hermanas* and the Costume Serial Drama as Quality Television

Concepción Cascajosa Virino

Seis hermanas (Bambú Producciones 2015–2017) may be considered one of the most innovative television fictions produced in Spain in recent years. It is an extremely ambitious daytime serial, both in narrative terms and as a representation of the Restoration period. Created by Ramón Campos and Gema R. Neira and developed by Verónica Fernández as script coordinator, *Seis hermanas* premiered on April 22, 2015 with a prime-time special that introduced the viewers to the Silva sisters, six young women living in Madrid in 1913, a time when women had little legal autonomy. After the sudden death of their father Fernando (Emilio Gutiérrez Caba), they decide to pretend that he is still alive in order to maintain control of the family textile factory, Tejidos Silva. In its regular afternoon slot on TVE1, state-owned Televisión Española's (TVE) main channel, the program followed the adventures of the six young women facing both personal and professional challenges. The two oldest sisters

C. Cascajosa Virino (✉)
Universidad Carlos III de Madrid, Getafe, Spain
e-mail: ccvirino@hum.uc3m.es

© The Author(s) 2018
D. R. George, Jr. and W. S. Tang (eds.),
Televising Restoration Spain,
https://doi.org/10.1007/978-3-319-96196-5_9

are Adela (Celia Freijeiro), an elegant and kind young widow who starts an affair with a married man, and Blanca (Mariona Tena), torn between the love of two brothers, banker and politician Rodolfo (Fernando Andina) and doctor and war veteran Cristóbal (Álex Gadea). The middle sisters are Diana (Marta Larralde), a strong-willed young woman who takes over the reins of the family factory while falling in love with the entrepreneur Salvador (Álex Adróver), and Francisca (Maria Castro), a talented singer who breaks all social barriers to succeed in her profession, but has to endure a marriage with the vicious and violent Don Luis (Cristobal Suárez). The youngest ones are Celia (Candela Serrat), a teacher, writer, and suffragist who learns to accept and openly embrace her homosexuality, and Elisa (Carla Diaz), a spoiled and immature girl who has serious difficulties finding her path in life (Fig. 9.1).

During its two years on the air, and through almost five hundred episodes, *Seis hermanas* featured a multilayered story in which the Silva sisters functioned as the link between different social strata, including the aristocracy, the haute bourgeoisie, the working class, and the poor living in the city outskirts. The social and political activity of the Silva sisters also included relations with the royal family, newborn political parties, the suffragist movement, the labor union movement and anarchist terrorism, drawing a well-rounded representation of a complex era with a

Fig. 9.1   *Seis hermanas* (Bambú, TVE, 2015–2017): Episode 1—the six Silva sisters

contemporary sensibility. In this chapter, *Seis hermanas* is analyzed as an example of the renewal process experienced by Spanish television fiction in recent years, during which the economic crisis has required the alteration of traditional production formulas to create series that might appeal to international audiences. In this sense, *Seis hermanas* is part of a recent and successful trend in both daytime serials and prime-time dramas that has taken the British costume drama as a key reference, aspiring to the category of so-called quality television. This chapter deals with three fundamental aspects of the series. First, it looks at *Seis hermanas* in the context of the contemporary trend of Spanish period serial dramas, and as one of Bambú's rare forays into this genre, in spite of the company's status as a leading independent producer in Spain. Second, the representation of the Restoration period in *Seis hermanas* is analyzed in terms of the mise-en-scène (including locations and sets) and historical accuracy. Finally, the reception of the series is considered, to see how a daytime costume serial produced in Spain attempts to reach a wide audience in the current fragmented and globalized television context. The argument of this chapter is that *Seis hermanas* uses the Restoration period as a generating framework for narratives focused on the struggle of a group of diverse young women finding their place in the world in a period characterized by a global crisis and political uncertainty, while offering above average production values and visually appealing settings. In this way, the series explores some of the most characteristic elements of the British costume drama, but with a progressive vision of social change.

THE DAYTIME SERIAL DRAMA IN SPAIN: *SEIS HERMANAS* AND BAMBÚ PRODUCCIONES

In the first two decades of the twenty-first century, the period serial drama has come to represent a significant part of television fictions produced in Spain. The production company Diagonal initiated this trend with the success of the regional serial *Temps de silenci* (2001–2002) on the Catalan public channel TV3. Later on, Diagonal transferred this model to the national market with the daytime serial *Amar en tiempos revueltos* (2005–2012) and the prime-time drama *La Señora* (2008–2010), both of which aired on TVE. These dramas were set during the dictatorships of Francisco Franco and Miguel Primo de Rivera, respectively. The success of *Amar en tiempos revueltos* demonstrated not only a wide interest among daytime audiences in narratives about the past, but also the possibility of offering a daily, fifty-minute period drama episode with high production value. According to Paul Julian Smith, "*Amar en tiempos revueltos* managed the twin, singular achievement of both investigating the particularity of Spanish history in a way accessible and relevant to local audiences while expressing that investigation in an attractive hybrid form, which drew on both Latin American and Anglo-Catalan expressive matrices" (2009, 139). In addition to its resounding commercial success, *Amar en tiempos revueltos* was the object of significant critical attention due to its remarkable narrative and thematic and visual quality, as well as the identifiable parallels with contemporary changes experienced by Spanish society.[1] *Amar en tiempos revueltos* was followed by *Amar es para siempre* (Diagonal, 2013–), which was broadcast on commercial channel Antena 3 after the production company Diagonal could not reach a contract agreement with TVE. By then, the rural-set *El secreto de Puente Viejo* (Boomerang TV, 2011–) had already debuted successfully with its first story arc, which takes place in 1902.

In April 2015, as a programming strategy aimed to compete with *El secreto de Puente Viejo* and *Amar es para siempre*, TVE premiered two new daytime serials set in the early years of the twentieth century, *Acacias 38* (Boomerang TV, 2015–) and *Seis hermanas*. Although both explored the life of the bourgeois class, they differed in fundamental ways. *Acacias 38* took the melodrama route, peppered with thriller touches, culminating its first narrative arc with the death by poisoning of the two original main characters before re-booting the story with new protagonists (a usual formula for long-running daytime serials). *Seis hermanas* opted for a different path, with more humor, further investment in the psychological development of the protagonists, and a greater interest in inserting their misfortunes into the relevant sociohistorical changes of the period.

Seis hermanas was only the second daytime serial produced by Bambú, the company founded in 2007 by screenwriter Ramón Campos and producer Teresa Fernández Valdés. At the new production company, Campos and Fernández Valdés were surrounded by a core group of close collaborators, including the head of development Gema R. Neira and director Carlos Sedes, who have accompanied them since their beginnings in Galicia. Through highly successful programs like the romantic drama *Velvet* (2014–2016), and failures, such as the pair's debut heist drama series *Guante Blanco* (2008), Bambú's series (almost always created by Campos and Neira) have offered a renewed approach to the traditional formulas of Spanish television fiction. Going against the model of the inter-generational drama that had become hegemonic after the arrival of private television, Bambú began to produce crime, romantic, and period dramas with young, strong leads and well-known veterans in supporting roles. Likewise, the producer's series stood out for their remarkably high production values; it is not accidental that talented visual storytellers such as Jorge Sánchez-Cabezudo, Alberto Rodríguez, and Manuel Gómez Pereira were often at the helm of their projects. According to Gema R. Neira, the need to innovate and offer a high-quality mise-en-scène has been essential since their first professional work for the Galician regional channel Televisión de Galicia (TVG):

> Desde que estábamos en Galicia decíamos: ¿Por qué técnicamente no avanzamos en este país? Con la calidad que hay en las series de fuera, ¿por qué siendo fácil hacer una luz buena seguimos poniendo los focos en el techo? Si cuento una historia, y quiero que esté bien, quiero que eso también se refleje visualmente.[2]

> (Neira 2017; Since we were in Galicia, we said: Why don't we advance technically in this country? Given the strong quality of foreign series, why is it that, given the ease of good lighting, we keep placing spotlights on the ceiling? If I am telling a story, and I want it to be good, I want that fact to be reflected visually as well.)

After Bambú's first period series *Hispania* (2010–2012), set during the occupation of the Iberian Peninsula by the Roman Empire, *Gran Hotel* (*Grand Hotel*, 2011–2013), their first approach to the Spanish Restoration, was a leap forward for the producers. The production value of *Gran Hotel* allowed the series to enter markets normally out of reach for Spanish fiction, such as the UK, where it was broadcast by Sky Arts 2 as "the Spanish *Downton Abbey*." According to *Radio Times*, "Such is the hunger for *Downton* that countries with little previous experience of period drama are hauling the lace out of their grandparents' chest" (Armstrong and Webb 2012). Ironically, what was a source of pride for its creators became a tool for negative criticism within the national press. In a review titled "Downton Hotel," television critic Alberto Rey was especially harsh:

¿Por qué nos hemos puesto a copiar (perdón, a parecernos a) una de las series más perfectas (¡y caras!) de los últimos tiempos? ¿Por qué no hemos escogido algo más sencillo y que, por otro lado, nos permita alejarnos más del original y demostrar un talento más allá de la reproducción?

(2011; Why do we have to copy [sorry, to resemble] one of the most perfect [and expensive!] series of recent times? Why didn't we choose something simpler and that, in addition, may allow us to move away from the original and demonstrate a talent beyond reproduction?)

Perhaps it was not a lost battle after all, especially if we take into account that, apart from being broadcast in sixty countries (including France, Russia, Germany, and the USA) and distributed in others by Netflix, *Gran Hotel* was remade in Italy, Mexico, and Egypt (as is further explored by Wan Sonya Tang in the present volume).

Seis hermanas was the next logical step in the creative evolution of Bambú. Their first daytime serial *Gran Reserva: El origen* (2013), a prequel to the prime-time series *Gran Reserva* (2010–2013), had been canceled after less than 100 episodes. However, Bambú's established relationship with TVE led to a new project that would portray the Restoration period in the same manner as *Gran Hotel.* In their time in Galicia, Ramón Campos and Neira had achieved great success with the series *A vida por diante* (2006–2007), the story of five women who must fight to get on with their lives after their sailor husbands die in a shipwreck. This narrative premise, a group of women facing adverse circumstances together without being defined by their male counterparts, was used again in *Seis hermanas*, although set in a past where that adversity was greatly defined by the specifics of the portrayed historical juncture. According to co-creator Neira: "Queríamos hacer una historia donde ellas fueran las protagonistas y que se demostrara la cantidad de cosas que no podían hacer por ser mujeres" (2017; We wanted to make a story where women were the protagonists and demonstrate the things they could not do because of their gender). In the development phase of the project, Neira and Campos were joined by Verónica Fernández, a respected playwright and screenwriter of period series such as *Cuéntame como pasó* (TVE, 2001–), and the script coordinator of daytime serials such as *Ciega a citas* (Big Bang Media, Cuatro, 2014), which was nominated for Best Telenovela in the International Emmy Awards. Fernandez's role in the development of *Seis Heramanas* is noteworthy; in fact, she appears as co-author of the first episode along with Campos and Neira. In her development of the show's original idea, the father died suddenly and the daughters made the decision to hide his death out of fear. If this fact were to be exposed, they would lose the most important family possession: the textile factory Tejidos Silva. The concept of inheritance, sanguine but also psychological, thus became a relevant topic in the serial, one that Fernandez had already explored intensely in previous works for film and television (Cascajosa Virino 2017, 158–159).

THE SPANISH RESTORATION AS A COSTUME SERIAL DRAMA

One of the most important elements of *Seis hermanas* is how it uses the British costume serial drama as its main referent. In one of the promotional videos for the series on TVE's website, co-creator Ramón Campos explains that one of the reasons why the viewer should watch *Seis hermanas* is because it is similar to great British series such as *Upstairs, Downstairs* (London Weekend Television, 1971–1975). Although in the last decade British fiction has largely disappeared from Spanish television schedules, during the 1970s and 1980s it was a programming staple for TVE, familiarizing viewers with a model of quality television centered around story lines with a literary basis, renowned actors and an elaborate mise-en-scène. The British fiction of those years was popular as a middlebrow quality product, establishing, as Tom O'Regan notes, the "international brand image of British television as a provider of a certain kind of content: middle-class fare skewed in various ways towards the maintenance and reproduction of a literary and cultural heritage" (2000, 304). As Barbara Selznick states in her discussion of costume drama as a quality product within a globalized television landscape:

> of course, the symbolic benefits include the cultural capital that will be gained by having watched a 'high quality' drama. The attributes and benefits connected with the heritage brand of British media combine to associate this brand with particular attitudes. These texts are sophisticated and mature programs for intelligent viewers. British historical costume dramas are often assumed to be high quality, high culture, and simply better than U.S. media. (2008, 81–82)

In this sense, it is essential to recall that *The Forsythe Saga* (BBC, MGM Television, 1967) was broadcast by TVE in 1971, garnering enough popularity to inspire a cycle of literary adaptations in which *La saga de los Rius* (TVE, 1976–1977) stood out. A 13-part serial based on the novels of Ignacio Agustí, *La saga de los Rius* was, at the time, one of the most expensive TVE productions (Peña Ardid 2010, 54–55). In the prime-time special debut of *Seis Hermanas*, titled "Derechos y deberes" (Rights and Duties), echoes of *La Saga de los Rius* are evident, starting with the choice of Emilio Gutiérrez Caba, one of the main actors of the 1967 serial, to play Fernando Silva, whose sudden death at the end of the episode sets the action in motion. Although based on an original idea, *Seis hermanas* references literary works by Jane Austen, Louisa May Alcott, Benito Pérez Galdós, and Emilia Pardo Bazán (as studied by Linda Willem in this volume).[3] Even if indirectly, *Seis hermanas* utilizes the legacy of the literary costume serial drama and its associated prestige as markers of quality entertainment.

The way in which *Seis hermanas* takes the British costume drama as a key reference has important repercussions. Many transformations have occurred in the daytime serial in Spain over the last two decades. Remarkably, it has turned into a privileged product in terms of ratings for the channels and also in terms of industrial stability for production companies. Writing in the wake of the success of *Amar en tiempos revueltos*, Hugh O'Donnell notes a particular trend in nationally produced daytime serials, particularly for TVE. They have evolved to exhibit a more sophisticated visual form:

> TVE's productions, on the other hand, seemed somehow more highly-strung. Much of this, it is true, appeared to be more a function of the mise en scène (broadly defined) than anything else: more grandiose interiors and occasionally exteriors, more beautiful actors and actresses, more flamboyant and more quick-change fashions, more overstated acting, even more saturated colors. (2007, 37)

The creators of *Seis hermanas* made a conscious choice to distance themselves from the Latin American *telenovela*, that is, "un drama más exagerado" (a more exaggerated drama) according to Neira, to be a more realistic form, a "*Gran Hotel* en forma de serie diaria" (2017; *Grand Hotel* in the form of daytime serial). She continues: "Quisimos apostar por una calidad técnica que diera un paso más de manera visual. Queríamos que pareciese casi un prime time." (We bet on improving the technical qualities of the show in order to take it a step further visually. We wanted it to look like a prime-time [program].)

Seis hermanas was launched with an hour-and-a-half prime-time special on April 22, 2015, the day before the series began its regular broadcast in the afternoons on TVE1. The first sequence presents the high society engagement party of Blanca Silva with Rodolfo Loygorri celebrated at the Casino de Madrid, an important liberal social club that came to represent the rise and consolidation of the bourgeoisie and the Restoration state. Located on the capital's Alcalá Street, the historic building featured in this prime-time special was inaugurated in 1910 and, although it belongs to the characteristic eclectic style of the period, has a beautiful and recognizable modernist façade. For a daytime serial marked by a rigorous production schedule, the initial offering set a standard that *Seis hermanas* would not be able to sustain in daily episodes. However, this fact was not an impediment for the creation of a very sophisticated production design, entrusted to Carlos Dorremochea, who has been in charge of the visual design of all Bambú series since their debut with *Guante Blanco*. He designed the interiors for *Seis hermanas* in two sets of 1100 and 700 meters in one of the Bambú production facilities in Pozuelo de Alarcón, while the recurrent exteriors (the Silva house and the main entrance to the textile factory Tejidos Silva) were built in another production facility on the outskirts of Madrid.

The construction of the interior sets was done such that the different rooms were connected, as they would be in reality. According to Dorremochea: "Lo normal es que los decorados se construyan en batería, pero el productor, Ramón Campos, quería una mayor profundidad, de tal forma que se vieran dos o tres estancias detrás, y eso se consigue construyendo la casa entera"[4] (Molinero 2015; Usually sets are built side by side, but the producer, Ramón Campos, wanted greater depth, so that two or three rooms could be seen in the background, and that can only be achieved by building the whole house). This construction system is more expensive. Consequently, in order to save some money for other locations, these sets were built in such a way that they could also be used as new locations just by changing some key elements—walls/panels, mirrors, and furniture, for example. In an interview about the sets of prime-time romantic drama *Velvet*, also designed by Dorremochea, Ramón Campos further developed his aesthetic ideas and production concept: "Lo que queda bien y bonito a simple vista no siempre queda bien en pantalla. Dame un decorado amplio, que si hay que reducir el espacio, ya se podrá hacer desde la cámara" (Redondo 2015a; What looks good and pretty to the naked eye does not always look good on-screen. Give me a large set, then if you have to reduce the space, you can do it using the camera). The set was large, and detailed in its design. In the hands of production designer Dorremochea, the narrative realism that Neira pinpointed as a key element of *Seis hermanas* was delivered through the extraordinary richness of a variety of elements such as lamps, porcelain figures, glasses, jars, pictures, books, kitchen utensils, and a long list of objects bought in flea markets and recycled from previous Bambú series such as *Gran Hotel* and *Velvet*.[5]

Due to the budgetary constraints of a daytime serial, many events in *Seis hermanas* were too expensive in production terms (e.g., a royal ball) and so took place off camera: They are recounted in the form of dialogues or narrated by journalistic chronicles read aloud by characters. Nevertheless, the serial is very careful in maintaining a clear spatial concept through establishing shots that recurrently precede the interior scenes. For this, different buildings in Madrid were carefully chosen as exteriors; all were built in the period portrayed in *Seis hermanas*. The textile factory Tejidos Silva is the "Joaquín Leguina" Regional Library, originally built between 1912 and 1913 to house the El Águila Brewery and whose Neo-mudéjar style is characteristic of many factories of the period. For the exterior of the house of the Loygorri family, the Hotel AC Palacio del Retiro was used. It was built in 1913–1914 by Jose Luis Oriol, an architect and businessman who, like Rodolfo Loygorri, also made his way into politics. He built this mansion, also known as the Oriol Palace, in a neighborhood in Madrid next to the Retiro Park, which welcomed the haute bourgeoisie and nobility of the time. As in the case of the Casino de Madrid, it is a building with a modernist façade. When the series began a story line that took place in a social club frequented by the haute bourgeoisie, the exterior used was the Military Casino, built in 1916 with a classic façade with modernist touches. Moreover, the series extends this quest for authenticity beyond the upper classes. When Celia moves to the popular neighborhood of Arganzuela to work as a teacher for children from poor families, the exterior of her apartment is a *corrala*, a characteristic architectural form of the popular classes of Madrid, with balconies overlooking an inner courtyard immortalized in the literature of Pérez Galdós and the television adaptation of his masterpiece *Fortunata y Jacinta* (TVE, 1980). For the house of Celia, the establishing shots used a real *corrala* in Salitre street, in the popular neighborhood of Lavapiés in Madrid.[6]

A second relevant aspect is the story's setting in the 1910s. According to Neira, this choice reflects an effort to constantly innovate. Undoubtedly, the Restoration period has attracted the attention of Campos and Neira before: the story of *Gran Hotel* began in 1905, while the first season of *Las chicas del cable* (Netflix, Bambú, 2017–), already in development at the time, takes place in 1928. For *Seis hermanas*, the intervening decade was chosen in order to distinguish the three series and imbue them with a separate period identity. For Neira, the choice of that decade in particular had much to do with the interest in finding a time full of conflicts in which the different Silva sisters could participate in a variety of ways: "Pensamos que era un momento un poco crítico. Políticamente las cosas estaban revueltas, empezaba a haber levantamientos de los trabajadores, y que eso lo íbamos a poder utilizar para las tramas de la fábrica" (2017; We thought it was a bit of a critical moment. Politically things were troubling, there were also labor movement uprisings, and we could use that for the factory story lines). It is essential to emphasize this aspect, since the series' story lines advance on two parallel paths: namely, the personal and professional lives of the Silva sisters and the political and social context of crisis. Thus, the series will ultimately be about the expansion of the vital universe of the six sisters once they are released from (and deprived of) the protective shield of their father Fernando. Although each of the sisters will explore a different social and economic sphere, three are especially important: Diana's world of business and commerce, Celia's left-wing political universe and Blanca's conservative political world.

Consequently, the tension between the Restoration regime and the forces of change is presented as the driving force of the narrative. A comparison between *Seis hermanas* and other daytime serial dramas reveals a striking presence of this notion of ideological conflict in the middle of sentimental conflict, so that the former always determines the latter. This approach is very obvious in the case of Blanca, whose heart is torn between her husband Rodolfo and her lover Cristobal. Despite being brothers, their characters and ideals could not be more different. Rodolfo is a banker who climbs the ranks of the Partido Maurista until he is appointed minister, representing how the nobility of the period tried to use liberal politics to retain power.[7] For his part, Cristobal returns from the Rif War reneging colonial policy and ends up being a member of an anarchist group.[8] Blanca, who in the first episodes seems obsessed with her public image and new marriage, develops a path of her own serving the Queen Victoria Eugenia and is made a baroness as a reward. Diana represents the emerging business class, willing to do anything to keep the family factory afloat, even spying for the British government to guarantee contracts. Celia is a suffragist teacher and writer who embodies progressive ideals. All her love stories are linked to an ideological struggle. Her lovers (the factory worker Petra, the nurse Aurora, and the seamstress Catalina) represent lower-class professions, so that the acceptance of their love by Celia, a taboo subject at the time, always aligns with the triple fight of Celia in favor of the workers, the poor and women.

No doubt, *Seis hermanas* seeks to present a feminist narrative, in which the protagonists, in the words of script coordinator Verónica Fernández,

> son mujeres que están en un lugar incómodo. El mensaje final de la serie es que no solo podemos elegir, es que debemos elegir. En el momento que nos ponemos en la posición de nuestras protagonistas, que son mujeres que quieren ocupar unos puestos que les están prohibidos, estamos yendo más allá de la época, luego es un planteamiento progresista.

> (2017; are women who are in an awkward place. The final message of the series is that choice is not an option but an obligation. When we put ourselves in the protagonists' position, women who want to hold positions that are forbidden to them, we are going beyond this time period, so it is a progressive approach.)

Perhaps, Celia is the moral compass of the series through her simultaneous defense of the rights of women and workers. However, the other women's stories are equally important: Francisca's attempts to free herself from a violent marriage, Diana's wish to be the new manager of the family business, and Blanca, who is ordered by the Queen to put together a nurse squad to help refugees from the First World War. It is striking that, through its feminist and progressive approach, *Seis hermanas* manages to distance itself from the view of costume dramas as a conservative genre. James Chapman notes, "The costume drama distances itself from the problems of the present through recourse to cultural nostalgia for the past. In particular, the lovingly recreated period mise-en-scène of the costume drama is seen as a safe alternative to the more agitational style of social realist plays and serials" (2014, 132). On the contrary, *Seis hermanas*, through its fascination with production elements and historical reconstruction, at no point conceals that it is representing an oppressive reality for its protagonists, who are engaged in a permanent struggle to achieve the positions to which they aspire. *Seis hermanas* is far from being an exercise in nostalgia. Proof of this is the recurring violence the protagonists face, from the horrific electroshock treatment that Celia undergoes to try to "cure" her homosexuality to the anarchist attack that almost destroys Tejidos Silva. In fact, precisely due to the violent content portrayed by *Seis hermanas* in a protected time slot for young viewers, TVE was reprimanded by the National Commission on Markets and Competition (Redondo 2015b). It is a violence of international agitation very much of the period in which the series' action unfolds: The outbreak of World War I following the assassination of Austro-Hungarian Archduke Franz Ferdinand in Sarajevo generated great anxiety in the protagonists after reading about it in the newspapers. The family business will profit from the war by making uniforms, but the factory will also be used by the Germans to store toxic materials to make gas bombs, which will later have unfortunate consequences for the workers. This representation of violence in the context of class conflict has been infrequent for Spanish television in the past few years, and even less so after the deep economic and political crisis that started in 2008. As a daytime serial drama with a fast production schedule, *Seis hermanas* enjoyed a freedom that it is not afforded to prime-time series.

THE RECEPTION OF *SEIS HERMANAS*: NICHE AUDIENCES IN THE GLOBAL CONTEXT

Bambú put a great deal of effort into instilling *Seis hermanas* with the kind of production values associated with prime-time programs, which was a key focus point during the promotion of the premiere episode and determined its reception. Critics got a first glimpse of *Seis hermanas* during its presentation at the FesTVal Primavera de Murcia, where the prime-time special was projected on March 24, 2015, almost a month before its premiere on TVE. With this pre-premiere, Televisión Española attempted to give great visibility to its two new daytime serials, *Seis hermanas* and *Acacias 38*, since in Spain fiction television reviewers focus almost exclusively on prime time and ignore daytime programming. In this case, the fact that Bambú was behind the series was significant since it allowed critics to make comparisons with the production company's previous series. This was the case in Mariló García's review in her blog for the *Cinemanía* website. While she highlighted the acting and some aspects of the mise-en-scène, she did not find it to be an especially original series, except for the main female characters: "Estas seis mujeres van a luchar por sus derechos, se van a enfrentar al qué dirán, quiero verlas como heroínas de verdad, anteponiendo sus intereses como mujeres pero también como hermanas, una lucha con la que, además, se haga historia, algo que he echado en falta en el piloto." (2015; These six women are going to fight for their rights, they will have to confront what other people think of them, I want to see them as real heroines, putting their interests as women first, but also as sisters, a struggle with which history is also made, something that I have missed in the pilot.) Writing for *El País*, Ricardo de Querol discussed the series in a similar fashion: "Tampoco es que esto sea un tratado de feminismo. Además hay cierta denuncia del clasismo, del puritanismo y de la hipocresía de una sociedad obsesionada con las apariencias. Pero por encima del mensaje hay drama, por ahora no tan lacrimógeno como otras propuestas." (2015; Nor is this a treatise on feminism. There is also a certain denunciation of classism, puritanism, and the hypocrisy of a society obsessed with appearances. But above any message there is drama, for now not as tearful as other projects.) At the same time, de Querol blamed TVE for its lack of originality in producing another period serial in an already crowded field. Generally speaking, the prime-time serial premiere succeeded in garnering greater attention than usual. However, Irene Lucas's review in the specialized blog *Los Lunes Seriéfilos* revealed both the dangers of trying to reinvent the daytime serial as a prime-time program, and the critics' own prejudices against the genre: "Sin darse cuenta, Bambú ha creado un híbrido de difícil clasificación, demasiado buena para ponerla de fondo mientras nos echamos la siesta, pero que quizá no esté a la altura para ocupar el prime time de la cadena pública." (2015; Without realizing it, Bambú has created a hybrid that is difficult to classify, too good to be on in the background while we have an afternoon nap, but perhaps not good enough to occupy the public channel's prime time.)

In terms of ratings, *Seis hermanas* was never successful. The first episode in the series' regular afternoon schedule had 700,000 viewers, a 7% share, compared to the better-rated *Acacias 38*, which exceeded a million viewers and around 10% share. However, the *Seis hermanas'* audience was very faithful, to the extent that the last episode had the same audience as the first, and each episode was regularly viewed by 600,000 viewers (Fórmula TV 2017). Additionally, *Seis hermanas* got more viewers from TVE's website, between 50,000 and 60,000 viewers just in the six hours following its afternoon broadcast, proving the particular appeal of the modernity of its arguments and characterizations (Lamelo 2016). *Seis hermanas* has been distributed internationally like other TVE series: The license rights have been sold on a country-by-country basis in Europe, and the series was broadcast in Poland (on the WP channel with the title of *Szesc siostr*) and Greece (on the EPT2 channel with the title of *Οι έξι αδελφές*). In Latin America, TVE Internacional broadcast the series. There are no data available to assess the success of the series in this region, but there is at least one relevant indicator. In the Facebook fan group *"Seis hermanas* Forever," the more than two thousand seven hundred members of the group reveal an important presence of users in Latin American countries such as Mexico, Uruguay, Argentina, Venezuela, Chile, Guatemala, and Colombia.

Part of *Seis hermanas'* international distribution has to do with the popularity of a single character: Celia, the sister who embraces her homosexuality. The narrative tries to combine an idea of acceptance of sexual diversity to a representation that is credible for the historical period. Thus, first Celia seeks medical help for what she considers a "disease" and as a result is subjected to painful electroshock treatments. But finally she accepts her attraction for women as part of her identity and starts a series of romances whose true nature must hide from society but not her sisters, whose reaction is one of understanding and acceptance. The representation of sexual diversity in the context of a period series is not completely new, but what is certainly novel in the daytime drama is that Celia is indisputably one of the protagonists, rather than a secondary character. This detail turned *Seis hermanas* into a cult series at the international level in the LGTBQ community. In the discussion forum "The L Chat," a section dedicated to the series was created on July 2, 2015, which is still active despite the fact that the series ended on April 2017, with 222 pages of messages and half a million cumulative visits. The blogger "natglee" (2017) has published on her Tumblr page "My Randomness," devoted to lesbian characters on TV, more than a hundred annotations, including captions, about Celia Silva and her story lines. On August 4 of 2015, a video titled "Celia & Petra 1" was uploaded on YouTube by the "Celistas" community, who edited each episode to focus on Celia's character and added subtitles in English. The videos reached between four thousand and nine thousand views on YouTube and later on the Dailymotion platform, until the community's dissolution on October 1, 2016 with the video dedicated to episode 312. On her blog "La Oveja

Rosa," the blogger and activist Alicia Rocafull began collecting testimonies from international viewers of the series with the title "Aureliers around the world." The title refers to a common practice among fans: merging the names of two characters that are in a relationship, in this case the nurse Aurora and Celia. On the blog, Rocafull reproduced testimonies of *Seis hermanas* fans from the UK, Panama, Colombia, Bosnia, Mexico, and Southeast Asia. The testimony of a Bosnian fan revealed that the representation of homosexuality in the historical context resonated especially with viewers from countries that are far from achieving the acceptance that the lesbian community has in Spain (where gay marriage has been legal since 2005): "Por esta razón Lamija no quiere que aparezca su nombre ni su fotografía en este artículo, porque ella misma me comenta que en Bosnia aún se vive la homosexualidad como en 1914." (Rocafull 2016a; For this reason, Lamija does not want her name or photograph to appear in this article, because she tells me that in Bosnia homosexuality is still lived as in 1914.)

Seis hermanas can be considered a special case in the development of television fiction in Spain: an ambitious daytime serial with top-notch production values similar to those of prime-time series. Inspired by the successes of British costume dramas, it had a clear progressive message about women's liberation and the acceptance of difference. These two aspects allowed the program to garner greater critical attention than is typical for the genre, and a loyal international audience within the LGBT community. At the same time, the decision to develop the story lines in the context of the outbreak of World War I allowed creators to broaden the stories' scope, and to provide an internationally recognizable historical background for the exploration of the liberal political system and the emergence of the suffragist and labor union movements. In this way, *Seis hermanas* deviated greatly from other recent iterations of the costume genre, since the psychological development of the characters and the exploration of the period were never subjugated to the romantic story lines. As a result, the representation of the Restoration period lacked the nostalgic elements often associated with period pieces since the six female protagonists were trapped in a world where they could hardly aspire to fulfill their desires for personal freedom. Nevertheless, the short life of *Seis hermanas* showed the limits of innovation in the context of serial television narratives, as the distinctions achieved by the show's historical engagement and high production values were not enough to connect with a broader audience.

Notes

1. See Galán (2007).
2. All the quotes by Gema R. Neira belong to this interview, unless otherwise noted.
3. Gema R. Neira and Verónica Fernández discussed these literary references in personal interviews conducted for this chapter. All the quotes by Verónica Fernández belong to this interview, unless otherwise noted.
4. A wide selection of pictures of the *Seis hermanas* sets can be viewed on the website of PROES (Producciones Escenográficas), the company that built the sets of the series and other Bambú products such as *Guante Blanco, Hispania, Gran Reserva, Bajo sospecha* and *Velvet*, available at: http://www.escenografias.es/index.php/es/ficcion/seis-hermanas (accessed June 18, 2017).
5. The author wishes to thank Verónica Fernández for the opportunity to visit the two interior sets in Pozuelo de Alarcón where *Seis hermanas* was shot. The visit took place on December 7, 2016.
6. A video made by the blogger and *Seis hermanas* fan Alicia Rocafull (2016b) shows the main exterior locations of *Seis hermanas*, including the specific address of each building.
7. Maurism ("Maurismo" in Spanish) was a conservative political movement established around the figure of Antonio Maura (1853–1925). It resulted from the fragmentation of the Conservative Party after Maura refused to accept in 1913 the terms of the "Turno Pacífico" (Peaceful Turn) between conservatives and liberals. Considered a precursor of the Spanish radical right, the movement was formed by young people from the aristocracy and the wealthy middle classes and tried to lead a conservative modernization based on an interventionist, nationalist, and corporative project. After its failure in the 1920 national elections, the Party split into different sections and started to lose its relevance.
8. The Rif War was a military conflict between the colonial power Spain and the Berber tribes of the Rif region (part of modern Morocco) which took place between 1920 and 1927. After seeing her colonial territories attacked by the same groups in 1924, France joined the fight and was a key ally in defeating the tribes and their leader Abd el-Krim in 1926. The early military losses and the unpopularity of the war were a source of instability during the Restoration period and are considered one of the main causes of the military coup of 1923.

BIBLIOGRAPHY

2015. "Seis hermanas Forever." Facebook Group. https://www.facebook.com/groups/SeisHermanasForever/. Accessed June 25, 2017.

2015. "Seis hermanas." *The L Chat*, July 2. http://s1.zetaboards.com/L_Anon/topic/5835831/1/. Accessed June 25, 2017.

2015. "YouSub." *Dailymotion*. http://www.dailymotion.com/desvla3. Accessed June 26, 2017.

Armstrong, Stephen, and Claire Webb. 2012. "*Grand Hotel*: Spain's Answer to *Downton Abbey*?" *Radio Times*, November 18. http://www.radiotimes.com/news/2012-11-18/grand-hotel-spains-answer-to-downton-abbey. Accessed June 10, 2017.

"Audiencias *Seis hermanas*." 2017. Fórmula TV. http://www.formulatv.com/series/seis-hermanas/audiencias/. Accessed June 23, 2017.

Cascajosa Virino, Concepción. 2017. "El guión como compromiso: la obra televisiva de Verónica Fernández." *Revue Iberic@l, Revue d'études ibériques et ibéro-américaines* 11: 153–165.

Chapman, James. 2014. "*Downton Abbey*: Reinventing the British Costume Drama." In *British Television Drama: Past, Present and Future*, edited by Jonathan Bignell and Stephen Lacey, 131–142. London: Palgrave Macmillan.

De Querol, Ricardo. 2015. "Feminismo retro contra Chicharito." *El País*, April 23. https://elpais.com/cultura/2015/04/23/television/1429785098_637363.html. Accessed June 23.

Fernández, Verónica. 2017. Interview with Concepción Cascajosa. Personal interview. Pozuelo de Alarcón, July 20.

Galán, Elena. 2007. "Las huellas del tiempo del autor en el discurso televisivo de la posguerra española." *Razón y Palabra* 12 (56). http://www.razonypalabra.org.mx/anteriores/n56/egalan.html. Accessed June 15, 2017.

García, Mariló. 2015. "*Seis hermanas: Mujercitas* en *Downton Abbey*." *Cinemanía*, March 25. http://cinemania.elmundo.es/blog/seis-hermanas-mujercitas-en-downton-abbey/. Accessed June 23, 2017.

Lamelo, Carles. 2016. *Televisión social y transmedia: Nuevos paradigmas de producción y consume*. Barcelona: Editorial UOC (Ebook Edition).

Lucas, Irene. 2015. "*Seis hermanas*: ¿sobremesa o prime time?" *Los Lunes Seriéfilos*, April 26. http://www.loslunesseriefilos.com/2015/04/seis-hermanas-sobremesa-o-prime-time.html. Accessed June 23, 2017.

Molinero, Patricia. 2015. "Un día de rodaje en *Seis hermanas*." *Mujer Hoy*, April 15. http://www.mujerhoy.com/corazon/paparazzi/rodaje-seis-hermanas-866676042015.html. Accessed June 18, 2017.

Natglee. 2017. "My Randomness." *Tumblr*. http://natglee.tumblr.com/tagged/Seis-Hermanas. Accessed June 25.

Neira, Gema R. 2017. Interview by Concepción Cascajosa. Personal interview. Pozuelo de Alarcón, July 20.

O'Donnell, Hugh. 2007. "High Drama, Low Key: Visual Aesthetics and Subject Positions in the Domestic Spanish Television Serial." *Journal of Spanish Cultural Studies* 8 (1): 37–54. https://doi.org/10.1080/14636200601148785.

O'Regan, Tom. 2000. "The International Circulation of British TV." In *British Television: A Reader*, edited by Edward Buscombe, 303–322. Oxford: Oxford University Press.

Peña Ardid, Carmen. 2010. "Las primeras grandes series literarias de la Transición: *La saga de los Rius* y *Cañas y Barro.*" In *Televisión y literatura en la España de la transición (1973–1982)*, edited by Antonio Ansón et al., 71–96. Zaragoza: Institución "Fernando el Católico".

Producciones Escenográficas, S. L. 2018. "*Seis Hermanas.*" http://www.escenografias.es/index.php/es/ficcion/seis-hermanas. Accessed June 18, 2017.

Redondo, David. 2015a. "Las verdaderas Galerías Velvet." *Cadena Ser*, February 23. http://cadenaser.com/ser/2015/02/23/television/1424702622_556860.html. Accessed June 18, 2017.

———. 2015b. "La CNMC advierte a TVE por unas escenas violentas de *Seis hermanas.*" *Cadena Ser*, December 17. http://cadenaser.com/ser/2015/12/17/television/1450363588_665831.html. Accessed June 19, 2017.

Rey, Alberto. 2011. "Downton Hotel." *El Mundo*, August 5. http://www.elmundo.es/blogs/elmundo/asesinoenserie/2011/08/05/downton-hotel.html. Accessed June 10, 2017.

Rocafull, Alicía. 2016a. "Aureliers por el mundo. Bosnia." *La Oveja Rosa*, May 3. https://laovejarosa.com/aureliers-por-el-mundo-bosnia. Accessed June 23, 2017.

———. 2016b. "Ruta por los escenarios reales de Seis hermanas." *La Oveja Rosa*, October 31. https://www.youtube.com/watch?v=DSbAc8wZ0Bs. Accessed June 17, 2017.

Selznick, Barbara J. 2008. *Global Television: Co-Producing Culture*. Philadelphia: Temple University Press.

Smith, Paul Julian. 2009. *Spanish Screen Fiction: Between Cinema and Television*. Liverpool: Liverpool University Press.

YouSub Español. 2015. "Celia Silva #Petrelia #Aurelia SubEng." *YouTube*, August 4. https://www.youtube.com/playlist?list=PLTC4eXzZwqr1gSA2jh-kQf1vul39cgO03S. Accessed June 26, 2017.

PART V

Sensing the Ending

CHAPTER 10

Commercializing Nostalgia and Constructing Memory in *As leis de Celavella*

María Gil Poisa

Between 2004 and 2006, Televisión de Galicia (TVG) broadcast three seasons of the fiction series *As leis de Celavella* (*Celavella's Laws*), co-produced with Voz Audiovisual, the second most important television production company in Galicia after the public network. Set in the 1920s, the plot of the series develops around a young lawyer, Don Pablo Veiga, who returns to his hometown after finishing his law studies and, due to unexpected circumstances, starts working as a private detective solving mysteries in the village. Created by Cheché Carmona and Pepe Coira, and co-directed by Gerard Gormezano, Jorge Coira and Carlos Sedes, the show received 19 Mestre Mateo Awards for its direction, production, screenplay, and acting.[1] The program, which continues to be rerun, was broadcast on Monday evenings in the coveted 10:30 p.m. prime time slot and received a 22% audience share on the first night (La Voz de Galicia 2005). According to the broadcaster's website,

M. Gil Poisa (✉)
Educational Services Abroad, Barcelona, Spain
e-mail: mgilpois@bates.edu

© The Author(s) 2018
D. R. George, Jr. and W. S. Tang (eds.),
Televising Restoration Spain,
https://doi.org/10.1007/978-3-319-96196-5_10

As Leis de Celavella é a primeira serie de intriga ambientada na Galicia de principios do século XX que emite a TVG. Na serie, de estilo costumista, retrátase un grupo humano cheo de posibilidades dramáticas e de comedia, mesturado coa riqueza do xénero de detectives.

(CRTVG; *As Leis de Celavella* is the first suspense series set in early twentieth-century Galicia broadcast by TVG. The show, with a *costumbrista* style, portrays a human group full of dramatic and comic possibilities, mixed with the richness of the detective genre.)[2]

Although TVG has recently produced other period dramas, like *Hotel Almirante* (Formato Producciones, 2015–) and *Vidago Palace* (Radiotelevisão Portuguesa, 2017–), and genre shows like *Matalobos* (Voz Audiovisual, 2009–2013) or *Serramoura* (Voz Audiovisual, 2014), *As Leis de Celavella* was the first Galician production set during the Restoration, and also the first to combine the costume drama with elements of fantasy and the thriller. Jorge Coira, an important name in Galician media and one of the directors of the show, states on the English version of his personal website that:

It was a very special project for several reasons: first, making a period thriller on that moment was something unique in Spain; second, every episode was like a small movie in which we had different narrative and aesthetic challenges; and third, it was obvious for all of us that the possibility of shooting something more elegant and fancy than usual was the reason why absolutely all the crew struggled to do their best. (2017)

Built around the collective character of an imaginary rural community, Celavella, the series presents a metonymical and nostalgic image of an almost forgotten rural Galicia, with the clear intention of faithfully representing the Galician experience in the first decades of the twentieth century. In his seminal work *On Collective Memory*, Maurice Halbwachs states, "the past is not preserved, but it is reconstructed on the basis of the present" (2008, 40). In this chapter, I examine how *As leis de Celavella* represents the past through the filter of present, reconstructing a collective memory for contemporary Galician television viewers. Through the inclusion of certain political elements and the elision of others, I argue, the series attempts to reshape the memory of the Restoration (1874–1931), especially the years of the Miguel Primo de Rivera dictatorship (1923–1930), by building fictional continuity between the political order of the period and the later national-Catholic regime of Francisco Franco (1936–1975). First, I examine how the series constructs a portrait of Galicia during the late years of the Restoration through a faithful recreation of the period that appeals to the audience's cultural identification and, consequently, appeals to an evoked nostalgia of a non-remembered moment. In addition to making a real effort to portray the daily life of a rural Galician community in the 1920s, the program often includes references to historical and political events that break with the characters' routine to fulfill the spectator's expectations for the detective genre, though notably without altering the daily life of the townspeople of Celavella. I consider how this unnatural imperturbability of the village and the inclusion of Franco as a character on the show, together with the omission of any reference to the historical Republican movements that led to the Second Spanish Republic, shape the idea of a peaceful continuum between the two dictatorships. Finally, I explore how the resulting portrait of the epoch subtly veils a revisionist idea of the Second Republic as an interruption between the two military regimes, mirroring Antonio Cánovas del Castillo's idea of the First Spanish Republic as an interruption in the history of Spain (Yllán Calderón and Jover Zamora 1985, 10),[3] and how the show creates a collective memory of this continuum.

THE STORY OF CELAVELLA

In *As leis de Celavella*, the protagonist, young womanizer Don Pablo Veiga (Manolo Cortés), is welcomed home by his mother, Dona Elvira (Margarida Fernández), an old-fashioned, upper-class widow, and his brother, Don Tomás (Salvador del Río), the local liberal-minded priest. Prior to her son's arrival, Dona Elvira fires the young servant Matilde (Eva Fernández), arguing that she is too attractive and might be a temptation for the young man; Matilde is replaced by her less appealing cousin Dora (Nuncy Valcárcel). Nevertheless, Pablo is still charmed by Matilde and hires her as his secretary. Once settled in his father's office, Pablo begins to be visited by the ghost of Belisario (Víctor Mosqueira), a peasant condemned to death by garrote 25 years prior for the murder of a young woman. The spirit claims he is innocent and implores Pablo to prove it. With the help of Sergeant Wenceslao (Marcos Viéitez), a member of the local Civil Guard, and his sidekick Blas (Avelino González), Pablo and Matilde set about to investigate the crime. On their quest, which spans the entire first season, they discover that some key members of the community are involved in the crime, such as Pombo (Antonio Mourelos), the local smuggler, and Laureano (Fernando Morán), the mayor. In the final episode of the season, the crime is solved and Belisario's innocence is made public, his spirit is released, and he disappears. At the same time, the local doctor of the village, Don Dionisio (Tuto Vázquez), is killed, and his spirit replaces Belisario's in Pablo's office, thus becoming the new advising ghost for the local detective. After the second season, the program's structure changes so that each subsequent episode follows a self-contained procedural structure in which Pablo and Matilde solve a single crime or mystery. Some of the quests are related to local issues, like the disappearance of the town's tax money or the murder of a woman predicted by a traveling illusionist. Other cases, though, are directly linked to the historical period, referring to events beyond Celavella. For instance, some of the mysteries Matilde and Pablo solve are the murderer of an anarchist activist and the disappearance of a Russian princess who supposedly visited the village after the Russian Revolution.

The townspeople of Celavella constitute a collective character, yet individually they also represent a set of stock social and regional types associated with Galicia, which originated in nineteenth-century *costumbrista* literature like *Los españoles pintados por si mismos* (1844–1845). The incidents recounted in each episode are juxtaposed with the personal relationships among the characters that add a comic dimension to the otherwise tense or unpleasant situations narrated. For example, characters like Dora and Blas relieve the tension by adding a lighter tone to the tragic situations lived by other characters, such as Matilde, who suffers under harsh personal conditions and adverse family circumstances throughout the program, like the imprisonment of her father, who is accused of trading contraband, and the absence of her brother, who has emigrated to Cuba. Likewise, the series uses the supernatural to achieve a similar comic effect: Ghosts serve as friendly advisors to the main characters, and so, the plot cannot be taken seriously, which according to Gary Edgerton is a common effect of historical television, often accused of telling unrealistic stories (2001, 7). The result is an eclectic portrait of the early twentieth century in rural Galicia mixed with the tradition of period, detective, and supernatural genres.

CREATING MEMORY, BUILDING HISTORY

It is key to distinguish between the concepts of history and memory before proceeding to address the televisual portrait of Galicia during the Restoration and the deployment of the tropes of memory in *As leis de Celavella*. In the production of *As leis de Celavella*, screenwriters clearly had to work with historical material instead of individual memories in order to create a plausible image of the period since they were not alive at the time of the Restoration. Lupicinio Íñiguez, Jose Valencia, and Félix Vázquez argue that "History [must be] constructed in such a way that not only those who were present at the sociohistorical moment of the events may have news of what really happened, but that a specific discourse may assure its future continuity" (2015, 240). History, therefore, does not reflect reality, but merely represents a certain discourse about the past, and the media plays an essential role in this process. Edgerton contrasts "professional history" as the work of historians, and "popular history" as the collective version of history presented in popular culture; he cites the key role of television as a "site of mediation" between the two (2001, 5). History does not reach people without effort, but memories can: People do not regularly read history books, but they do watch television (Edgerton 2001, 1). It is here where mass culture has an essential role because popular history can actually replace a current memory of a period of history for the audience.

Edgerton refers to postmodern historiographers like Hayden White, whose arguments relate to the academic treatment of historical evidence and demonstrate that the past is narrated from the present and, therefore, it has always already passed through a filter (2001, 5). In other words, every piece of history we produce, either professional or popular, is the narration of the past from the present; thus, it is liable to be studied from the present. In his study of Mario Camus's television adaptation of *Fortunata y Jacinta*, David George observes the inherent presentism of the representation of the Bourbon Restoration (in this case, the period's foundational moment) in television period series (George 2009, 155). The same can be said of *As leis de Celavella*, since its representation of history, as an interpretation of the past, can also be read as a reflection of the contemporary context in which the program was produced. At the same time, the historical projections of a specific perception of the period represented can also drive the construction of new memories for audiences, since they can pick and choose aspects of those institutionalized narratives and reinterpret them through their own experience or lack of it: If the spectator does not have any reference for the period, the media product may be the only memory the person can recall.

For Halbwachs, collective memory is the construction of a shared past based on the discussion of personal memories among the individuals. According to him, individuals build frameworks through their perception of a number of elements (time, space, and order) imposed by the group, and the collection of all those aspects is what is perceived as reality. These constructed frameworks of reality intersect, shaping a general perception of the world for the individual, and they create, the scholar notes, "the collective framework of memory … the result, or sum, or combination of individual recollections of many members of the same society" (Halbwachs 2008, 39). When those references change, individuals forget those frameworks because they are now focused on some other aspects of reality, recollecting different elements that construct new frameworks. Again, Halbwachs notes, "Society represents the past to itself in different ways: it modifies its conventions. As every one of its members accepts these conventions, they inflect their recollections in the same direction in which collective memory evolves" (2008, 172–173). As previously stated, media can aid in the construction of such a collective memory through the dissemination of elaborated images; if the receptors of popular history can adapt them to their individual reality frameworks, then the points where those frameworks intersect will eventually become a collective memory of the portrayed period. As I argue below, when a series like *As leis de Celavella* overlaps the audience's current cultural references (Galician culture in this case) with a historical representation, a collective memory can be created by the reproduction of those referential frameworks that, presented to a large audience through mass media, can produce consensus.

In their introduction to *Memory and Political Change*, Aleida Assmann and Linda Shortt consider memories as narratives that can be activated in different debates, claiming their part in public dialogue. The authors further describe the process of memories becoming history, that is, being institutionalized, by linking them to people's lives. According to the authors, once there are no living witnesses of the period or the event, historians appropriate existing narratives and make them part of a collective imagination (Assmann and Shortt 2012, 9). Therefore, the process of building collective memories of a time period is different for those who lived it versus for those who did not. For a historical event or period, those who were not alive at the time cannot remember it directly and therefore are missing an imaginary, which makes their memories easier to construct. When dealing with historical fiction, the product is in some way attempting to build a representation of history for its audience and potentially constructing a new memory. In portraying the Restoration, *As leis de Celavella* paints an image of the historical period through the use of mass media, aided by the lack of individual experiences, since the audience cannot link the period to a personal memory.

When mediating between spectators and history, media create a dominant vision of the past by preserving and passing that version to future generations (Neiger et al., 4). For authors like Ana María Castillo Hinojosa, Núria Sumelio Solà, and María Jesús Ruíz Muñoz, televisual historical representations introduce questions of history of current general interest to a public debate (2012, 668). However, sometimes those products aim to do quite the contrary—instead seeking to supply definitive answers to the questions proposed by the public debate— by building a dominant vision of that past. In *As leis de Celavella*, the show recovers a period of history, the dictatorship of Primo de Rivera, less present in contemporary Spanish collective memory than more recent times, and links it to one still present in the national memory, the Francoist dictatorship. In this fashion, fiction potentially builds new, universally accepted memories of a moment that is not remembered, thus avoiding the need for debate. In this case, I argue, the show addresses the audience from the perspective of a memory that does not exist but potentially could: a historical continuum between both twentieth-century Spanish military regimes, Primo de Rivera's and Francisco Franco's. The sequencing of mediated memories is also relevant for this construction. Lupicinio Íñiguez, Jose Valencia, and Félix Vázquez discuss the process of remembering as "a semantic ordering of events" (2015, 238). The transmitted order of past events is meaningful because it has an impact on the receptor's interpretation of the sequence that builds history, which then shapes memory. In the case of *As leis de Celavella*, although the audience knows the actual order of the historical events, by omitting one element (the Republican movements) and portraying the character of Franco during the previous dictatorship of Primo de Rivera, the show effectively creates a new memory linking the two regimes.

However, since every memory has an emotional component, in order to build memories, mass media need to establish some identification with the audience. When dealing with history, nostalgia as the sentimental yearning of the past is one of the means fiction uses to establish identification with the audience. Mordechai Neiger, Oren Mayers, and Eyal Zandberg consider media "inventors of memory," adding that "nostalgia appeals toward a non-existing past" (2016, 8), a past that is not personal, especially when it was not lived and cannot be remembered individually. If the spectator perceives the product as close to his or her own personal experiences, those televised contents will relate to actual memories in such a way that the whole internal ideological discourse of the program can be accepted as true. Thus, if different spectators' memories become more similar through the building of that nostalgia to the point of reaching an agreement or common point, the personally created memory becomes collective because it evolved from an independent individual's memory to a consensual one for the whole group. When evoking a time that is not remembered by the audience, the Restoration, *As leis de Celavella* creates a collective, fictional memory of the moment.

NOSTALGIA AND THE REPRESENTATION OF HISTORY

The portrait of Galician culture and society in *As Leis de Celavella* appeals to the present-day audience's sense of regional identity, and this cultural identification imbues the show both with a sense of verisimilitude and a feeling of nostalgia for a non-remembered period. In *As leis de Celavella*, the constructed image of the Restoration in Galicia dialogues with earlier televisual depictions of the period, like Gonzalo Suárez's *Los pazos de Ulloa* (TVE, RAI, 1985), but incorporates a new sense of identity for twenty-first-century Galician spectators due to its production values. This reimagining of a verisimilar non-remembered past of the region, together with the imperturbability of Celavella and its inhabitants' lives, contributes to the depiction of a community that seemingly lives outside of history, separated from the rest of the world in time and space; the resulting seclusion indirectly builds for the audience a bubble of nostalgia for a time they have not experienced.

The series attains a high degree of verisimilitude by incorporating references to historical events or elements that contextualize fictional events within a broader time frame for the audience. A recurring motif of the program is references to technological progress that symbolize the advance of modernity and provide signposts for understanding and locating the temporal setting of the narrative universe of *Celavella*.[4] Science and rationalism are two key concepts of Restoration culture and society, and the series introduces both through an internal debate among the community. The discussion usually splits the characters between conservatives, like Laureano's wife Leocadia (Ana Santos), who are presented as superstitious and religious, and who reject the introduction of technology into the community; and progressives, like Laureano's son Paquiño (Carlos Fernández) or the doctor Don Dionisio (Tuto Vázquez), who decide to embrace modernity. Through this dichotomy, Paquiño is constantly shown—as the youngest character and embodiment of the future—as ahead of his time, since he is frequently imagining different apparatuses and technological possibilities that serve as ironic winks to the modern audience, such as a small wireless phone that could fit into a pocket.

Despite the arrival of technology to the village, it does not really change anything in the townspeople's lives, but rather promises a perpetual potential for change that never happens. Contemporary scientific advances, such as the use of fingerprints and the spread of technological novelties like the telephone, might potentially reverse the backwardness of the village, but ultimately fail to do so. A controversial instance is the arrival of the movies to Celavella. Though the residents embrace the novelty by religiously attending the weekly projections, they create an argument within the community since some of the town's citizenry view it as immoral to be seated together in the darkness. Once again, modernity and immobility clash in the form of technology encroaching on or contradicting the practices of tradition. Interestingly enough, the presence of history in the whole series' plot is formally highlighted through the use of historic audiovisual documents and imitations of silent film pieces, giving the actual footage a contextual function within the series and helping to establish historical references for the audience. At the same time, it symbolizes the way in which the town is anchored in the past: Progress reaches Celavella, but the town does not necessarily progress as a result. Thus, it is a place represented as forever locked inside an eternal memory; although modernity visits the village in different ways, the town and its people never get to change, embodying a spiral of immobility that reinforces the general idea of the historical continuum proposed by the show.

All the while, elements of the mise-en-scène aid not only to locate the show temporally in the past, but also to link it to the present audience's regional identity and experience. The portrayal creates a collective memory framework by immersing the story in a familiar cultural environment that reinforces the narrative of memory (Neiger et al. 2016, 5). When spectators identify with the characters' way of life, the resultant image of the period is more likely to be internalized through the feeling of belonging to the group. In this sense, *Celavella* aspires to verisimilitude and identification by reflecting essential aspects of what is popularly perceived as Galician identity. This is seen, for instance, in the case of the name and setting of the village. Both are imaginary but clearly plausible; thus, the place becomes representative of the entire Galician countryside. The name is fictional but very similar to existing towns—Celavella makes a clear reference to the important town of Celanova in Lugo. The shooting location in Betanzos is also well known and easily recognizable in numerous exteriors, although the camera avoids any emblematic sights in order to avoid connection to any specific part of Galicia. Additionally, the village gathers all the traditional representative features of a small Galician town, such as the main plaza, the church, or the aristocratic *pazo* (palace). Interestingly, the program does something other Galician fictions usually avoid: Instead of a seaside locale, Celavella is landlocked, even though the coast is much more popular than the more rural internal Galicia. This setting helps to reach a part of the population not often addressed in Galician mass media and serves to reinforce the identification with a broader part of its audience.

In this Galician setting, socioeconomic and cultural stereotypes are used to link past and present, and therefore also to build memory. The presentation of the social structure of Celavella is based on the classic image of *cacique* society and linked to the corrupt electoral system inherited from the nineteenth century that persists in the region to this day. This mode of reproducing local cultures is commonplace in fictional series produced for regional televisions throughout Spain—in this case, through elements such as the construction of the characters as Galician natives by their dialects, accents, and way of life (Martínez Hermida 2002, 239). As a token gesture, the characters speak standard Galician, avoiding some commonly used Hispanicized terms, but they try to replicate how people actually spoke at the time. Also, the language on the show is used to categorize characters—in terms of social class, for instance. The language used, for example, by Don Tomás, the educated priest, is much more elaborate and literary than that of Blas, the Civil Guard, who is characterized as rather uncouth and uneducated.

Along the same lines, other aspects, such as autochthonous surnames (Moure, Veiga, Pombo, or Bouzas), common professions, and other economic activities associated with Restoration Galicia, such as peasant farming and smuggling, help to identify the story as Galician and so reinforce the representation of the period and the verisimilitude of its projected image (Martínez Hermida 2002, 239). Elements like regional costumes (whose use actually started in the nineteenth century), traditional food, and literature from the *Rexurdimento* (Galician literary intellectual movement from the second half of the nineteenth century) are also emphasized on the show. Regarding the costumes, only the working class in Celavella, especially women like Matilde and Dora, wear what are now considered traditional outfits designed for peasants. Both Matilde and Dora, and sometimes Leocadia (the mayor's wife), consistently cover their heads with the traditional *pano* (scarf) to avoid showing their hair, whereas women from different origins or social classes, like the more open-minded pharmacist Inés (Camila Bossa), or upper-class Dona Elvira, only do so inside the church. The two working-class girls also wear several layers of undergarments, *saias* (traditional skirts), and *mantelos* (large aprons), as well as traditional shirts and *dengues*, medium-sized capes covering their shoulders. Women's outfits are therefore linked to the persistence of tradition in the historical context, but at the same time they reflect a moment of change in the national mentality. As a case in point, the whole village makes a big deal when those sartorial codes are broken by young bourgeois Inés, who, after visiting Paris, starts wearing trousers. Traditional male Galician costumes are not often shown in the program, but there are also not that many examples of working-class males in the plot since the main male characters are either of the middle class (the lawyer, the pharmacist, or the mayor) or a profession that requires some sort of special dress (like the Civil Guard or priests).

Similarly, food also provides an interesting reflection of class divisions in the show; while upper middle-class families like the Veigas are usually portrayed eating more expensive dishes, such as chocolate or fish, working-class characters eat inexpensive traditional Galician food, like *caldo* (simple soup made with potatoes, turnip tops, and animal fat) or *empanada* (traditional pie made with cheap meat or fish, depending on the part of the region). As the ending of the series confirms, these class differences do not change in Celavella, confirming the immutability of the town. After three seasons, and despite several attempts by characters like Matilde and Pablo to break class barriers and establish new relationships, the town remains the same, with every villager wearing the same fashions and eating the same cuisine from the first to the last episode.

Finally, the program also offers insight into the cultural and intellectual life in early twentieth-century Galicia by introducing into the plot several figures associated with the *Rexurdimento* (Galician Renaissance) widely known to local audiences. Contemporary authors like Eduardo Pondal, Manuel Murguía, and Rosalía de Castro are occasionally mentioned by the well-read characters, and the plot even uses one canonical poet of the period to develop a romantic relationship between the characters. Wenceslao, the chief of the Civil Guard and head of the masonry in the village, courts Inés through the poems of Manuel Curros Enríquez, who was a mason himself. At the same time, the program includes as part of the mise-en-scène issues of the nationalist journal *Nós*, which was funded by conservative nationalist leader Vicente Risco, served as the platform for some key authors of the moment (such as Ánxel Fole and Ramón Otero Pedrayo), and was an essential piece of the *galeguismo* intellectual movement, which sought to preserve Galician culture through strengthened regional institutions. By combining these recognizable historical and local elements together in *As leis de Celavella*, the series appeals not only to a feeling of nostalgia for a past that the spectator cannot remember, but also to the constant sensation of permanence that the program seems to promote.

IMMUTABILITY AND CONTINUUM

The sense of stability is partially represented in the series through the constructed image of a peaceful village where nothing ever changes. Although the echo of 1920s revolutionary movements like anarchism, Galician *revoltas labregas* (peasant riots), or even the Russian Revolution, are included in some episodes at the core of the plot, these are exceptions and never directly affect the villagers' lives in the long term. Celavella, illustrating Miguel de Unamuno's notion of *intrahistoria* (2017), is surrounded by historical events and political references that have no impact in the town, perpetuating the timeless atmosphere of a place that does not move with the world. Although the characters in the program face historical events like the visit of a Russian princess fleeing the 1917 Bolshevik Revolution, anarchist attacks in the town, and the visit of North African war hero Francisco Franco, after every episode the villagers seem to forget those moments, and everything remains the same in Celavella. When depicting the place as an unperturbed environment, Celavella metonymically represents the dictatorship of Primo de Rivera as a polarized and convulsed moment during which, however, nothing really changes. The apparent immutability of the town reflects the well-known adage from Giaccomo Lampedusa's novel *Il Gattopardo*: all must change, so that all can remain the same. Although different things happen in Celavella, at the end of the day, life there always remains the same. While the Restoration reached its most polarized and agitated period in the late 1920s, the image projected by the series is one of imperturbability, reinforced by the peacefulness of the village and its residents. Furthermore, the lack of change results in the suggestion of a historical continuum between the two Spanish military dictatorships in the twentieth century: The short mandate of Primo de Rivera, between 1923 and 1930, is bridged to that of Francisco Franco, such that both are grounded in the Restoration. In Celavella, the system of peaceful cohabitation of liberal and conservative parties conceived by the architect of the Restoration, Antonio Cánovas del Castillo, is built into the image of pacific stability and continuity of the rural community.

Returning to the idea of history, especially popular history, as a narrative of the past written from the present, the writers of *As leis de Celavella* choose to include or omit specific historical elements in building a coherent plotline. Most notable in this regard is the absence of Republicanism, which would ultimately bring down the Restoration system in 1931. No doubt, the Second Spanish Republic is a key historical moment in understanding present-day Spain, but for a part of contemporary Spanish right-wing movements inspired by Cánovas's idea of "continuar España," the Republican period is considered an interruption of one single historical moment formed by both dictatorial regimes (Boyd 2008, 141). By overlooking the Republican movements but including others such as regionalism or anarchism, the show avoids making any reference to the coming Second Republic and, at the same time, presents an image of Franco as a promising figure for Spain by introducing him as a hero of the colonial wars in North Africa. With these narrative decisions, *As leis de Celavella* develops the figure of Franco as a capable young leader and links him to Primo de Rivera's regime, leaving out any trace of the future rupture with the military regime that actually happened with the Republican government.

The character of Franco is introduced in the show through his role in the war. The second season of *As leis de Celavella* begins with references to the Rif War (1920–1927).[5] The colonial conflict is commented upon by the village people when, in episode 17, they refer to the young Franco as "un xeneral de Ferrol que colleu moita sona" (a general from Ferrol who became really famous). Here, the series introduces the idea of an imperial Spain, one that Primo de Rivera actually rejected despite the support he obtained from a part of the "Africanistas," when in Celavella many of the villagers defend the war without thinking of its consequences.[6] Despite the fact that not everyone in Celavella agrees with the war—some like Don Pablo reject the military occupation and read it as a unnecessary step backward in the modernization of the country—the characters talk about and read the news about the war out loud in public spaces, like the local tavern, praising the virtues of the young general. In claiming such a collective position, the show presents for the first time an image of Franco as a respected general and leader of Spain's colonial adventures in North Africa. The image is reiterated later in episode 33 (set in 1925), when he appears as a character in the plot developed around his visit to A Coruña (episode 33). The historical image of the notorious figure is softened when he is presented merely as charismatic and heroic; the program emphasizes his personal link to Galicia by presenting him as a sort of a national hero to people in the town. In the show, Franco is at first presented as a slightly upsetting character who suffers from personal traumas and insecurities,[7] but once those issues are overcome, the character appears empathetic and is almost revered by the villagers as an admired leader: "É o xeneral máis novo de Europa, o máis duro e disciplinado" (He is the youngest general in Europe, the harshest and most disciplined). Even though at the moment represented on the show Franco was not yet the dictator he would later become, when filtered through the present of the audience, the two identities are inevitably conflated. The Restoration is a period that had not been frequently revisited by the media before this moment, as the essays in the present volume elucidate, and consequently, the construction of a suggested sequence of events in *As leis de Celavella*'s representation of the 1920s can function as the construction of a potential collective memory.

The static image of the Galician Restoration that the series provides through ideas like immovable tradition and unsuccessful progress creates for the audience of *As leis de Celavella* an impression of verisimilitude and a nostalgic identification with a non-remembered past. By linking this historical representation to the audience's cultural identity, the show potentially creates a new collective memory of the represented period. In a village where everything happens but nothing changes, the spirit of Cánovas's "continuar España" hangs over a community surrounded by history and events that remains, nonetheless, unaffected by them. Instead, the townspeople are destined to watch progress systematically pass by their lives, overtaking the village's reality without changing it. In that timeless bubble of immutability, the setting of Primo de Rivera's regime merges with the later Francoist dictatorship through the appearance of Franco himself, portrayed on the show as an admired leader. The program establishes a vague link between both dictatorial periods, suggesting a continuum between them: If nothing ever changes in Celavella, the regimen may not be able to change either. This fictional continuity creates a framework that is nevertheless as verisimilar as possible, building nostalgia for a non-remembered history as a potential new collective memory.

NOTES

1. The main awards in Galicia for audiovisual productions, given by the Academia Galega do Audiovisual.
2. For this and all subsequent quotes, any translation from Spanish or Galician is the author's.
3. Architect of the Bourbon Restoration, Antonio Cánovas del Castillo, was a Spanish politician, member of the Unión Liberal Party and Prime Minister of the country, alternating with the progressive Mateo Sagasta.
4. This same idea is developed in the present volume by Wan Tang, in her analysis of Antena 3's TV series *Gran Hotel*.
5. Armed conflict started by the revolts of autochthonous tribes in the region of Rif, in Morocco, between the Berber population and colonial Spain.
6. Doña Elvira, one of the main characters, says the war and the military men "lévanlle civilización ós mouros" ("bring civilization to the moors").
7. He is clownishly nicknamed the diminutive "Paquito."

BIBLIOGRAPHY

Assmann, Aleida, and Linda Shortt. 2012. "Introduction." In *Memory and Political Change*, edited by Aleida Assmann and Linda Shortt, 1–17. New York: Palgrave Macmillan.

Boyd, Carolyn P. 2008. "The Politics of History and Memory in Democratic Spain." *The Annals of the American Academy of Political and Social Science* 617: 133–148.

Castillo Hinojosa, Ana María, Núria Sumelio Solà, and María Jesús Ruíz Muñoz. 2012. "La reconstrucción del pasado reciente a través de la narrativa televisiva. estudio comparativo de los casos de Chile y España." *Comunicación: revista Internacional de Comunicación Audiovisual, Publicidad y Estudios Culturales* 10: 666–681.

Coira, Jorge. 2017. "The law of Celavella (As Leis de Celavella)."http://www.jorgecoira.com/en/traballos/tv/celavella/. Accessed August 19, 2018.

Unamuno, Miguel de. 2017. *En torno al casticismo.* Madrid: Alianza Editorial.

Edgerton, Gary R. 2001. "Introduction: Television as Historian: A Different Kind of History Altogether." In *Television Histories: Shaping Collective Memory in the Media Age,* edited by Gary R. Edgerton and Peter C. Rollins, 1-18. Lexington: University Press of Kentucky.

George, David R., Jr. 2009. "Restauración y transición en la Fortunata y Jacinta de Mario Camus." In *Historias de la pequeña pantalla: representaciones históricas en la televisión de la España democrática,* edited by Francisca López, Elena Cueto Asín, and David R. George, Jr., 53–73. Madrid: Iberoamericana.

Gormezano, Gerard, Jorge Coira, and Carlos Sedes. 2003–2004. *As leis de Celavella.* CRTVG.

Halbwachs, Maurice. 2008. *On Collective Memory.* Chicago: University of Chicago Press.

IMDb. 2017. "As leis de Celavella". IMDb. http://www.imdb.com/title/tt0451530/awards?ref_=tt_awd. Accessed December 14, 2017.

Íñiguez, Lupicinio, Jose Valencia, and Félix Vázquez. 2015. "The Construction of Remembering and Forgetfulness: Memories and Histories of the Spanish Civil War." In *Collective Memory of Political Events: Social Psychological Perspectives,* edited by James W. Pennebaker and Becky Banasik, 237–253. New York: Psychology Press.

La Voz de Galicia, Redacción. 2005. "«As leis de Celavella» se impuso el lunes a «CSI»." March 5. https://www.lavozdegalicia.es/noticia/television/2005/05/03/as-leis-celavella-impuso-lunes-csi/0003_3693686.htm. Accessed December 14, 2017.

Martínez Hermida, Marcelo A. 2002. "Contexto de ficción e series de televisión en Galicia." *Grial* 40: 235–243.

Neiger, Mordechai, Oren Mayers, and Eyal Zandberg. 2016. *On Media Memory: Collective Memory in a New Media Age.* Houndmills, Basingstoke, Hampshire: Palgrave Macmillan.

Yllán Calderón, Esperanza, and José María Jover Zamora. 1985. *Cánovas del Castillo, entre la historia y la política.* Madrid: Centro de Estudios Constitucionales.

CHAPTER 11

"Felices años veinte?": *Las chicas del cable* and the Iconicity of 1920s Madrid

Leslie J. Harkema

The pilot of the Netflix original series *Las chicas del cable* (*Cable Girls*) is set against the backdrop of an historic event: the first international telephone communication between Spain and the USA.[1] On October 13, 1928, US President Calvin Coolidge spoke with King Alfonso XIII in a brief conversation that reinforced diplomatic ties and paid tribute to Spain's imperial legacy in the Americas. Evoking the achievements of the Spanish explorers of the New World, Coolidge heralded the expanding reaches of the new technology of transnational telecommunication.[2] The Spanish monarch responded warmly to the President's words, while seated in a large room on the third floor of Madrid's Telefónica building, located on Calle Pi y Maragall (now Gran Vía). Still under construction at the time, the Telefónica building would soon become an emblem of Madrilenian modernity.

The reenactment of this momentous phone call in the last minutes of the first episode of *Las chicas del cable* carries its own symbolic charge, as the series represents another first for US–Spain collaborations

L. J. Harkema (✉)
Yale University, New Haven, CT, USA
e-mail: Leslie.harkema@yale.edu

© The Author(s) 2018
D. R. George, Jr. and W. S. Tang (eds.),
Televising Restoration Spain,
https://doi.org/10.1007/978-3-319-96196-5_11

221

in media. This show is the first Netflix original produced in Spain, and with its opening episode, Spanish television officially joins the expanding transnational network of the digital streaming media provider. Today as in 1928, technology facilitates and reinforces ties between the USA, Latin America, and Europe.[3] With *Las chicas del cable*, Spanish production company Bambú Producciones affirms a partnership that follows on the success its other period dramas *Gran Hotel* (2011–2013) and *Velvet* (2014–2016) have enjoyed on Netflix after their initial distribution by Antena 3. *Las chicas del cable* not only shares directors (Carlos Sedes, David Pinilla) and writers (Ramón Campos, Teresa Fernández-Valdés, Gema R. Neira) with both of these series, but also features actor Yon González (*Gran Hotel*) in another leading role, and chooses a geographical setting less than 200 meters down Gran Vía from the Hotel Cibeles, the model for the Galerías Velvet in *Velvet*.

The similarities among all of these shows led one reviewer for *El País* to declare that *Las chicas del cable* represents "más de lo mismo" (Marcos 2017; more of the same), and indeed, this most recent series seems to repeat a tried-and-true formula found in both *Gran Hotel* and *Velvet*. This formula, ubiquitous among Spanish series set during the Bourbon Restoration, as well as the later twentieth century, uses a given historical period as the backdrop for an impossible or forbidden love between main characters belonging to different social classes. This is the case of the lowly waiter Julio and the hotel owner's daughter Alicia in *Gran Hotel*, and that of seamstress Ana and her lover Alberto, heir to the fashion enterprise at the center of *Velvet*. In *Las chicas del cable*, the analogous romance is between Francisco (González), son-in-law to the owner of the Compañía de Telefonía (modeled on the Compañía Telefónica Nacional de España, created in Madrid in 1924) and Alba (Blanca Suárez), his long-lost childhood love who appears at the company under an assumed identity in the first episode of the series. Although the recycling of narrative conventions in this setup is clear, *Las chicas del cable* soon complicates the idealized, fairy-tale notion of "love against all odds" that characterizes its predecessors. As I argue here, this complication arises from the series' nuanced engagement with the historical period in which it is set.

To be sure, it would be impossible to reduce the 1920s in Spain to a mere backdrop. Spanish cultural imagination reserves a special status for this decade, known as *los felices años veinte* (the Happy Twenties). Seen from the perspective of the twenty-first century, the 1920s are remembered as the height of Spain's prolonged Belle Époque and one of the last, shining moments of freedom and lightheartedness before the outbreak of the Spanish Civil War and the forty dark years of dictatorship that followed the conflict.[4] The final decade of the Restoration has become fixed in cultural memory (and, to an extent, in popular imagination) as a time like no other before or since: the time when Federico García Lorca, Salvador Dalí, and Luis Buñuel coincided at the Residencia de Estudiantes (Student Residence); the era of the avant-garde and the *nueva mujer*; and a brief moment when Spain (represented by the synecdoche of the capital, Madrid) managed to be modern and progressive, and to synchronize its cultural watch with the rest of Europe. Insofar as it represents a Spain that was "of its time" (as opposed to "belated" or "unmodern"—terms so frequently used to describe the country before and after), the decade in which *Las chicas del cable* is set is iconic of contemporaneity itself.

Yet is this iconicity well founded? In semiotics, iconicity refers to a resemblance between form and meaning. An icon embodies that which it signifies. Can *los felices años veinte*, as a decade, be iconic? What do the most famous figures (Lorca, Dalí) and ideas (modernity, avant-gardism, transgression, freedom) associated with these years leave out of the picture? To what extent can a past era embody the contemporary, or speak to contemporary audiences? These are questions that arise when one watches *Las chicas del cable*. What differentiates this series from other Netflix hits set in the Restoration period (and moreover, from the bulk of Spanish cultural production dedicated to remembering the 1920s) is that it embraces the notion of 1920s Madrid as a place and time of intense *presentness* in order to imagine it not as a lost paradise—a past present frozen in time by the imposition of war and dictatorship—but as an era as uncertain, as riddled with injustices and deception as any, including our own. It does this principally through its focus on working women who struggle for autonomy in a misogynistic society, frequently suffering discrimination, manipulation, violence, and abuse. The feminist outlook of the program causes it to scratch beneath the veneer of this iconic period in Spanish history, much as the AMC period drama *Mad Men* (2007–2015) did in the US context, with its depiction of the advertising world of 1960s Manhattan.[5] This critical posture and the series' historical references allow it to offer a complex vision of the 1920s as a time when modernity could be both liberating and oppressive, when women's rights were advancing but still extremely limited, and when, though the Second Republic was not far off, Spain was ruled by both a king and a dictator. The analysis that follows addresses how the series achieves this complexity in its first season, which aired on Netflix in the spring of 2017.

In Search of a Reunion with the Contemporary

Both in terms of presentation and content, *Las chicas del cable* clearly strives to connect with contemporary audiences. The show's soundtrack, made up completely of twenty-first-century music, recalls Baz Luhrmann films like *The Great Gatsby* (2013) or *Moulin Rouge!* (2001) in eschewing period-specific songs and opting for the sounds of contemporary pop culture. While the romance mentioned above between Francisco and Alba serves as a primary plotline (one to which I will return later in this essay), the series primarily pitches itself as a show about the lives of four women working as telephone operators in the "big city." The foursome is composed of Alba, who is known to her fellow *telefonistas* (operators) as Lidia; Ángeles (Maggie Civantos), a married woman struggling to fulfill the roles of wife and mother while also rising through the ranks at the switchboard or *centralita*; Carlota (Ana Fernández), a general's daughter who shuns her aristocratic family out of a desire to support herself and be independent; and Marga (Nadia de Santiago), a wide-eyed emigrant from rural Spain adjusting to the fast-paced life of the capital. This basic premise evokes the conceptual framework of the HBO hit *Sex and the City* (1998–2004), signaling the Spanish series' investment in portraying independent, modern women and the bonds of female friendship that they form to support one another in a world built by and for men. Over the course of the first eight episodes, the program examines a number of issues relevant to twenty-first-century public discourse. Among these are domestic violence (Ángeles in particular suffers physical and psychological abuse from her husband) and an exploration of gender and sexuality (as Carlota finds herself unexpectedly attracted to her supervisor at the *centralita*, Sara, and begins an affair with her that ultimately extends to include Carlota's boyfriend, Miguel).

These formal gestures and thematic points of contact with twenty-first-century culture might lead to accusations of presentism from those who view them as efforts to titillate and boost ratings that compromise the series' pretentions to historical accuracy.[6] In fact, however, *Las chicas del cable* uncovers similarities between the 1920s and the 2010s through an engagement with historical context that often surprises with its rigor. Beyond the short haircuts and flapper-style dresses of the leading actors that evoke the "Roaring Twenties" for Spanish and North American audiences alike, several strategic references to historic figures and places serve to anchor the series in time and approximate it to specific cultural contexts. Some of these references are easily comprehended by both Spanish- and English-speaking audiences, such as when Carlota quotes Virginia Woolf in the opening episode. Others pertain specifically to the Spanish context. In episode five, the lawyer and politician Victoria Kent makes an appearance when the women seek legal recourse against Ángeles's abusive husband—and they find they have none. As an icon of feminist history in Spain,[7] Kent links the series to the most progressive feminist circles of the period. Another link appears with the show's depiction of the Lyceum Club, where Carlota and Sara attend lectures on women's rights. This women's club, founded in 1926 and frequented by Kent, María de Maeztu, and other well-known figures such as Zenobia Camprubí, María Teresa León, or Concha Méndez, serves as the setting for key scenes in *Las chicas del cable*. It is there that the romance between Carlota and Sara begins to bud, and later on a police raid on the Lyceum lands Sara in jail. While Sara is in prison, a fellow inmate tells her about a group of students who have been arrested for taking off their hats in the middle of Puerta del Sol. This is a clear allusion to the circle of female artists and intellectuals known as "las Sinsombrero."[8]

By mentioning these people and places, *Las chicas del cable* situates its story within, or better, just alongside the orbit of the most progressive women of 1920s Madrid: the elite group that attended the Residencia de Señoritas, founded as the women's version of the Residencia de Estudiantes in 1915, and later participated in the activities of the Lyceum Club. Over the last several decades, the work of many scholars in the USA and in Spain has brought increasing attention to the writers, artists, and thinkers that made up this exceptional group of women.[9] Most recently, their history has achieved widespread visibility in Spain through a made-for-television documentary and an exhibition at the Residencia de Estudiantes. The documentary, titled *Las Sinsombrero*, aired on Televisión Española on October 9, 2015, and discussed the lives and work of several of these women (Concha Méndez, María Teresa León, Ernestina de Champourcín, Rosa Chacel, Josefina de la Torre, María Zambrano, Maruja Mallo, and Marga Gil Roësset). Tània Balló, one of the directors of the documentary, subsequently published a book by the same title. Later in 2015, the Residencia de Estudiantes celebrated the inauguration of the exhibition *Mujeres en vanguardia. La Residencia de Señoritas en su centenario (1915–1936)*, which remained on display in Madrid for several months and has since travelled to Alcalá de Henares, Santander, León, Cáceres, Málaga, and Valladolid, among other locations across Spain ("Mujeres" 2016). Though indirectly, *Las chicas del cable* can be seen to engage in dialogue with the exhibition, the documentary, and with the academic research that informs them. In a sense, though its main characters are fictional, it extends the work carried out in these other fora, that is, the work of recovering the experiences of women who have been overlooked by history. Recovery has in fact been the framing metaphor for many accounts of the artists and intellectuals of the 1920s, beginning with the reopening of the Residencia de Estudiantes in the post-Franco era. The reedition of Margarita Sáenz de la Calzada's classic study of the Residencia, published to celebrate its one-hundredth anniversary in 2010, includes a prefatory note that states, "Desde su refundación en 1986, uno de los aspectos fundamentales de la actividad de la Residencia de Estudiantes ha consistido en recuperar y difundir su tradición intelectual" (2011, 12; Since its re-founding in 1986, one of the fundamental aspects of the activity of the Residencia de Estudiantes has been the recuperation and dissemination of its intellectual tradition). The emphasis on recovery also appears in the opening paragraphs of Balló's book, where the author invokes a title that has become nearly synonymous with the 1920s in Spain, and with the Residencia: the "Generation of 1927." She writes,

> Todos conocemos la Generación del 27. Tan popular grupo cultural da nombre no solo a una de las nóminas artísticas más excepcionales de la historia cultural española, sino que también identifica el devenir de unas décadas clave de nuestro país (1920–1930).
> Durante los cuarenta años de dictadura que siguieron a la Guerra Civil, gran parte de los ilustres nombres de aquellos jóvenes intelectuales y artistas que protagonizaron ese *boom* de libertad y creatividad, que culminó con la proclamación de la Segunda República (1931–1939), fueron silenciados. (17)

> (We all know about the Generation of 1927. This recognized cultural group not only gives its name to one of the most exceptional artistic cohorts of Spanish cultural history, but also represents the history of key decades for our country [the 1920s and 1930s].
> During the forty years of dictatorship that followed the Civil War, most of the illustrious names of the young intellectuals and artists that led that burst of freedom and creativity, which culminated in the proclamation of the Second Republic [1931–1939], were silenced.)

Balló goes on to assert that even when some members of this lost generation returned to Spain after Franco's death, only the stories of male artists and intellectuals—the canonical members of the so-called Generation of 1927—were recovered. She presents the objective of her book (as in the documentary) as that of rediscovering the women who have been left out of this picture. *Las chicas del cable* could be seen as an extension of this project, one that widens its purview and shifts its focus to consider the lives of working women at another remove from the elites of the "Generation of 1927".

There is more going on here, however, for this shift in focus allows the series to interrogate the prevailing notion of the 1920s that ties it so closely to this legendary group of writers. When Balló extends the denomination "Generation of 1927" to account for whole decades of the nation's past, she appeals to the group's iconic status—that is, to the way its particular history has shaped contemporary understandings of the decades before the Civil War in general. Yet the version of the past that equates the 1920s with the "Generation of 1927" originates not so much in the 1920s itself as in memories of the period composed and constructed during the forty years coinciding with Franco's dictatorship, both within and from outside Spain. As a result, the decade is tied to the history of the Second Republic, the Civil War, and Republican exile, and more or less disassociated from the Bourbon Restoration. Historian Eduardo González Calleja offers one explanation for this separation by pointing out that the dictatorship of Miguel Primo de Rivera differentiated the period between 1923 and 1930 from what came before and after it:

[L]a dictadura de Primo de Rivera ha gozado de una discreta fortuna historiográfica, "emparedada" entre los ensayos parlamentaristas de la Restauración y la Segunda República (cuyas circunstancias—tan diversas— de nacimiento, evolución y crisis han centrado gran parte de las discusiones académicas sobre el siglo XX español), y oscurecida en su ambiguo autoritarismo por el régimen más longevo y represivo de nuestra historia contemporánea: la dictadura del general Franco.

(13; The dictatorship of Primo de Rivera has had a muted historiographical fortune, "sandwiched" between the parliamentary experiments of the Restoration and the Second Republic [whose—very different—origins, evolutions, and crises have been the subject of most of the academic discussions about the twentieth century in Spain], and overshadowed in its ambiguous authoritarianism by the longest

and most repressive regime of our contemporary history: the dictatorship of General Franco.)

While Spain was still ruled by the Bourbon line throughout the 1920s,
Primo's interruption (or culmination) of the course of Restoration politics marked a shift that ultimately brought the period to an end. Juan
Pablo Fusi has argued that Primo's dictatorship effectively dissolved the
Restoration while at the same time appearing as the inevitable result of
the oligarchism and *caciquismo* that had plagued the Restoration and
prevented it (in the view of the *fin-de-siècle* thinker Joaquín Costa) from
truly modernizing and democratizing Spanish political structures (Fusi
2012, 201). Notably, this political dimension of the decade is almost
entirely absent from the cultural accounts that have shaped contemporary ideas about *los felices años veinte* in popular imagination. The avant-
garde aesthetics of Dalí, Lorca, or Buñuel and the progressivism of the
first years of the Second Republic retrospectively obscure the social complexities of the decade, allowing those looking back upon it in the wake
of the Civil War and Francoism to view it as an idyllic, carefree time of
youth, innocence, and freedom.

One of the most influential sources for this postwar idealization of
the 1920s is the autobiography of José Moreno Villa, *Vida en claro* (Life
Made Clear, 1944), where the exiled poet and painter recalls the years he
spent living at the Residencia de Estudiantes (along with García Lorca,
Dalí, and Buñuel) as time spent "En presencia de la eterna juventud"
(In the presence of eternal youth). In Moreno Villa's description, the
Residencia is idyllic and set apart, both from the rest of Madrid and from
historical time. The site of learning and camaraderie becomes a poetic
Arcadia, forever lost with the outbreak of a war that, even as Moreno
Villa writes, threatens to "intrude" on his memories.[10] This nostalgic
vision also appears in works by several of Moreno Villa's contemporaries
and fellow exiles, such as Rafael Alberti's memoir, *La arboleda perdida*
(The Lost Grove) and María Teresa León's autobiography *Memoria de
la melancolía* (Memory of Melancholy), where this writer refers to herself and her fellow exiles as "Nosotros, los del paraíso perdido" (1999,
36; We, the people of the lost paradise). León is speaking most directly
here of the Republic, but the view of the prewar period as a lost paradise certainly extends to the 1920s. In Moreno Villa's account and that
of Dámaso Alonso in his essay "Una generación poética, 1920–1936,"
the most idyllic era seems to have been the early years of the decade.[11]

Notably, these are the years before the onset of what Alonso calls "el demonio de la política" (the demon of politics)—the radicalization of ideological oppositions that would eventually lead to war (Alonso 1975, 670).

The view of art as apolitical and "pure" that is so often associated with these writers has colored the view of the decade of the 1920s in general, casting it as a peaceful time free of political strife. This is, in part, why Shirley Mangini is able to downplay the importance of the dictatorship of Primo de Rivera in her analysis of the women intellectuals of the decade, writing that "[a] pesar de la dictadura, los años veinte gozaron de cierta magia cultural y social" (2001, 30; in spite of the dictatorship, the 1920s possessed a certain cultural and social magic). Such a statement overlooks the political impact of the Rif War in Morocco (1920–1926), Primo's clashes with intellectuals, and the protests against his regime led by young university students, both men and women.[12] To be sure, the injustices of Primo's dictatorship fade in comparison with the repression of the Franco era, and the earlier regime did promote the modernization of the country, its institutions, and its infrastructure (telecommunications included). Yet by and large, the dominant image of the 1920s in contemporary Spanish culture conforms to a literary historiographical model that has traditionally opted to portray the years when Primo was in power as a tranquil, prelapsarian time, in keeping with its idealization of the decade as prior to the "fall" into ideological division and civil strife in the 1930s.

The difference between this dominant, nostalgic view of the 1920s and the one offered by *Las chicas del cable* can be illustrated by a comparison of narrative techniques in the television series and the documentary *Las Sinsombrero*. Both rely on a narrating voice to frame their depictions of and reflections on the past era. In *Las chicas del cable*, an older Alba speaks in voice-overs, looking back through time and explaining the struggles of her sex in the 1920s. In *Las Sinsombrero*, this role is filled by the voice of Concha Méndez, recorded in an interview from 1981. Each of these voices offers retrospective commentary, yet while Méndez fondly recalls "la atmósfera de la generación del veintisiete" (the atmosphere of the generation of 1927) as "algo único que ha habido en el mundo" (something unlike anything else in the world), the narrating Alba (like her on-screen character) is clear-eyed and unsentimental. At the very beginning of the first episode of *Las chicas del cable*, her words sketch out the historical and social context of the series with a clear emphasis on the inequalities suffered by women during the decade: "En 1928, las mujeres éramos algo así como adornos que se llevaban a las fiestas para presumir de ellos. Objetos de poder sin opinión ni decisión" (In 1928, we women were like jewels that one would wear to a party to show them off. Objects of power with neither voice nor vote). At the end of the episode, as the trans-Atlantic phone call between Alfonso XIII and President Coolidge is being administered by one of the *telefonistas*, Alba's voice-over returns:

> Un día para la historia. El triunfo de las comunicaciones. El mundo en manos de una mujer. Una telefonista. Todos celebraban este hecho insólito sintiéndose parte de un nuevo mundo. Aunque algunas ya empezaban a comprender que ese nuevo mundo no era tan idílico ni tan sencillo como habrían deseado.

> (A historic day. The triumph of telecommunication. The world in the hands of a woman. A telephone operator. Everyone celebrated this remarkable event, feeling themselves to be part of a new world. Although some of us were already beginning to realize that this new world was not as idyllic nor as simple as we would have wished.)

This final statement, which pointedly singles out the difficulties faced by women amidst a general atmosphere of celebration, sounds as a challenge to the vision of the 1920s that has dominated Spanish cultural history since the immediate postwar period.

Triangulating the Past–Present Relationship

Alba's words at the end of the pilot signal to viewers of *Las chicas del cable* that the series will not offer a simple re-encounter with 1920s Madrid. Its presentation of this time and place as deeply contemporary serves not to create a reassuring reunion with a progressive pre-Franco Spain, but to make it possible to evaluate the historical period anew; the recovery that it carries out is less celebratory than investigative. As the series makes use of narratives of false identity, deception, and blackmail to create intrigue and hold its audience's interest, it ultimately poses the question: To what extent is the "idyllic" vision of the 1920s handed down to democratic-era Spaniards itself a deception? The encounter between the present and the dominant, mythologized notion of the 1920s is complicated by the juxtaposition of the myth with other accounts of the past.

The most prominent way in which *Las chicas del cable* challenges the idealization of the 1920s in the Spanish cultural imagination is through its direct representation of sexism and misogyny, from structural inequities to domestic violence. Its depiction of the lethal danger faced by Spanish women almost a century ago resonates with the contemporary in an unsettling way, as it engages a topic discussed frequently in current Spanish news and made visible throughout the Hispanic world in the twenty-first century with the hashtag #niunamenos. The theme of violence against women emerges in the very first scenes of the pilot, as Alba and her friend Gimena leave a high-society party. They have stolen jewelry from the party's host and now plan to sail off to Argentina. But as they chatter excitedly about finding freedom in South America, they come upon precisely the person they want to escape: A former lover of Gimena's blocks the street in front of them, brandishing a gun. A charged exchange with this man (who would rather kill Gimena than relinquish her) ends disastrously, with Gimena and her pursuer dead, and Alba unjustly accused of murder. Now under the power of a corrupt policeman, Alba escapes her own death sentence by agreeing to steal for him. Thus it is that she arrives at the Compañía de Telefonía to apply for a position as an operator, calling herself Lidia and planning to rob the company's safe.

The violent encounter at the opening of *Las chicas del cable* is a harbinger of things to come. Of the four lead female characters, Ángeles deals most directly with verbal and physical abuse. Her husband, Mario, pushes her to leave her job at the *centralita* in order to stay at home with their daughter, in accordance with the traditional role of the "ángel de hogar" (angel of the hearth). When Ángeles goes against his wishes and accepts a promotion at the telephone company, Mario takes her home and beats her severely. With no legal recourse to divorce, Ángeles makes plans to escape to Barcelona with her daughter, but even this escape route is blocked when Mario intercepts her just as she boards her train.

Ángeles's situation is representative of the experiences of many women outside the elite minority of freethinking circles like those of *las Sinsombrero*. As Antonio Gil Ambrona notes in his analysis of violence against women during this period in Spanish history, "si dejamos de lado a las clases privilegiadas, o al reducido sector de mujeres embarcadas en la defensa de unas ideas políticas impregnadas de feminismo, y descendemos al terreno de la realidad social, el panorama es ciertamente desolador" (2008, 421; if we set aside the privileged classes, or the small sector of women involved in the defense of political ideas inspired by feminism, and descend to the ground level of social reality, the panorama is quite heartbreaking). Gil Ambrona stresses that married women were at a particular disadvantage in the 1920s, for while Primo de Rivera allowed unmarried women and widows to vote in municipal elections, married women were represented only by their husbands. While cultural production like the silent film *La malcasada* (1926, based on the novel by Carmen de Burgos) added force to the push for the legalization of divorce, this would not occur until 1932. In *Las chicas del cable*, even upper-class women like Carlota are subject to violence if they refuse to obey men. Carlota's father threatens her and goes to great lengths to ensure that she returns home and remains under his control; we eventually discover that he has used his contacts with the police to organize the raid on the Lyceum Club that results in Sara's arrest. Alba likewise finds herself at the mercy of men: first Beltrán, the corrupt police officer who blackmails her with the threat of charging her with the murder of Gimena and her husband, and then Francisco, who pays off her debt to Beltrán in a gesture that, rather than romantic, comes off as manipulative.

The relationship between the independent, wily Alba and the dashing—but domineering—Francisco emblematizes the series' questioning of the idea of a re-encounter with an ideal past. As I have noted above, this central narrative thread is itself a story of reunion. When we first meet him, Francisco is second-in-command to the owner of the Compañía de Telefonía, but we soon learn that he first came to Madrid with Alba, when they were adolescent sweethearts. (In the first episode, a flashback shows them stowing away on a train and discussing their dreams for the future together.) Like Ana and Alberto in *Velvet*, Francisco and Alba have known each other since childhood, and their love is challenged by circumstances beyond their control. Upon arrival in the capital, they are immediately separated when Alba chases after a man who steals her suitcase. While Francisco searches for her, Alba finds refuge in a brothel, whose owner raises her to fend for herself in Spain's patriarchal and duplicitous society. Francisco eventually marries into the powerful Cifuentes family, while Alba remains on the fringes of society and becomes a skilled thief. The setup for her re-encounter with Francisco is complete.

Yet the reunion brings more ambivalence than anything else. Alba is by now a fiercely independent woman, unwilling to burden or endanger Francisco with her problems—but also, and more fundamentally, unwilling to surrender her autonomy. The emphasis that the series places on the misogyny of early twentieth-century Spain deepens this ambivalence, as does the presence of Carlos, Francisco's brother-in-law and best friend, who meets Alba under her guise as Lidia. Carlos, though a participant in his sexist culture, is also young, wide-eyed, optimistic, and enthusiastic. Born into the well-to-do Cifuentes family, he lacks all of the cynicism that Francisco has acquired through trying life experiences. Carlos is immediately fascinated by the new *telefonista* and boldly initiates a persistent flirtation with her. Though Alba/Lidia rebuffs his advances at first, he eventually wins her over, by the penultimate episode of the first season they are engaged.

The inclusion of two legitimate love interests for Alba distinguishes *Las chicas del cable* from *Gran Hotel* or *Velvet* and complicates the way the series deals with, and thematizes, memory and the past. "Las memorias" (Memories) and "El pasado" (The Past) are in fact the respective titles of episodes two and five of the first season. Francisco, a figure from Alba's past, represents a known and established order, while Carlos stands for innovation, the future, and openness to change. Together, the two men embody a contrast between innocence and experience. Carlos, the younger child in his family, infantilized and belittled by his father, plays the part of a carefree, entitled, well-to-do young man, a *señorito*, yet he also displays drive and ambition. He dreams of revolutionizing the family business, and throughout the first season of the series he works to develop a prototype of a rotary telephone.[13] Francisco, by contrast, is responsible and worldly. His role of authority at the telephone company gives him power and control, and it is clear that he has grown accustomed to this status. The ease with which he lies to his wife about Alba, together with his expectation that Alba will be willing to leave her own life and run away with him, hints at a selfishness and machismo not present in Alba's memories of him. Ultimately, Carlos's novelty, energy, and openness cast Francisco in a new light. He provides a point of contrast that triangulates the relationship between the long-lost lovers and allows for a critical re-evaluation of their past in relation to their present.

Another prominent triangulation of romantic relationships occurs in the case of Carlota, Sara, and Carlota's boyfriend, Miguel. Carlota's unexpected attraction to Sara initially threatens her romance with Miguel, but in the end she is not forced to choose between the two of them. Instead, their threesome provides an opportunity for *Las chicas del cable* to explore non-binary sexuality and shifting gender identity—especially in Sara, who appears trying on Miguel's clothes in the eighth episode. While their ménage-à-trois in episode six is certainly included for sex appeal, it need not be seen only as an effort to titillate contemporary audiences. In fact, it challenges hegemonic notions of sexuality and enacts a re-encounter with sexual practices that, as Maite Zubiaurre has argued, were forgotten or repressed during the Franco period. Zubiaurre's documentation of erotic culture in early twentieth-century Spain indicates that "deviant" sexual practice was in fact widespread in Spanish culture during these years, and cut across divisions of both class and ideology (2012, 1). Where the Carlota-Miguel-Sara story line may cater to twenty-first-century sensibilities, then, is in its presentation of sexual liberality as linked to progressive politics.

Carlota, Sara, and Francisco are all linked by yet another narrative thread that undermines the idealization of the 1920s by highlighting the precariousness of the political order in Spain during this decade. Early in the series, we learn that the Compañía de Telefonía has agreed to spy on some telephone calls for the government, as there is fear of a coup d'état. Francisco informs Sara of this arrangement and charges her to select operators who will listen in and transcribe calls. When Carlota's father attempts to have her fired from the company, she gets her job back by agreeing to become one of these spies. The inclusion of this story line, while adding a layer of intrigue to the story, also serves as a subtle reminder that the regime that ruled Spain in 1928 had itself come to power through a coup: Miguel Primo de Rivera had established his dictatorship by leading a military takeover of the government in September of 1923. By the late 1920s, Primo's position was weakening and multiple attempts to unseat him were planned. *Las chicas del cable* develops its representation of these political battles through the character of Carlota's father, a general known as "El Halcón," who is in fact colluding with other military personnel to plan an uprising. Given the setting of the series in fall 1928, this is likely based on the failed coup attempt led by conservative José Sánchez Guerra in January, 1929.

Though Primo is not mentioned by name in the first season of *Las chicas del cable*, the show's allusions to the complexities of Spanish government in the 1920s also differentiate its representation of the decade from a historical narrative that often prefers to overlook the political context in order to focus on culture. The series does not shy away from political entanglements, but instead highlights the less-than-transparent dealings of the Spanish government in its manipulation of the telecommunications industry. In this way, it highlights continuity with the earlier Restoration period, which, despite its appeal to democratic politics and ordered sharing of power by conservatives and liberals, was plagued by corruption. Within the context of Primo's dictatorship, the idea that the telephone company would spy for the government does have a degree of historical grounding. The Compañía Telefónica Nacional de España (CNTE) was a nationalized company and held a monopoly on telecommunications in Spain. This is acknowledged in the first episode of *Las chicas del cable*, when Alba's narration describes the company as "la única compañía de telefonía del país" (the only telephone company in the country). Formed in 1924 after the International Telephone and Telegraph Company (ITT) acquired the Compañía Peninsular de Teléfonos, the CTNE achieved this monopoly by winning a competition that was, in fact, rigged in its favor (Pérez Yuste 2007). Though it is not clear how involved Primo was in this manipulation, its outcome was engineered to the mutual benefit of his government and the CTNE, as well as to the North American company that controlled it. This last historical fact reveals yet another point of connection between 1920s Madrid and twenty-first-century television, for with *Las chicas del cable*, another US company—Netflix—is also expanding its reaches in Spain.

In its critical engagement with the iconic status of 1920s Madrid in the Spanish cultural imagination, the first season of *Las chicas del cable* departs from other recent period dramas set during the Restoration. This is perhaps appropriate, given the unique historiographical status of the Primo years that González Calleja highlights. Trading a conventional tale of "love against the odds" for a layering of love triangles and deception that at times recalls film noir (Alba is certainly a potential *femme fatale*), its depiction of *los felices años veinte* challenges the rosy, nostalgic image of the decade that has been preserved since the Civil War, first in Republican memoir and later within the Spanish cultural establishment. The series' treatment of duplicity and corruption ties its story to the legacy of the Restoration and presents the iconic modernity of 1920s Madrid as deeply ambiguous. In this, the inaugural season of *Las chicas del cable* also suggests possible analogies with the present of a democratic Spain also ruled by a Bourbon king, where political corruption is rampant and a longstanding two-party system has entered into crisis.

A comparison with yet another recent television program offers a final indication of *Las chicas del cable*'s departure from the most common treatment of the decade in contemporary Spanish culture. When the Televisión Española series *El Ministerio del Tiempo* dedicated an episode to the 1920s at the end of its first season, it selected the setting of the Residencia de Estudiantes and featured García Lorca, Buñuel, and Dalí.[14] The choice was foreseeable in a series whose premise imagines a department of the Spanish government dedicated to preserving the official historical record. While *El Ministerio del Tiempo* zooms in on the icons of 1920s Spain, *Las chicas del cable* trains its vision just beyond these figures and spaces, and ultimately forces a reflection on the decade's iconicity itself.

Notes

1. The pilot aired on April 28, 2017.
2. "This western hemisphere, discovered by the wonderful Spanish navigators, has always been indebted to your nation," Coolidge stated, before going on to affirm that "our friendship with the great nations of the South brings us even closer to their Mother Country" (Transcription in Pérez Yuste and Salazar Palma 2003, 1742).
3. Netflix expanded to Latin America in 2011, and to much of continental Europe in 2014 (McDonald 2016, 212). It reached Spain in October of 2015 (Marcos 2017).
4. This perception of the prewar period is exemplified in Fernando Trueba's 1992 film *Belle Époque*, set in 1930.
5. While *Mad Men*'s alliterative title names male executives and *Las chicas del cable* focus on female subordinates, both shows confront the pervasive sexism of their respective periods head-on. By contrast, *Velvet*, although set in roughly the same chronological moment as *Mad Men*, presents a much more passive view of 1960s Madrid, evincing a notable reluctance to discuss social issues or politics—or indeed, acknowledge the dictatorial rule of Francisco Franco during the years it depicts. Jerome de Groot (2011) has studied the treatment of nostalgia in *Mad Men* as a tool the series employs to interrogate national history.

6. De Groot challenges such a distinction between the official history of professional historians and that of others who "access" the past by non-scholarly means in the introduction to his book *Consuming History*. On televised costume dramas, he writes, "they can invoke complex models of historical subjectivity, confound expectations, and consider key political issues of the past in order to educate the viewer. As a consequence, they are not dry, conservative mythmakers and (...) are flexible and innovative" (184). On presentism and its obverse, pastism, see López (2009, 12).

7. It should be remembered here that Kent opposed women's suffrage in the parliamentary debates of 1932, clashing with her colleague Clara Campoamor and arguing that too many Spanish women would simply vote as the Catholic Church instructed them and thus endanger the Republic. The fact that Kent, and not Campoamor, appears in *Las chicas del cable* speaks to the ways in which her more radical leftist politics have made her seem the more modern or contemporary of the two, despite her controversial stance on women's suffrage.

8. On the Lyceum Club, see Mangini (2001, 88–91), Balló (2016, 26–32), and Fagoaga (2015). No raid was ever carried out at the club, but the inclusion of a raid in *Las chicas del cable* does reflect the fact that the club and its members were attacked verbally and criminalized by conservative Spanish society and the press (Mangini, 90–91). Similarly, while the original *sinsombreros* (in Maruja Mallo's telling, they included Mallo herself, Margarita Manso, García Lorca, and Dalí) were not arrested, they were unequivocally shunned. Mallo described the indignation they provoked as stemming from a transgression of gender norms, by which they seemed to represent a third sex, "tercer sexo" (Balló et al. 2015).

9. See, among many other publications, Mangini (2001) and Kirkpatrick (2009).

10. When his thoughts move to the war and the last days before the Residencia closed, Moreno Villa writes, "Es inevitable esta intrusión de las horas finales en el relato. Me propongo hablar de 'la eterna juventud', pero se me presentan nubarrones de los últimos días. Días en que la juventud se había dispersado" (2011, 109; This intrusion of the final hours upon the story is inevitable. I set out to speak of 'eternal youth,' but the dark clouds of the final days rise up before me. Days when that youth had dispersed). On Moreno Villa and the Residencia, see Harkema (2017, 91–136).

11. In his essay, Alonso identifies a turning point around the year 1927, when the emphasis on poetic purity (and, one might read, the purity or innocence of the young artists) gave way to growing political concerns and politically engaged art.

12. On Spanish culture and the intellectual community during the Primo dictatorship, see González Calleja (2005, 294–302). Another Bambú Producciones series, *Tiempos de guerra*, released on Antena 3 in the fall of 2017, takes the Rif War as its setting, thus potentially expanding Spanish television's critical engagement with the 1920s. The Televisión Española series *La señora* (2008) also addresses the final decline of the Restoration through references to the Jaca Revolt of 1930.
13. Rotary technology was indeed introduced in Spain in the 1920s and in fact already available in Madrid by the end of 1926. See Cabezas (1974, 69–70).
14. The episode, titled "La leyenda del tiempo" (The Legend of Time), aired on April 13, 2015. An episode in the second season of *El Ministerio del Tiempo*, "Separadas por el tiempo" (Separated By Time) also engages with *Las Sinsombrero*. As in other efforts by Spanish cultural institutions to recover the memory of the 1920s, the series turns first to the most well-known male figures of the period and then proceeds to consider women's experiences as a secondary gesture.

BIBLIOGRAPHY

Alonso, Dámaso. 1975. "Una generación poética (1920–1936)." In *Obras completas*, 4: 653–476. Madrid: Gredos.
Balló, Tània. 2016. *Las Sinsombrero. Sin ellas, la historia no está completa.* Barcelona: Espasa Libros.
Balló, Tània, Manuel Jiménez Nuñez, and Serrana Torres. 2015. *Las Sinsombrero.* RTVE. http://www.rtve.es/alacarta/videos/imprescindibles/imprescindibles-sin-sombrero/3318136/.
Cabezas, Juan Antonio. 1974. *Cien años del teléfono en España. Crónica de un proceso técnico.* Espasa Calpe: Madrid.
Campos, Ramón, and Gema R. Neira. 2017. *Las chicas del cable.* Netflix. https://www.netflix.com/title/80100929.
de Groot, Jerome. 2009. *Consuming History: Historians and Heritage in Contemporary Popular Culture.* London and New York: Routledge.
———. 2011. "'Perpetually Dividing and Suturing the Past and Present': *Mad Men* and the Illusions of History." *Rethinking History* 15, no. 2: 269–285.
Fagoaga, Concha. 2015. "La relación del grupo de señoritas de la Residencia de Estudiantes con el Lyceum Club." In *Mujeres en vanguardia. La Residencia de Señoritas en su centenario (1915–1936)*, 318–329. Madrid: Publicaciones de la Residencia de Estudiantes.

Fusi, Juan Pablo. 2012. "España 1808–1939: La debilidad del estado nacional." In *Historia mínima de España*, 187–227. México: Colegio de México.

Gil Ambrona, Atonio. 2008. *Historia de la violencia contra las mujeres. Misoginia y conflicto matrimonial en España*. Madrid: Cátedra.

González Calleja, Eduardo. 2005. *La España de Primo de Rivera. La modernización autoritaria, 1923–1930*. Madrid: Alianza.

Harkema, Leslie J. 2017. *Spanish Modernism and the Poetics of Youth: From Miguel de Unamuno to La Joven Literatura*. Toronto: University of Toronto Press.

Kirkpatrick, Susan. 2009. *Mujer, modernismo y vanguardia en España: 1898–1931*. Madrid: Cátedra.

León, María Teresa. 1999. *Memoria de la melancolía*. Barcelona: Galaxia Gutemberg.

López, Francisca. 2009. "Introducción: El pasado en la pequeña pantalla." In *Historias de la pequeña pantalla: Representaciones históricas en la televisión de la España democrática*, edited by Francisca López, Elena Cueto Asín, and David R. George, Jr, 9-25. Madrid and Frankfurt am Main: Iberoamericana/Vervuert.

Mangini, Shirley. 2001. *Las modernas de Madrid*. Ediciones Península: Las grandes intelectuales españolas de la vanguardia. Barcelona.

Marcos, Natalia. 2017. "'Las chicas del cable', más de lo mismo." *El País*. https://elpais.com/cultura/2017/05/01/television/1493639584_181942.html.

McDonald, Kevin, and Daniel Smith-Rowsey, eds. 2016. *The Netflix Effect: Technology and Entertainment in the 21st Century*. New York and London: Bloomsbury.

Moreno Villa, José. 2011. *Memoria*. Edited by Juan Pérez de Ayala. México and Madrid: El Colegio de México/Residencia de Estudiantes.

Pérez Yuste, Antonio. 2007. "La creación de la Compañía Telefónica Nacional de España en la Dictadura de Primo de Rivera." *Cuadernos de Historia Contemporánea* 29: 95–117.

Pérez Yuste, Antonio, and Magdalena Salazar Palma. 2003. "Scanning Our Past from Madrid: Celebrating 75 Years of Madrid-Washington Telephone Service." *Proceedings of the IEEE* 91, no. 10 (October): 1738–1742.

Residencia de Estudiantes. 2016. "Mujeres en vanguardia." *Residencia de Estudiantes*. http://www.residencia.csic.es/expomujeres/sedes.htm. Accessed September 28, 2017.

Sáenz de la Calzada, Margarita. 2011. *La Residencia de Estudiantes. Los residentes*. Madrid: Publicaciones de la Residencia de Estudiantes.

Zubiaurre, Maite. 2012. *Cultures of the Erotic in Spain, 1898–1939*. Nashville: Vanderbilt University Press.

CHAPTER 12

The End of the Restoration: A Vision from the Early Second Republic in *14 de abril. La República*

Iván Gómez García

On April 14, 1931, the Second Republic was proclaimed in Spain. Republican candidates had won in 41 provincial capitals in the municipal elections two days before, although the rural areas of the country continued to be conservative and reluctant to change. The proclamation brought to a close the long period known as the Restoration, which was plagued by various institutional crises in the first decades of the twentieth century. Many of the problems that beset the economic and social structures of the country had gone unresolved, and the advent of what promised to be a true democracy signaled a fresh hope for many. This moment of change and transformation serves as the backdrop for the 2011 Televisión Española (TVE) series *14 de abril. La Republica* (Diagonal TV, 2011). The first season is set in the months following the April 14 proclamation, and the story line by and large focuses on the tensions wrought by the imperfect and incomplete agrarian reforms pursued by the nascent

I. Gómez García (✉)
Universitat Ramon Llull, Barcelona, Spain

© The Author(s) 2018
D. R. George, Jr. and W. S. Tang (eds.),
Televising Restoration Spain,
https://doi.org/10.1007/978-3-319-96196-5_12

241

Republican government in an attempt to address the legacies of the earlier regime. It depicts the emergence of conservative political factions, driven by a nostalgia for the old order, who resist the sweeping changes pursued by democratic cadres who attempt to modernize the country. All in all, the series does not achieve a high degree of historical accuracy and ultimately shirks debate, but as I will argue, it does offer television viewers a snapshot of the acute social and political problems that had become entrenched during the final decades of the Restoration, and which would cause constant crises throughout the Republican period.

In this chapter, I study *14 de abril. La República* in terms of its representation of history and how it explores the characters' experiences of the new period and their perceptions of the new Spain they were in the process of creating. I show how the series reveals the desperate nature of the situation in Spain in 1931, by alluding to the fundamental and unresolved problems of the Restoration that led to the political and social divisions that came to the fore during the years of the Republic. I attribute the historical inaccuracies of the drama, and its reluctance to engage in a true debate about the contemporary legacies of the Republic to two factors: First, the depiction of political content is weakened by the tendency toward melodrama inherent to the prime-time television format. Second, the drama is set in a polemical period of Spanish history, around which there remain considerable historiographical, ideological, and political controversies.

The first season of *14 de abril. La República* aired on TVE between January and April of 2011. Originally conceived as a sequel to the successful *La Señora* (Diagonal TV, 2008–2010), with which it shares some characters such as Encarna Alcántara (Lucía Jiménez) and Hugo de Viana (Raúl Peña), the first thirteen episodes cover the first year of the democratic regime, from autumn of 1931 to September of 1932. A second season, which continues from 1932 up to the outbreak of the Civil War in 1936, was to be aired the following year, but was never broadcast. One wonders why this is so, and whether this is another case of political pressure and censorship deciding the fate of a series. Quite apart from any accounting and financial issues which may have delayed the release of the sequel, its fate is at least partly connected to being set in a highly complex and enormously controversial period of history.

Historical dramas set in the complex periods of the Restoration and the Second Republic are nothing new to TVE. Following the death of Francisco Franco in 1975, a number of series were produced for Spanish television, including *Curro Jiménez* (TVE, 1976–1978); *Fortunata y Jacinta* (TVE, 1980), an adaptation of the famous novel by Benito Pérez Galdós; *Los gozos y las sombras* (TVE, 1981), based on the work by Gonzalo Torrente Ballester; *La forja de un rebelde* (TVE, 1990), an adaptation of an essential work by exiled Republican Arturo Barea; and *Los jinetes del alba* (TVE, 1991), based on the work of the same name by Jesús Fernández Santos.[1] These dramas, almost all adaptations, also wrestled with the history of the country and some of them, such as *La forja de un rebelde*, which dealt with the Rif War, the Republic and the Civil War, covered a lengthy chronological period. TVE thus has a track record in this type of production, even if it had never taken on a drama which provided such a detailed depiction of the historical panorama of the Spanish Second Republic. *La República* can be seen as an attempt to fill this gap, especially as the first season, composed of thirteen episodes lasting more than an hour each, covered the relatively short period of just over a year following the proclamation of the Republic.

THE DAWN OF A NEW POLITICAL SYSTEM

The Republic was proclaimed at a difficult time of crisis and division. The previous Spanish political system of the Restoration had failed, as King Alfonso XIII had been incapable of discovering viable solutions for a country which, since the beginning of the twentieth century, had shown all the symptoms of economic and social collapse after a succession of alternating but equally ineffective governments, an ineffectual dictatorship, and a ridiculous colonial war. Spanish philosopher José Ortega y Gasset was of the opinion that the Spain of the early Restoration and the Regency had a structure, but the Spain of the twentieth century, covering the final period of the Restoration, lacked a backbone (Ortega y Gasset 1922). The turn of the century signaled the emergence, and the grudging acceptance, of uncontrollable processes of modernization that rocked the foundations of conservative societies as they witnessed with considerable astonishment the emergence of the masses in public life.[2] Ortega y Gasset was not looking nostalgically at the past but rather watching in amazement as those who had had no voice until the beginning of the new century burst onto the political scene with energy and determination. The emergence of these new forces was not without its risks.

Spain's pride had been wounded after the loss of Cuba in 1898, but the political crisis it precipitated soon passed. Other issues, such as long overdue agrarian reform, slow and uneven industrialization, political corruption and rural poverty, were more pressing. These problems that had gripped the country throughout the Restoration remained hidden, unresolved, and entrenched. The dictatorship of Miguel Primo de Rivera at the Restoration's end was a disaster in general terms, as the reforms he promised did not materialize, and onto the scene burst new political actors who were ideally suited to giving voice to the discontent of the masses. Predominantly anarchists, trade unionists, and socialists, they were all struggling to occupy the political space and to be heard in this new, profoundly unequal society. And against them stood the conservative politicians, capitalists, the moneyed classes, and the ever-present landowners.

The complex backdrop against which the Second Republic was proclaimed provides not only the historical setting for the 2011 TVE series but also contextualizes the show's range of deeply polarized characters covering the entire ideological spectrum of the times. On the one hand, there are the landowners, the De la Torre family headed by Agustín (Héctor Colomé) and Leocadia (Cristina de Inza). Their close family friend, the military conspirator Hugo de Viana (Raúl Peña), is godfather to Beatriz (Ursula Corberó), one of the daughters of the family. And then there is Mercedes (Mariona Ribas), the fiancée of the De la Torre family's eldest son, Fernando (Félix Gómez) who at the outset is in a somewhat ambiguous situation, estranged from his parents. All part of the conservative block, they are nostalgic for the old order of the Restoration, and their political positions, their words and their actions reveal their wish to turn back the clock, to destroy the Republic and undermine its values. The modernizers, on the other hand, include Encarna (Lucía Jiménez), socialist politician, and activist for equal rights and women's suffrage, Ventura, the anarchist (Fernando Cayo), Alejandra (Verónica Sánchez), a modern woman from a poor background who is employed in the Republican Ministry of Agriculture, and Amparo (Marta Belaustegui), the communist conspirator whose aim, curiously, is also to bring down the Republic. Between the two camps are the day laborers, pawns caught in the middle between two worlds and two forces that they cannot understand: the masters (the past) and the unions and anarchists (the future).

The series clearly differentiates the two blocks; indeed, a key part of its dramatic structure lies precisely in the somewhat simplified opposition among characters. But, are the characters in the series truly representative of two different ways of understanding the Spain of the time? In a certain sense, yes: the confrontation between the holdovers from the old social order of the Restoration and those who desired the new order of the Republic definitely existed historically, and this can be seen in various episodes. But on the other hand, the series prefers to highlight hostilities and employ melodrama in the relationships between characters rather than delving deeper into the historical facts to explain the reasons for these social differences and the class struggle which would end up bringing down the Republic.

The series begins in autumn 1931 *in media res*, and it opens with an agricultural dispute. Agustín de la Torre, the family patriarch, has decided not to cultivate his land in order to put pressure on a government which he considers to be fundamentally illegitimate. His decision provokes first concern and then outright rejection by the day laborers who work his land. Shortly afterward, we discover that the De la Torre family's finances are at risk and that their delicate situation is the result of the lengthy economic crisis in Spain, all of which reflects the historical reality. The dictatorship of General Primo de Rivera had shown signs of deterioration well before 1931. 1930 brought the crisis to a head, and on January 28, Primo de Rivera resigned, precipitating yet another institutional crisis in a long series that had afflicted the country since 1917 (González Calleja et al. 2015, 31). The subsequent government of General Dámaso Berenguer faced a polarized ruling class, an army split into various factions, and an obsolete structure of social control (González Calleja et al. 2015, 31). The hopes generated by the turn of the century had been dispelled by the debacle of 1898, and ushered in a prolonged period of social upheaval, ineffective government, political repression and class inflexibility. By the 1920s, it became clear that the Restoration system was unable to respond to the emergence of the masses onto the political and social scene, and this inescapable reality announced a fundamental change in the nation (González Calleja et al. 2015, 31).

But it was not only the masses that were responsible for ushering in the Republic, although they were an essential contributing factor. It should be remembered that the declaration resulted from the municipal elections of April 12, 1931, which, based on their extent and size, do not seem to be a sufficient mechanism to define, clarify, or proclaim the constitution of the state by today's standards.[3] But the Restoration, and in particular the Primo de Rivera dictatorship of the late-1920s, was in its death throes. Ucelay Da Cal and Tavera García make the shrewd observation that republicans, constitutionalists, and liberals (both old school and new) all had a certain inclination toward insurrection (1994, 123). This is relevant to any discussion about whether the shift from the dictatorship to the Republic, and therefore the dissolution of the Restoration regime, was a genuine political revolution or not. Recent historical studies emphasize the revolutionary dimension of the process and highlight certain characteristics such as the discredit into which the previous regime and its political leadership had fallen, the government's perceived illegitimacy, and the boom in political writing at the time. What happened in Spain in 1930 was highly unusual. The attitude of protest and the rejection of Primo de Rivera's dictatorship were shared not only by the unions, left-wing parties, non-unionized workers, intellectuals and students, but also by some of the old Restoration élite and part of the army (González Calleja et al. 2015, 35). Even the monarchy aroused little affection, as shown by the fact that major and rising figures of the time, such as General Sanjurjo, did not lift a finger to defend Alfonso XIII, who was forced into exile following the proclamation of the Republic, first to Paris and ultimately to Rome.

In *14 de abril*, these complex elements, which can be deduced from both the enthusiastic, robust activism of Encarna and the misgivings of Agustín de la Torre, are not presented openly. Some of them can be glimpsed in the character of Fernando de la Torre, Agustín's modern son, who is presented initially as a lover of the nightlife and cabarets of Madrid, and is perhaps one of the students or sons of "good" families who no longer supported the dictatorship of Primo de Rivera. In the series, the advent of the Republic creates a deep divide between those who support it and those who fear it. Almost always according to their social background, the characters adopt positions either in favor of or against the new regime, although Fernando moves between the two blocs, and anarchists such as Ventura and the communist Amparo only support the Republic outwardly, in reality intending to destroy it and establish a political order of a different kind. Agustín, on the other hand, is a conservative who is totally opposed to agrarian reform and the redistribution of the land and its revenue. The landowner is suffering economic hardship for the first time in his life and is under pressure from other large landowners to join with those of his class to protect their common interests.

Historically, the first Provisional Government after the declaration of the Republic attempted to fight against the excesses of the large landowners and issued a decree on May 7, 1931 which made it obligatory to cultivate the land. The law generated immense resistance and conflict, and in many parts of Spain it was ignored (Preston 2011, 38). The South was particularly troubled, as were conservative strongholds such as Salamanca. Positions hardened and, as far as they were able, each side created mechanisms to defend the interests of their class. The landowners had associations, money and close links to power, especially locally, while the day laborers saw socialist trade unions and anarchism gain prominence. The series attempts to reflect this ongoing struggle. Take, for instance, the character of Ventura, the anarchist who is constantly prepared to organize the day laborers, who early in the series are portrayed as being little more than puppets in the hands of the anarchist union CNT. The portrayal is superficial and simplistic and does little justice to the enormous range of situations at the time and the existence of an intermediate class of farmers who had their own small property or land to farm. The rural world is presented reductively, although it is crucial to any understanding of the historical period depicted. After all, the votes of the peasant class, which changed over time, were decisive in the web of electoral alliances woven throughout the period (González Calleja et al. 2015, 667).

The series seems to imply in its early episodes that the proclamation of the Republic automatically situated all characters on one side or the other of the political spectrum, each with their reasons and arguments. But this is, at best, another example of a partial and somewhat biased account of what was happening at the time: Many of these positions were formulated over a greater period of time than that enveloped by the series, dating back to the Restoration. While there were also those, especially of the Spanish right wing, who did not give the Republic the slightest chance, a number of sectors changed sides or opinions time and again. However, such nuances are generally lacking in the characters of the series who greet the proclamation as if they all knew exactly what to do going forward; this is clearly far from the historical truth. For instance, the 1932 Agrarian Law, in general terms, did not meet the aspirations of workers and the rural working class, and faced many insurmountable obstacles from the start (Robledo 2011, 81). The cumulative effects of so many years of rural backwardness were so complex that the successive governments of the Republic had to deal with a change in political loyalty by the rural working class, who moved increasingly to the right as the problems became ever more pressing.

The New Social Actors:
The Characters and Their Values

The De la Torre family is a good example of what Jordi Gracia called the "stagnant, rancid bourgeoisie," a holdover from the Restoration who drifted aimlessly through the last years of the Republic, anxious and penniless (2004, 148). Money motivates Fernando's nuptials with Mercedes, as marriage between the two is the condition for a loan from Mercedes's father, a conservative banker. It is a curious kind of blackmail with a melodramatic flavor that Fernando finally accepts, despite being in love with Alejandra and not the woman who is to become his wife.

Episode 6, titled "The Trail of Secrets," tackles one of the reasons for the delicate financial position of the De la Torre family. It turns out that that the family had what were called "Philippine bonds," shares in a business based in the Philippines, whose management had been entrusted to the Society of Jesus. With the loss of the colonies and the Jesuits' problems with the new Republican government—which would culminate with their expulsion from the country in 1932—the bonds lose all their value. The story likewise shows that some of the landowning bourgeoisie were closely linked to the Church, and this provides another reason for their resistance to change and modernization.

For others, the Republic meant both a rupture and fresh hope: a break with the Restoration, as associated with the endemic backwardness of Spain and its old values, and the promise of progress. There is something of this in Fernando's modern and carefree attitude at the beginning of the series, in the political commitment of Encarna, and in the violent and utopian activism of the Ventura. It can also be appreciated in the tensions generated by the love between Fernando and Alejandra, as Alejandra is the daughter of day laborers (adopted, as it will later emerge). Nevertheless, there remains a considerable degree of resistance to modernization. The political conservatism of Restoration Spain, which persisted and festered in a part of the social fabric, was enshrined in the constitutional laws of the time. For instance, Article 11 of the 1876 Constitution not only establishes Catholicism as the official religion of the State, but also tacitly justifies discrimination against other faiths (Torres del Moral 2015, 190). While the constitution does provide for a certain degree of religious freedom, the intimate relationship between Church and State is fully sanctioned by the document's wording. Jordi Gracia observes how Spanish liberalism failed in its drive to modernize by not adequately addressing the question of religion (Gracia 2004, 148). Persistent religiosity not only explains some of the fears of the Spanish right; it also explains that of liberal Catholics who were likewise horrified by the burning of convents and the religious persecution unleashed by the proclamation of April 14. This topic, however, is not presented explicitly in the first season of the series. The May 1931 burning of convents and the persecution of clerics in Madrid, so present in the memory of the Spanish right, is nowhere to be found in the drama. The fourth episode does show a church being burnt, but this is the result of an attempt to hide certain documents held in its archives sought by a mysterious customer of Don Agustín. We might conclude that this distortion of the facts sacrifices history in favor of melodramatic elements of the plot.

One issue closely connected to the presence and power of the Church is the role of women in public life, which increased greatly under the Republic and thus is reflected through the various female characters of *14 de abril*. As Chicharro-Merayo has pointed out, the series introduces "particularly noteworthy innovations in terms of the representation of women" (2012, 509). The advent of the Second Republic made notable advances in the recognition of women's rights: The first divorce law in Spain was passed in 1932, and women like Teresa Claramunt, Maria Cambrils, and Victoria Kent contributed to changing the way the country viewed women and their ability to handle positions of responsibility. Various women stood out on the political scene: Clara Campoamor founded the Unión Republicana Femenina (Feminine Republican Union) in 1931; Victoria Kent figured on the voting lists of the Popular Front; and Dolores Ibárruri, popularly known as la Pasionaria, became a distinguished leader of the Communist Party (Álvarez-Uría 2013, 638). In the series *14 de abril*, it is Encarna who best represents these political and social changes. Encarna leaves her family in Asturias to travel to Madrid in response to the call of the Socialist Party. The first of her struggles, and one of the most important, is for women's suffrage. She is seen in Madrid in front of a large auditorium, preparing to argue in favor of the vote and the participation of women in public life. Encarna, then, is a character who clearly represents the new republican values and she promotes her beliefs even among women who, paradoxically, do not believe in women's suffrage.

In another example, Fernando is torn between Alejandra, who represents the future and progress, and Mercedes, who stands for the past and
tradition. Fernando's opposite is Jesus Prado (Alejo Sauras), the kind-
hearted day laborer who is ready to come between his sister Alejandra
and *Señorito* (young master) Fernando, as he is pejoratively called by
the laborers. The female characters are intriguingly nuanced: Alejandra
works in the Ministry of Agriculture, which had been almost impossible for a woman previously. Mercedes is not a schemer but rather a victim both of circumstances and of her social background. This makes it
difficult to pursue her affair with Jesús, with whom she falls hopelessly
in love despite his status as a peasant. The clichéd story of star-crossed
lovers unfolds throughout the season and forms the basis of the dramatic structure. Although it may appear that Alejandra's and Mercedes's
only importance is in their shared passion for the same man, Alejandra
demonstrates her complete commitment to the Republic and to her
work in the Ministry of Agriculture when she is asked by Encarna to
hide some important documents during the Sanjurjo military coup in the
tenth episode.

Another strong woman is Amparo Romero, the proprietor of the El
Alemán cabaret. Amparo is an enigmatic figure, a kind of Spanish Mata
Hari who is tasked with providing vices and pleasure to whoever can pay
for them. She is one of the most independent characters in the series,
with few family ties. Nor does she raise the slightest flicker of interest or
desire from the male characters of the series, and the person with whom
she gets along best is her partner Paco "the Blonde" (Vicente Romero),
a kind of gangster with ill-formed political convictions. Amparo appears
first as Ventura's main ally, but is soon revealed as a communist agent,
presumably from the Soviet secret police. She is a tough, modern, bisex-
ual woman who in the second episode states that "la República se tiene
que derrumbar desde lo más alto" (the Republic must be brought down
from the very top). She is in dealings with a shady figure, Gonzalo de
Castro/Lázaro Ortiz, a secret government agent to whom she filters
information about the anarchists, which ends up frustrating the assassination attempt on President Niceto Alcalá Zamora in the fifth episode.
This frustrated assassination attempt, a complete fiction with no basis
in historical fact, is used to generate an excellently executed, tense, and
well-resolved action scene that ends in a shootout, with the death of an
anarchist and the escape of the injured Ventura. Once more, melodrama
trumps historical accuracy.

In the first episode "The Decision," we see a mischievous and happy-go-lucky Fernando living the Madrid highlife in Amparo's German-inspired nightclub, one of the most important locations of the season. Right at the beginning of the series, the cabaret is described by Fernando as "el mayor santuario de Madrid, que como pueden ver no es ninguna iglesia" (the largest sanctuary in Madrid, which, as one can see, is no church). Later, in the tenth episode it is revealed that Amparo had been sent to Berlin as a communist agent where she discovered that a cabaret can be an excellent place to acquire information. It is in her cabaret that we are introduced to an entertaining song which sums up the attempt to transcend the values of the Restoration. The song, sung in German and used as a leitmotif in other episodes, is openly sensual. It tells of a passionate love story in which the woman sings to the lost lover she wishes to win back. It is heard for the first time in the series just after Encarna makes a toast in the cabaret, "a la salud de las mujeres con conciencia" (to the health of women with a conscience), marking the series' feminist tone as a departure from previous Restoration values.

La República also incorporates the figure of a plotting army officer. Hugo de Viana (Raúl Peña) is an officer connected to the De la Torre family who is involved in the *sanjurjada*, the historic coup d'état which General Sanjurjo carried out with the support of several monarchist politicians and army officers. The coup failed and Sanjurjo was arrested and condemned to death, although in the end he was pardoned. He went into exile in Lisbon where he remained in wait of a better chance to try to overthrow the government. Meanwhile, the fictional Hugo is wounded in action and becomes addicted to morphine, provided in this case by a solicitous Amparo. He is tortured and taciturn, a representative of the old order and strongly opposed to the modernization being undertaken in part of the Republican army.

In sum, the series clearly depicts the existence of a conservative and reactionary Spain opposed to the Republic, which sought to cripple, if not destroy it outright. At the same time, it also exposes the presence of another group of enemies of the Republic: the radical left, principally anarchists and communists. The anarchists from the CNT are portrayed rather stereotypically and the series also takes a superficial look at the FAI in episode 9. Here, the De la Torre family refers to the historic events at Castilblanco on December 31, 1931 in which four *guardias civiles* were lynched by a riotous crowd. However, no further details are given. Considerable effort is made in the series to show the fear the upper classes had of the Republic and new social actors of the time, particularly those operating among the working classes, but then these threats, like the anticlerical violence, are not shown on-screen nor detailed. What is clear is that all the characters, with their diverse values and attitudes toward what is happening in the country, adopt positions which are to a great extent determined by their sense of belonging or proximity to either the rural or urban environment, though this opposition is far from being well delineated in the first season. It is unclear where the De la Torre estate is located, although it is understood to be near Madrid. The day laborers, Jesús and Alejandra and their father Antonio Prado (Álex Angulo), belong to the rural world, whereas Fernando, Amparo, Ventura, and Hugo are more comfortable in Republican Madrid. Encarna comes from a rural background in Asturias, the epicenter of the miners' struggle which would be brutally put down in 1934, but her political activity takes place in Madrid. This is logical: Conservatism is rural while republicanism is an urban phenomenon. Madrid, which was branded by some of the writers of the Generation of '98 as a traditional and backward provincial capital that was inward-looking and a hotbed of the worst examples of reactionary culture, had turned into a city in which the fate of the country would be permanently in play (Castillo 2010).[4] But we never see Madrid in all its magnitude and complexity during the first season. We see the Spanish Parliament in the frustrated coup against the president Alcalá Zamora; we lose ourselves regularly in El Alemán, and we attend a number of gatherings in fashionable cafés. But the hubbub of the streets, the problems in the neighborhoods, the geographical distance between the classes, the poverty and the insecurity of some areas of the city are all missing. Historically, Madrid was a city for conspiracy; there, a communist agent like Amparo could go undetected or an anarchist on the run could just disappear. It was also a place where double agents could hatch their plots, but in most episodes of *14 de abril*, the city is just an inert backdrop that contrasts with the meticulous artistic direction or the visual work on interiors undertaken by the series' creative team.

Additionally, the series hardly shows what was going on elsewhere in the country; apart from the rural locale of the De la Torre property, only Asturias has a certain presence. It is Encarna's homeland and is also mentioned halfway through the series when news arrives in the capital of a tragic Asturian mine explosion that causes a number of deaths. Furthermore, the story begins with the arrival at the De la Torre household of the Asturian servant Ludi (Mónica Vedía), who had previously served the Márquez family in *La Señora*. She enters service with the De la Torre family and falls in love with Don Agustín's legal assistant, Rafael Mesa (Guillermo Ortega), but she is never fully developed as a character. The vicissitudes she goes through demonstrate the hardship suffered by those who lived in the provinces or in the countryside, girls obliged to serve in affluent houses in the capital just to be able to survive, but little more. Thus, Ludi's presence marks the stark division between urban and rural development, further commenting upon the troubled legacy of the Restoration period.

The creators of the series clearly have chosen to work within the well-trodden paradigm of the "two Spains," which is based on the idea that there were two opposed and irreconcilable visions of what the country should be. The first stages of the series reveal how the Restoration had failed to present an idea of the country as inclusive and robust that would appeal to the different interest groups of the time, who instead remained entrenched in their opposing ideological positions. As Archilés and García Carrión state, "There is little doubt that in the Spain of the Restoration there was no attempt at any time by the state to construct or recognize a multicultural identity" (2012, 486). In fact, it appears that the Restoration failed to articulate even the most basic national identity and it is possible that this was responsible for the slow modernization of the country. Archilés and García Carrión (2012, 487) refer to Eugene Weber to account for this. According to Weber (1976), modernization processes erode traditional identities (especially rural ones) and the state tends to work toward this end by reinforcing institutions such as education.

In the series, the dialectic between the rural and the urban worlds focuses almost exclusively on the problems generated by the agrarian reform that the new Republican government was trying to introduce. The reform that was anathema to the landowners gave hope to the impoverished day laborers, but this hope would soon evaporate. For people like Encarna, it represented a radical change, the proof that even one of the most entrenched and intractable problems, debated endlessly during the Restoration, might finally be solved. Fernando, in his own way, remains hopeful for a better future, whereas Hugo de Viana has given up on the future and seeks to recover a now obsolete past with his military plots. Alejandra also expresses her trust in the Republic and in a brighter future, while Mercedes is tied to her social status, without which she would not be who she is.

In the Spain of 1931, class interests are inseparable from landowner-ship and semifeudal labor relations. This is how the De la Torre family lives. They are landowners, not industrialists, and against change. So are the day laborers such as Jesús and his father, to a degree. With no strong identity other than the one forged through years of submission and semi-slavery, they let themselves be carried away by Ventura, who prom-ises them a better world through direct action, something that is histori-cally questionable, as the CNT stopped preaching direct action once the Republic had been proclaimed. When, in opposition to Agustín, Leocadia and Fernando persuade the day laborers to return to work, somebody, presumably other landowners (although it could likewise have been an extreme left-wing cell seeking to provoke a confrontation between lab-orers and landowners), sabotages the harvest by pouring lime on the seed. This shows how little loyalty existed between and even within social classes, an unmistakable sign of an ill-articulated social fabric little given to acknowledging difference. This can also be seen clearly in the char-acter of Hugo de Viana and his officer co-conspirators, or in the series' first two episodes when the *Guardia Civil* are seen acting more as Agustín de la Torre's private guard than as defenders of public order.

Some of the social relations portrayed in the series are characterized by the master–servant relationship, so central to traditional Spanish cul-ture. Leocadia is the lady of the house and has no qualms in acting as such. The female servants are, to a certain extent, anchored in the past, with highly limited or simply nonexistent personal autonomy. Similarly, Mercedes could be independent but is not. We do, however, see some new social models, in personal relationships and even within fami-lies. Encarna leaves her family in Asturias to serve her party in Madrid; there are other characters from an intermediate professional class such as the law student and clerk Rafael Mesa, and there are women who have prospered through education and professionalization such as Alejandra, who is committed to the agrarian reform. Education has enabled her to advance socially and she is a modern, progressive woman. On occasions, however, as pointed out by Chicharro-Merayo (2012, 519), her charac-ter seems to respond more to our own contemporary expectations than to the reality of the times.

Beyond these criticisms, nonetheless, it is possible to state that some-thing was indeed changing in social relations and this could be seen especially in urban contexts, as is portrayed in the series. A new elite claimed power and a revitalized professional class ascended socially, while salaries improved and more people could be emancipated from strictly defined class boundaries. These changes had been taking place slowly, at least since the final stages of the reign of Isabel II (Otero Carvajal 2005, 28), when the old structures based on hierarchical power over subordinates had begun to break down, something that can be seen in some of the characters in the series and their relationships. There is a curious moment, in episode 10, when Agustín tries to convince a Jesuit to help his son Fernando to enter politics. The idea of the patriarch is to defend his class interests from within the new system. On the one hand, this is his way of prolonging his traditional dominance by other means, but on the other hand it implies that he recognizes his failure and the fact that he can only defend his privileges through politics. Physical force appears no longer to be a viable option for someone like Agustín in 1932. He even expresses his many doubts when Hugo de Viana tells him about the planned coup d'état. The failure of the coup strengthens the Republic, while it also demonstrates that characters like Alejandra and Encarna are completely committed to republican values. The approval of the Agrarian Reform Law on September 9, 1932 leads the Ministry of Agriculture to issue expropriation orders which, in the series, will affect the properties of the De la Torre family. Once again new legislation crosses the family and gives them yet another reason to hate a new order that for many now provided hope of a redistribution of farmland. The first season of the series concludes with a confrontation between the day laborers who have seized some land following the expropriations and a *Guardia Civil* who does not hesitate to shoot into a crowd of the workers infiltrated by the unions who are organizing and controlling them. It is noteworthy that this finale ends with this explosion of violence, as tradition and progress clash, and class conflict comes to a head.

OLD AND NEW MORAL VALUES

In recent years, Spain has witnessed the emergence of a right-wing revisionism which has not been shy about its desire to condemn outright the Republican period between 1931 and 1939, including the years of the Civil War. The central argument of this revisionism has been the hackneyed phrase "cada uno tiene sus razones" (each side had its reasons) and the affirmation that the military coup of Franco, Mola and the other plotters was the consequence of a period of disorder which made the republican régime illegitimate and unsustainable.[5] The Spanish right, led by the Popular Party, has always been reluctant, and on occasions even refused, to accept that the Franco coup was exactly that, an illegitimate act against a legally established government. Denigration of the Second Republic has led to a renewed legitimization of the July 18, 1936 coup as a tough but necessary reaction to the mismanagement of the Popular Front (Reig Tapia 2017, 135). To defend this controversial position, the argument goes that the republican regime had collapsed into chaos, and to back up this argument adherents name a battery of problems which took place during the years of the Republic, such as the Sanjurjo plot and 1932 attempted coup, the Asturias revolution in October 1934, problems with Catalonia and the proclamation of the State of Catalonia by the Catalan president Lluís Companys, the workers' strikes and the political violence in the streets of Barcelona and Madrid.

Viewed from this angle, many have seen the refusal to broadcast the second season of *La República* as a maneuver by the Popular Party to prevent the screening of a controversial television product set in a period about which the party and its leaders remain uncomfortable. Of course, we must recognize that the economic crisis was responsible for the paralysis and modification of many TVE productions. Several series already filmed were not screened, as television accounting rules make it obligatory to account for the cost of a series once it is broadcast, even if it has already been paid for. There were also delays in the broadcasting of important series such as *Isabel* (Diagonal TV, 2011–2014) or *Los misterios de Laura* (Ida y Vuelta P. F., 2009–2014), but they were not canceled. In February 2011, Ramón Moreno, spokesperson of the Popular Party in the parliamentary committee that oversees RTVE, directly criticized *La República* for, in his opinion, reopening old wounds (De Luna 2017). Given that he stated this position in parliament, one can only assume that his criticism was the official position of the Popular Party, and nothing seems to indicate that this might have changed. It is important to remember, moreover, that the series was authorized and broadcast originally while the PSOE, presided by José Luis Rodríguez Zapatero, was in power. For these reasons, the absence of the second season of *La República* led a number of journalists to refer to the series as the "series silenced by the PP" (Jabonero 2016). The broadcast of the first episode on January 24, 2011 achieved an excellent 19.2% share with a total of more than 4 million viewers. The remaining episodes did not garner such numbers, but viewership remained stable at around 17% on average, or 3.5 million views, which for a 2011 show is a more than respectable result. The numbers warrant the continuation of the series, particularly as the rest of the episodes had already been filmed. The second season was due to be screened in January 2012, but at the end of 2011 the PP won a landslide victory in the general election. This seems to have sealed the fate of the series and explains why it was consigned to oblivion. Nevertheless, Fernando López Puig, who is responsible for the series at TVE, remains hopeful, stating that "I don't know when, but we will see it at some point, because it is a great product" (in Miguélez 2016).

As a casualty of political machinations, *14 de abril* is not an isolated case. Other series have suffered the same fate, and almost all of them deal with historical facts related to the Civil War, the Second World War or the troubles in the Basque Country. The miniseries *Tres días de abril* (Boomerang, TVE, 2010), which deals with the crucial days (April 12–14, 1931) leading up to the regime change and the declaration of the Second Republic has still not been shown. Antón Reixa, the producer, noted that the people responsible for the product at TVE were involved in all production stages and were happy with the final cut, so he suspects that the decision not to broadcast the series was political (*Zeleb* 2017). Another similar case is *La Conspiración* (ETB, TVE, 2012), although here the drama focuses on the final stages of the Second Republic, the military plot and uprising led by Mola and Franco and the effects of the insurrection. The series was broadcast by ETB, the Basque television channel who co-produced it, but not by TVE. And there are further cases, such as the miniseries *Volveremos* (Brutal Media, TV3,TVE, 2011), about the republican Spanish soldiers who fought with the well-known 9th company, or *El precio de la libertad* (BlogMedia, ETB, TVE, 2011), about the life of the ETA activist Mario Onaindía, which was broadcast by ETB but not by TVE.[6]

We may ask why products set in historical periods now long past raise broadcasting issues. The Restoration is long gone, but series set in that period do not seem to have suffered the same broadcasting or censorship issues as those set in the Second Republic. Perhaps the distance from the events is sufficient. But it may be that the tendency to think about dramas set in the Restoration in romantic or melodramatic terms makes them less controversial for television. It is completely different when the focus is on the Republican era and the problems it inherited from Restoration are observed from the perspective of a present in which the aspirations for democracy and modernization pursued during both periods have supposedly been realized. Returning to these historical issues will doubtless continue to pose a very real political problem as the issues have not been settled or overcome, and on so many occasions have served as weapons in the struggle between the political left and right. And this ties in with the idea that as a melodrama and a historical drama, the series *14 de abril* alludes to a range of questions related to identity and society that are actually more closely related to the context of production than to the historical period represented on-screen (Costa-Alruzu 2003). Any series, and indeed any television program, has an inherent socializing function, such that far from being an innocuous or insignificant product, *La República* takes a stand in a debate which is not yet resolved, or at the very least, remains so controversial that every new drama is seen more as a problem than as an opportune or necessary contribution to dialogue (Chicharro-Merayo 2012, 509).

Christelle Colin argues that this series embodies a Republican ideology as it represents the various different left-wing utopias of the time in some detail (2017, 126). It is true that the character of Fernando is attracted to Alejandra and toward the defense of Republican values, and it is also true that Encarna is an essential and strong character within the series. But, I would argue, there remains a lack of definition in the show's narrative thrust, which suggests that if the series' historical recreation was intended to bolster Republican ideals, it does not do so convincingly. The drama, I conclude, is strapped by the antinomy of political options, in the rather simplistic "each side had its reasons" referred to earlier, and by a degree of vagueness that is a direct result of the suppression of the second season of the series. The broadcast of the missing episodes on TVE or via another platform would allow viewers to make a better judgement about the cultural and political implications of *14 de abril. La* República, and more importantly, about the lasting impressions of the Restoration and the Second Republic for contemporary Spain.

NOTES

1. For a more exhaustive account, see Cascajosa Virino and Zahedi (2016, 57–62). The authors explain the changes caused, for example, by the adoption of the 1980 Radio and Television Statute, while they also explain the history of television in Spain from a comparative perspective. They accurately highlight issues about which there is still considerable controversy, such as the role played by TVE in constructing the Spain consisting of Autonomous Regions.
2. See Blom (2010).
3. The result of these elections is still debated today. Questions remain over which block should have received some of the votes for parties whose affiliation was less obvious, and historians continue to discuss the reasons for and the effects of the proclamation. One of the most recent contributions to the debate comes from Álvarez Tardío and Villa García (2017).
4. Other 1898 liberals, in an unexpected lurch to the right, would end up calling Republican Madrid *Madridgrad*, a term which would have undoubtedly tickled Agustín de la Torre or Hugo de Viana (see Castillo 2016). *Madridgrad* or *Madridgrado*, in Spanish, is a play on Soviet period names for St. Petersburg and Volograd, Leningrad and Stalingrad respectively; politicians on the right and also some liberals talked about Madrid this way to criticize leftist parties, soviet sympathizers, and intellectuals with close ties to the Soviet Union.
5. The main exponents of this revisionist thinking have been Pío Moa and César Vidal, who have emphasized their role as "demystifiers" and guardians of a supposed historical truth, which in their opinion has been subject to major bias and attack by left-wing historians. The role of Moa and Vidal as historians is highly questionable, and they have come under considerable criticism from the academic world for the content of their work.
6. The terrorism of ETA, its origins, development, causes, and consequence have always been one of the most complex and controversial subjects for Spanish drama. While this series does not deal directly with either the Republic or the Civil War, it does deal with a set of historically traumatic events and political problems whose roots go deep into the profound divide which opened up with the victory of Franco in 1939 and the establishment of a lengthy dictatorship.

BIBLIOGRAPHY

Álvarez Tardío, Manuel, and Roberto Villa García. 2017. *1936. Fraude y violencia en las elecciones del Frente Popular.* Barcelona: Espasa.

Álvarez-Uría, Fernando. 2013. "Mujeres y política. Las políticas de las mujeres en la España de la Segunda República y la Guerra Civil." *Papers. Revista de sociología* 98 (4): 629–646.

Archilés, Ferran y Marta García Carrión. 2012. "En la sombra del Estado. Esfera pública nacional y homogeneización cultural en la España de la Restauración." *Revista Historia Contemporánea* 45: 483–518.

Blom, Philipp. 2010. *Años de vértigo. Cultura y cambio en Occidente 1900–1914.* Barcelona: Anagrama.

Cascajosa Virino, Concepción, and Farshad Zahedi. 2016. *Historia de la televisión.* Valencia: Tirant lo Blanch.

Castillo, Fernando. 2010. *Capital aborrecida: la aversión hacia Madrid en la literatura y la sociedad del 98 a la posguerra.* Madrid: Polifemo.

———. 2016. *Los años de Madridgrado.* Madrid: Fórcola.

Chicharro-Merayo, Mar. 2012. "*14 de abril, La República*: La intrahistoria española desde la ficción televisiva." *Palabra Clave* 15 (3): 505–523.

Colin, Christelle. 2017. "14 de abril. La República (2011): De la historia a la memoria utópica." *Cultura de la república. Revista de análisis crítico* 1 (abril 2017): 118–127.

Contreras, José Miguel, and Manuel Palacio. 2003. *La programación de televisión.* Madrid: Síntesis.

Costa-Alruzu, C. 2003. "I Am Not a Feminist… I Only Defend Women as Human Beings: The Production, Representation, Consumption of Feminism in a telenovela." *Critical Studies in Media Communication* 20 (3): 249–269.

De Luna, Manuel. 2017. "Las *líneas rojas* de TVE." *El Periódico*, June 18. http://www.elperiodico.com/es/tele/20170618/lineas-rojas-tve-6103004.

Frades, Jordi, and Virginia Yagüe. 2011. *14 de abril. La República.* http://www.rtve.es/alacarta/videos/14-de-abril-la-republica/.

González Calleja, Eduardo, Francisco Cobo Romero, Ana Martínez Rus, and Francisco Sánchez Pérez. 2015. *La Segunda República Española.* Barcelona: Pasado & Presente.

Gracia, Jordi. 2004. *La resistencia silenciosa. Fascismo y cultura en España.* Barcelona: Anagrama.

Jabonero, Daniel. 2016. "Cinco años de 'La República' en TVE: la serie que silenció el PP." *Bluper.* http://bluper.elespanol.com/noticias/cinco-anos-la-republica-tve-serie-callo-pp.

Miguélez, Xabier. 2016. "En algún momento veremos *La República*". *El Confidencial.* http://www.vanitatis.elconfidencial.com/television/2016-09-06/fernando-lopez-puig-serie-la-republica-se-vera-tarde-temprano_1255693/.

Ortega y Gasset, José. 2006. *La España invertebrada.* Barcelona: Espasa Calpe.
Otero Carvajal, Luis Enrique. 2005. "Las ciudades en la España de la Restauración, 1868–1939." *España entre repúblicas 1868–1939*, 27–80. Guadalajara: VII Jornadas de Castilla la Mancha.
Preston, Paul. 2011. *El Holocausto Español. Odio y exterminio en la Guerra Civil y después.* Barcelona: Random House Mondadori.
"Series que no han sido emitidas en TVE por motivos ideológicos." 2017. *Zeleb. Público,* March 21. http://www.zeleb.es/tv/series-vetadas-en-tve-por-motivos-ideologicos.
Reig Tapia, Alberto. 2017. "La derecha española y la Segunda República: Neofranquismo e historia." *Cultura de la república. Revista de análisis crítico* 1 (April): 129–148.
Robledo, Ricardo, ed. 2011. *Historia del Ministerio de Agricultura 1900–2008.* Madrid: Ministerio de Medio Ambiente, de Medio Rural y Marino.
Torres del Moral, Antonio. 2015. *Constitucionalismo histórico español.* Madrid: Editorial Universitas.
Ucelay Da Cal, Enric, and Susanna Tavera García. 1994. "Una revolución dentro de otra: la lógica insurreccional en la política española 1924–1934." *Ayer. Violencia y política en España* 13: 115–146.
Weber, Eugene. 1976. *Peasants into Frenchmen: The Modernization of Rural France, 1870–1914.* Stanford: Stanford University Press.

INDEX

© The Editor(s) (if applicable) and The Author(s) 2018
D. R. George, Jr. and W. S. Tang (eds.),
Televising Restoration Spain,
https://doi.org/10.1007/978-3-319-96196-5

268   INDEX

S
Salamanca, Amaia, 95, 96
Salvador, Santiago, 53
Sancho, Rodolfo, 3, 120, 134
Second Republic, 17, 56, 123, 167,
    207, 217, 223, 227, 228, 241,
    242, 244, 249, 256–258. *See also*
    Republicanism
Sedes, Carlos, 95, 186, 205, 222
Seis Hermanas, 15, 16, 46, 139–141,
    143, 148, 149, 151, 152, 156,
    157, 183–186, 188–199
Sexism, 14, 17, 223, 231. *See also*
    Gender inequity; Women
Social class, 60, 104, 132, 140, 142,
    214, 222. *See also* Class conflict
Social justice, 6, 64, 70, 135, 171
Social media, 2, 13, 83, 85, 94, 197.
    See also Twitter
Sorolla, Joaquín, 38, 39, 46, 111
Spanish Civil War, 5, 17, 223, 227,
    242, 243, 255, 257, 259
Spanish history, 1, 2, 4, 5, 11, 14, 78,
    80, 96, 99–101, 186, 223, 231,
    242
Spanish television
    history of, 28
    study of, 12
Spousal abuse, 15, 140, 157. *See also*
    Domestic violence
Spousal infidelity, 15, 140, 145, 148,
    184. *See also* Marriage
Stock characters, 17, 174, 208
Streaming services, 9, 11, 26, 94. *See
    also* Netflix
Superheroes, 179

T
Teatre del Liceu, 53, 60
Technology, 14, 52, 95–98, 100,
    102–104, 107–109, 111, 112,

171, 173, 213, 222, 238. *See also*
    Period technology; Transmedia
TECMERIN, 11
Telecommunications, 221, 230, 235.
    See also Telephone
Telenovela, 8, 15, 28, 33, 111, 163,
    165–168, 170, 171, 174, 177,
    179
    history of, 33
    Latin America and, 15, 190
Telephone, 97, 104, 105, 108, 213,
    221, 224, 230, 231, 233–235
Televisió de Catalunya (TV3), 13, 52,
    55, 56, 58, 62, 63, 68, 70, 71,
    167, 185, 257
Televisión de Galicia (TVG), 16, 111,
    187, 205, 206
Televisión Española (TVE), 1, 4, 6–9,
    12–14, 23, 24, 26, 27, 29, 33,
    35, 37, 38, 40–45, 52, 54, 56,
    58, 62, 77, 78, 81–83, 85, 87,
    121, 122, 124, 131, 135, 152,
    163, 167, 183–186, 188–190,
    192, 195–197, 212, 225, 236,
    238, 241–244, 256–259
Thriller, 94, 103, 186, 206
Tragic Week, 5, 53, 71
Transition to democracy, 5, 7, 8, 25,
    26, 36, 45, 52, 57, 120
Transmedia
    active users of, 78, 82
    gamification and, 78, 90
    interactivity of, 78, 82, 84, 85, 89
    media platforms and, 13, 54, 81,
        85, 87
    storytelling and, 13, 78, 82, 83, 87,
        89
    videoblogs and, 85
Triangulation, 234
Tristante, Jerónimo, 79, 83
Twitter, 13, 40, 78, 83–85, 87